Mediumistic Romance

NOTHING IS BY CHANCE

ZIBIA GASPARETTO

BY LUCIUS

Translation into English:
Nicole Castillo Paredes
Lima, Peru, July 2023

Original Title in Portuguese

"Nada É por Acaso"

© Zibia Gasparetto, 2005

Reviewer:

Katerine Torres

World Spiritist Institute
Houston, Texas, USA

E–mail: contact@worldspiritistinstitute.org

About the Medium

Zibia Gasparetto is a Brazilian spiritual writer. She was born in Campinas. She is married to Aldo Luis Gasparetto and has four children. According to her story, a night in 1950 she woke up and began to walk around the house speaking German, a language that she didn't know. The next day, her husband bought a book about Spiritism to study together.

Her husband assists the spiritual association Federação Espírita do Estado de São Paulo, but she has to stay at home. On one occasion, Gasparetto felt a severe pain in her arm which it begins to move around without control. After Aldo gives her a pencil and paper, she begins to write quickly. Writing her first novel "And Love Won" signed by a spirit called Lucius. The manuscript was typed. Gasparetto showed a Historian professor of São Paulo University, who was interested in Spiritism too. Two weeks later, she receives the confirmation that her book will be published by LAKE Editorial. In her late years, Gasparetto used her computer four times a week to write stories dictated by her spirits.

She wrote usually at night for one or two hours. "They [Spirits] are not available, to work many days per week", she explains. "I don't know why, but each one of them just appears once a week. I try to change but I couldn't" As a result, she used to have one night a week, which each spirit communicated with her.

See the last available books of Zibia Gasparetto translated in English at the end of this book.

CHAPTER 1

Marina hurried her pace, pushing past passers-by to make her way. She was late. She still had to stop by two banks before they closed and deliver the documents to Dr. Moura's office. Those were confidential and she had been recommended to take the utmost care, and they should be delivered directly to him.

She checked her wristwatch and sighed tiredly. Why did she has to do everything herself? At the law firm where she worked there were other employees, but Dr. Olavo, her boss, seemed to have eyes only for her. Whenever there was an important document or a more complicated transaction at the bank, she was the one to go.

- You go, he decided. - I know you'll do everything right.

She would go. She began working in that office after she entered law school. She had struggled a lot to pay for her studies. Her family lived in Sorocaba, in the city of São Paulo. Ofelia, her mother, was a seamstress and her younger brother Cicero was in high school.

Her father had left the family when Ofelia was still pregnant with Cicero and never looked for them again.

When Marina decided to go to college in São Paulo, Ofelia was against it:

- It's just the three of us, she said sadly. - What will we do if you go away too?

- I'm not leaving, Marina answered in a firm voice. - I need to earn more money to pay for my studies.

- You could keep working at Jose's pharmacy and study something else.

- I want to get ahead in life, mum. I want to be somebody. I don't want to stay behind a counter all my life. I'm going to continue my studies and graduate.

- Nonsense! You're already twenty years old. Soon you'll get married and put your studies aside.

Marina pressed her lips together and said angrily:

- Not me! I'm going to take care of my life and I'm not going to look for someone to give me trouble. Think about it, mum: I am going to make a career for myself, earn a lot of money and take you both to São Paulo. Cicero will also need to continue his studies.

- I earn enough to live. Why else?

- You do what you can. But you have supported us all our lives. The time has come when I can help provide for the household.

Ofelia smiled.

- You have good intentions. But it's going to take time before you can help with the expenses. How much do you think you can earn in São Paulo? Then you'll have to support yourself. It won't be easy.

- I'll handle it. Bete wrote to me. She's living in a boarding house, and it's not expensive. I'll work in the pharmacy until I get paid and then I'll go to the boarding house. Classes won't start until next month. Meanwhile, I am looking for a good job.

- I don't like you being out there by yourself. You don't know anyone.

- I can look after myself.

There were no arguments that could change her mind. She received her salary and moved into the same boarding house where her friend Bete lived. Interested in a career in law, she looked for a job and managed to get hired by Dr. Olavo Augusto Resende's office. He led a group of lawyers who worked in the civil area.

Marina began modestly as an assistant. Wanting to progress, she tried hard to learn what she could, taking an interest in the group's business and doing more than was asked of her. Educated, intelligent and, above all, shrewd, Marina knew how to deal with people. The lawyers in the office soon realized they could count on her, glad to be free of dealing with them and entrusted her with the most complicated matters, she would be at ease.

As Marina advanced in her studies, her expenses increased, making her situation difficult. This problem, however, was alleviated by the salary increases she received as an incentive to complete the course.

It had been six months since Marina had graduated, and she wanted more. Olavo had promised her some small cases so that she could start winning the trust of her clients. He told her:

- In our profession, patience is needed. The name is important. You're good, you've learned a lot in these years here, but nobody knows you. You need to make a name for yourself.

She continued working as before, and the cases did not come. At the office, she was the one doing most of the legal work, writing petitions, following up on cases, analysing them, suggesting measures, attending hearings, talking to the opposing party's lawyers or the clients and their opponents.

He worked more than before. Having finished her studies, she stayed late. She often took cases to read at weekends.

Seeing her overwhelmed with work, Bete shook her head in annoyance:

- They are exploiting you. Not only you stay late every day, but you also bring work for the weekend? Don't you think that's too much?

- I need to get experience. It's my advantage.

- Meanwhile they pay you little and make money at your expense.

- Don't be mercenary! I like to work. I do it for myself, not for them. One day I'll have everything I want.

- If it doesn't end before then. Today there's a dance at the club where Carlos is a member. He invited us. Wanna go?

- You go. I'd rather stay here.

- You're no good at all. Marcelo is crazy about you. He usually goes to that club.

- I'm not interested.

- He's a great catch! If it was me, I wouldn't play hard to get.

- It's yours.

- I don't understand you. You don't date, you don't go out, you just work. That way you'll be an auntie.

- I don't care. Marriage is not in my plans.

- That's awful! Don't even joke about that. When someone I like comes along, I'll get married right away. I can't wait to have a family, to be happy.

- Well, not me. Marriage won't give me a future. I want to achieve more and take care of my life.

Marina arrived at the bank and looked discouraged at the long line at the teller. She went to talk to the manager. She smiled, chatted, told a story she had made up on the spot and got him to quickly assist her. She was used to these kindnesses. She knew she was beautiful, elegant, and had a nice body. Her golden-brown hair, her deep green eyes, her delicate dark skin, her straight and well distributed teeth, the two dimples that formed when she smiled and especially her irresistible personality guaranteed good service wherever she showed up.

She went to the other bank and to Dr. Moura's office. He was not there and she did not want to give the document to his secretary. It was a very important contract. It was at her insistence that Dr. Olavo had started to take on cases in the business area.

Marina thought that big business deals happened all the time in companies. To participate in them was to obtain more profit in less time. Evictions, inheritances and family problems, besides being time-consuming and laborious cases, were less profitable. At first Olavo was not very interested, but later he ended up taking on some cases in this area.

Sitting on the soft sofa in the twilight of the afternoon, Marina felt the pleasure of enjoying those moments of rest. She looked at the magnificent paintings on the walls, at the crystal vase filled with fresh, fragrant and artistically arranged flowers, at the fine and tasteful furniture, and could feel the softness of the carpet under her feet.

- Dr. Moura will be late. Are you sure he has to be here?

The secretary was standing in front of her.

- Yes, I'm sure. It was Dr. Olavo's request. Is he coming?

- Yes, he will. But we don't know when.

- If he comes, I'll wait.

- Can I get you a coffee or a soda?

- Coffee, please.

Marina took the coffee and put the silver-coated porcelain cup on the tray on the small table. Placing some magazines at her disposal, the secretary said:

- Make yourself comfortable – and retired to the other room.

Whether it was because she was tired, or the softness of the sofa, or the dimness of the room, Marina leaned back and without realizing she fell asleep. She dreamed she was in a green field, full of flowers and birds singing happily. She walked through the green meadows with pleasure and joy, pleasantly inhaling the nice perfume coming from the flowers. Suddenly, she stopped. A woman was approaching. Her beautiful young face attracted her. Where did she know her from?

- How are you, Marina? - she asked.

- Fine. Where do we know each other from?

- It's been a long time. You don't remember.

- I remember I know you, but from where?

- From other lives.

-Other lives? What do you mean?

- Have you forgotten that you've lived on Earth before? You must remember reincarnation.

- I don't think it exists.

- You'll remember when the time comes. I came to see you because I need your help. You promised, and I expect you to keep your promise.

- Me? Help? What can I do?

- Soon, many things will change in your life. It's all right. Remember: there's nothing wrong. There is no mistake.

Marina woke up still hearing her voice repeating this sentence and was startled to realize that the secretary was standing in front of her saying:

- Dr. Moura called and said that he won't be coming back to the office today.

- I am sorry. I guess I nodded off... It's so nice here, I couldn't resist. What time will he be here tomorrow?

- After ten. He has a meeting with an important client at half past ten.

- I'll be here at ten. Thank you.

Marina left. It was already dark and the streets were still busy. She felt hungry and decided to eat something and go home. It was after seven o'clock, she would not go back to the office. She was tired.

She went into a full cafeteria. She found a table, sat down, ordered a sandwich and a guarana. While she ate, she thought about improving her finances. The money she earned allowed her to leave the boarding house and rent a small flat in Largo do Arouche, which she furnished slowly but tastefully. It was her corner. There she felt like the owner of her own life. Everything had been achieved with her own money, and this small victory gave her the certainty that she could achieve much more. She only needed to find out how.

Immersed in her intimate thoughts, Marina didn't even notice the interested looks of the boys watching her. Not that she was indifferent to male harassment. On the contrary: she enjoyed exchanging glances, flirting, chatting when she met someone interesting, but nothing more than that.

Her attitude aroused more interest, and she was constantly harassed, receiving numerous invitations, which she accepted when she felt like relaxing a little.

Bete couldn't accept it. If only it had been her! So many invitations, so many handsome guys, intelligent men, and Marina was indifferent, as if it was nothing. She didn't understand how she, acting this way, was so successful.

Marina paid the bill and left, and as she drove home, she kept thinking about how to get what she wanted. She began to suspect that she was wasting her time at Dr. Olavo's office. She had learned a lot with them, but now she was starting to think differently and think that they could make much more progress if they modified some aspects that she thought were outdated.

In recent times they had become complacent and did not intend to grow, to open up other areas of activity. They were tired, old, limited. For them, what they had was enough. They were not motivated to make greater efforts.

"If I stay there, I'll be stuck too," she thought.

She thought of looking for a job in the legal department of a large company. That way she could progress until she had the money and fame to open her own law firm.

She arrived home, looked around the small flat and decided:

- 'Right tomorrow I'm going to look for another job. I have enough knowledge to get something better. And I am sure I will find it.

CHAPTER 2

Sitting in a luxurious living room, Marina waited. She had prepared herself for the occasion. She had bought elegant clothes, gone to the hairdresser, and felt very well receiving admiring glances from the people she passed by. She was going to be interviewed again to get a new job.

It had been more than a month since she had started her search. She had been to several interviews, she had talked to managers, she had filled out applications. She was asking for a high salary. She needed to value herself. She didn't intend to leave Dr. Olavo if it wasn't for a rewarding salary and a place where she could progress.

She was in talks with a group formed by a chain of companies. She had been interviewed twice and now they called her in for a conversation in the president's office. Beforehand, they wanted to know everything about her life: family, health, aspirations. She provided the information, amazed at the details they asked her. But she did so willingly. She was very interested in getting that job. She realized that there she could get where she wanted to go.

- Miss Marina, please come in.

She stood up and followed the elegant secretary. She entered a large and luxurious room, decorated with extreme good taste. Curious, she looked at the desk, behind which was seated an elegantly dressed woman whose face was not unfamiliar to her. Where had she seen her?

- Please sit down, miss – she said.

Marina tried to recover from her surprise. She hadn't expected to find a woman. She settled down and waited.

- My name is Adele, she said in a deep, polite voice. - I've been reading your file and I have a proposition for you.

- Yes, ma'am.

- First, I must tell you that what we are about to discuss is strictly confidential. Promise me, whatever happens, whatever your answer is, you will keep it absolutely secret.

- I'm a discreet person. You can trust me. I won't say anything to anyone.

- I chose you because it seemed to me that you have all the qualities I am looking for the task we are about to begin. However, I need your promise, without which we will end our business now.

- All right, you have my word. I promise I will not tell anyone about what is happening here.

Adele sighed, stood up and walked slowly and thoughtfully around the room, choosing the words for what she was going to say. Marina felt her curiosity sharpen. What was she going to propose?

Was it some kind of shady deal? The information she had about that group was the best. They were highly respected people in the market. Now she remembered where she knew Adele from. It was from the social magazines, where she was always shining and considered one of the most important women.

- I need your help to solve a delicate personal problem. I know you want a job. I can get you that and much more. I also know that you are ambitious and can't accept a modest life. If you accept what I am going to propose, you will receive a sum of money that will make you independent. You will be able to live comfortably for the rest of your life.

Marina did not miss a word. Adele continued:

- My husband died at the beginning of last year. Half of his shares in our companies belong to me and my only daughter. The other half would belong to the male child. As I did not have a son, and neither did my daughter, after three years of my husband's death, the assets will go to my brother-in-law.

He is part of the group. With these shares, he will become the majority shareholder and I will have to leave the presidency.

Marina listened with interest. Adele was silent for a few moments, then she continued:

- That would be a disgrace, because he, besides having no competence, is unreliable, having been kept here only in consideration of his grandfather, who was the founder of the company and left these determinations in his will thinking with this to prevent our business from falling into the hands of strangers.

Adele paused briefly and, noticing that Marina was listening attentively, continued:

- My daughter has been married for five years and has no children. As I said, it has been a year and a half since my husband died. If she were to have a boy, everything would be all sorted out.

- But she still might.

Adele shook her head and said sadly:

- Maria Eugenia is sterile. She will never be able to have children. Two months ago, we were sure of that. To try to solve this problem, I made a plan. At first, she refused, but now, faced with the facts, she's agreed. It's our only chance to preserve our business, as we've always done. That's why we need your help. We have a year and a half to figure this out.

- I don't understand. What can I do?

- I have it all planned out. You'll quit your job and move to a place only we know. There, you will sleep with my son-in-law. I want you to have this child for Maria Eugenia.

Marina stood up as if driven by a spring.

- What? Me?

- Yes, you're a healthy, intelligent, cultured, good-natured, beautiful, competent and ambitious girl. You will be the ideal mother for my grandson.

- You're going too far. This will never work. I can't do such a thing. Why would I?

- Don't get ahead of yourself. You'd have a nine-month isolation, but then you'd be free to do as you please and you'd have my help and protection. Besides, I'll give you a million dollars.

Marina let herself fall back into her armchair, frightened. A million dollars! When she caught her breath again, she objected:

- 'That will never work. What if it's a girl?

- I've thought about that. But it's the only alternative; we have to try and take the risk. I hope it's a boy.

- You don't have to do that. You can adopt a newborn baby and register it as your daughter's. No one will find out. There are single mothers who can't raise their children and who would give in to you.

- I thought of that. This boy will inherit all our shares. The future of our business will be in his hands. I can't risk adopting a child from unknown parents. My son-in-law is an intelligent man full of qualities, healthy, lucid. That's why I selected a woman like you. I am sure that you will produce a being capable of shouldering this responsibility.

Marina stood up, worried:

- Even so, I don't think it will work out. I can't do it. It's against my principles.

- You are different from the girls we interviewed. You don't dream of getting married and giving up everything for your husband, like most of them. You will make a sacrifice for a few months, and then you will have everything you want for the rest of your life. I will give you a million dollars whatever the outcome of our contract. It is a good deal for you, and it would be helping us a lot.

- You said your daughter has agreed. And your son-in-law? Does he know?

- Yes. He was reluctant, but finally agreed to cooperate.

- Still, it seems impossible.

- You don't have to answer me now. Go home, think it over. I'll give you two days to decide. During the time you are on recess, while you wait for the child to be born, you will be in a beautiful house, with all the comforts, you will have a large allowance to spend on whatever you want. Do you drive a car?

- I have my license, but I don't have a car.

- You'll get one in your name as soon as you agree.

Adele came up to Marina and held her tightly in her arms. Looking into her eyes, she said in an emotional voice:

- Please! This is a personal favour for which I will be grateful for the rest of my life. Promise you'll look at my problem with sympathy.

Marina felt her body tremble. The magnetism of this woman was almost irresistible. She began to understand why she held that position and was so famous.

- Certainly. Your proposal is tempting, but I need to think about it. I don't think I am up to what you are asking of me. How do you intend to make them believe that the child is your daughter's legitimate son?

- It's easy. She'll wear a fake belly. As time goes by, she'll make her belly bigger. No one will suspect. When the time approaches, she'll go wherever you are. When the baby is born, she will pick him up and return with him. As for the doctors, it is easy to invent a trip abroad, to see a specialist. Don't worry about that, it will be easy. I have everything planned. Your task will be to go to the agreed place, get to know Henrique and stay there until the birth. Then you will be free to continue your life.

- That sounds crazy to me. It will never work! I can't do something like that.

- Don't get ahead of yourself. Although it involves your personal life, this is a business deal, after which, once the parties are satisfied, everything will go back to normal. If you refuse, you'll regret it, I'm sure.

Marina felt dazed. She needed to breathe. She decided to leave and came back:

- All right, I'll think about it.

- Remember: you promised. Not a word to anyone.

- You can trust me. This is a story my family can never know. Take care, ma'am.

- See you in two days. I'll be waiting.

Marina left quickly. Once outside, she took a deep breath. That couldn't be true. It sounded like a story from a movie. Adele was crazy. She would never agree. To have a relationship with a married man, with his wife's consent, to bear his child, was the stuff of psychologically ill people. She wouldn't even have to wait for the two days to refuse.

She decided to go home. She had no head for work. Adele's words, her delicate perfume, her emotional gaze, could not leave her memory.

In spite of the unusual, the proposal was tempting – a million dollars! Even if she got a good job, if she worked hard, it would be impossible to get so much in such a short time.

She did not want to get married. A child! How would she feel? She shrugged. He wouldn't be hers. He would have another family, but he would certainly be very rich. He would live a good life, maybe better than she could offer him, if he really was hers.

Adele had made it clear that it was all just good business, win-win. She had also said that she would be grateful to her for the rest of her life.

Adele was a strong woman; she knew what she wanted. In business, you had to dare, and that plan was a daring one. It might not be a boy, but still, she wanted to try.

Adele was so determined, so sure of herself, that Marina began to think there were odds that the plan would work out. If it was a boy, she would have solved her problems. There was a fifty per cent chance.

It had been two months since Adele had been looking very carefully for the woman to bear her grandchild. If she refused, surely another would accept. It was a lot of money at stake.

Marina remembered the meticulous interviews she had conducted. To have been chosen for this partnership made her proud. It was a case of trust. But she couldn't accept it.

She decided to forget the matter. It was already decided. Two days later, when she saw Adele again, she would definitely say "no". She must have other candidates; she would soon find a replacement.

She felt hungry and remembered that she had not eaten lunch. She looked at the clock: it was past seven. She took a shower and went to the kitchen to prepare something to eat. Then took a book, stretched out on the sofa and tried to read. But Adele's face, her living room, her look, her words came back to her mind, and she couldn't understand what she was reading.

It was useless to try to read. She had to admit that Adele's proposal had messed with her head.

A million dollars... What would she do with that much money? She would buy a nice flat and open a law office. It would be a nice, beautiful place, different from the place where she worked. Modern furniture, pictures on the walls, flowers. A friendly, nicely dressed, pretty receptionist who knew how to welcome clients. An efficient and dedicated secretary, a young man for the street services.

She would buy a good house for her mother. She would no longer let her sew on demand. Maybe she would bring her family to live in São Paulo. In this case, instead of a flat, she would buy a good house, in a middle-class neighbourhood, where Cicero could have access to a good school. That would be wonderful!

Suddenly Marina remembered that she had decided not to accept the offer. A doubt began to bother her: would it be fair to refuse and let her mother continue sewing, and let her brother have his horizons limited, without attending a university?

Nevertheless, she did not feel inclined to accept. In two days, she would say "no" to Adele. Let her find someone else.

Marina thought that, having decided the matter, she could rest, but she was wrong. That night, she had trouble sleeping. And when she did, she had a terrible nightmare. Because she slept badly, she woke up late the next morning.

When she entered the office, Dr. Olavo was already impatiently waiting for her.

- What happened to you? I've been waiting for half an hour. I have an important hearing this afternoon, I came early to better study the details of the case, and you didn't show up.

- You could have picked up the case notes from the file. They're up-to-date.

- I don't like to go through the file. Then it's your job. You should be here on time. I'm never this early. You'll see that you're late every day.

He was being rude, and Marina tried to control herself. She had always fulfilled her obligations, worked overtime, took her files home, and now he was complaining that she was half an hour late. It was unfair, and she barely contained her indignation.

She took a deep breath, picked up her notes from the file, and returned to Dr. Olavo's room. He picked up the documents, skimmed through them, then said:

- I recall that I had a statement made last week that should be attached to the file. It seems that you didn't.

- Of course, I did, doctor.

- Well, it's not here.

Marina picked up the documents, leafed through them and handed them back, saying:

- Here it is, doctor.

- Ah well... You don't file in order. That's why I couldn't find it.

- Is there anything else you need, doctor?

- Shouldn't you have summarized the arrangements and given an opinion?

- It was not possible, because yesterday this folder was not in the file. I was informed that Dr. Mario had picked it up to study it. He will accompany you to the hearing.

- Because of that, I will have to read the whole text.

Marina left the room in a rage. It seemed as if she was seeing Dr. Olavo for the first time. She was tired and not in the mood to work. She looked for her secretary and said:

- I'm not feeling well. I'm going home.

- In that case, you should go to the doctor.

- I have a headache. If it doesn't get better, I'll go anyway. Tell Dr. Olavo, please.

Without waiting for an answer, she left. She needed to think better. Suddenly, that office seemed ugly, sad, unpleasant. The people who worked there were mediocre. That place had no future.

She remembered Adele's office and sighed. Everything there was beautiful. It would be good to work in a place like that, amid so many beautiful and tasteful things.

She walked around the city, looking at shop windows, trying to forget her worries, but she couldn't. When she was tired, she had a snack, then she went into the cinema. The movie was good, but she dozed off, because she was very sleepy.

She left the cinema and went home. She entered the flat, looked around, and thought: why did everything seem different to her? Even that flat, which she had rented as a conquest, now seemed small, ugly, sad.

She turned on the radio, sat down and tried to read. But she felt restless, agitated, she couldn't stop thinking about Adele. She went to bed and finally managed to sleep. She was very tired.

The next morning, it was past ten o'clock when Dr. Olavo arrived at the office. He called Marina, handed her a folder with some recommendations, and then asked for information about a client. Marina didn't remember the case, to which Dr. Olavo said:

- I don't know what is happening to you. You are inattentive, without interest. Yesterday you left me in the lurch without any more. I would like you to explain yourself.

- I am sorry, doctor. Yesterday I wasn't well, but today I got better.

- It doesn't seem like. You used to be active, now you don't pay enough attention to your work.

Marina could not contain herself:

- That's not true. Since I joined here, I have made an effort to attend to everything you need, working overtime, taking files home. Yesterday, just because I had a bad night and was half an hour late, you treated me badly.

- If you want to earn money in your profession, you need to become a good professional. Thanks to us, you have this chance, but of course we have our conditions.

- By the way, doctor, since I got my degree, you have been promising me small claims, but nothing so far.

- It's just that you are not ready yet.

- In that case, why do all the cases in this office go through me, have my opinion and most of the time you do what I say?

- What is this? Are you insinuating that we are taking advantage of you? How absurd! That's what you get for helping others. Do me a favour!

Marina's face flushed with indignation:

- You're the one saying that. I only meant that I am already prepared to work for myself.

- In that case, you can go. You are fired!

Marina left and still heard Dr. Olavo say to his secretary:

- I want to see where she's going to hit. I'm sure she'll come back running to apologize. I'll only accept if it's on my terms.

Marina gathered her belongings and left. Her head hurt. She went into a coffee shop and asked for some water. She had a bad taste in her mouth.

What was happening? Why were things suddenly not working well? She needed to think and cool down. Of one thing, she was sure: she would not return to Dr. Olavo's office. His last words were still ringing in his ears. She would show him that she didn't need them to live. She had prepared herself, studied hard, dedicated herself, knew that she had a good performance.

She bought the newspaper and went home. Maybe she should look for another job, at least until she could save money to open her own office.

She ate a snack, then sat down on the sofa and started reading the newspaper. She couldn't find anything interesting. There were two lawyers looking for a girl to do general office work. The salary was insignificant and would not be enough to pay for her expenses. After all, she had graduated, she was competent.

The telephone rang. Marina answered: a woman's voice asked:

- Are you Ms. Marina?

- Yes.

- This is Marcia, Dr. Adele's secretary. I'm calling to confirm your appointment with her, tomorrow at ten o'clock.

Marina shivered. She had to go.

- You can make an appointment. I'll be there.

She thanked her and hung up. Then she let herself fall back in her chair, thinking. She had thought of saying "no", but now, in the situation in which she found herself, perhaps she should have a closer look at that proposal.

She remembered Adele's words:

- Time passes quickly. Soon you will be free, with a good financial situation, and I will be grateful to you for the rest of my life.

Despite this, she didn't have the courage to accept. It seemed to her that she was prostituting herself, selling her body. Adele had made a point of saying that it was just a business. Looking at it this way, one could say it was an excellent business.

For the rest of the day, Marina couldn't think of anything else. At night, she went to bed late. Her body ached, as if she had been carrying stones all day.

She remembered her mother's words:

- When you have a problem, and you don't know what to do, think of God, put it in his hands. Everything will work out.

How long had it been since she had prayed? Not that she was a non-believer, but most of the time she was so involved with work that she forgot to pray.

She took a deep breath and felt she needed help. Her head was confused. She mumbled a prayer, asking for clarity to decide what was best. Finally, she fell asleep.

She dreamed that she was walking in a very flowery and fragrant garden. She met a woman with a pleasant physiognomy. She was sure he knew her.

- My dearest! It's time to do what you promised me. Don't forget what we agreed.

- I'm confused. I don't remember anything.

- I will revive your memory.

They talked, and finally the woman said:

- Now you must go. Remember that you must be guided only by the universal laws. Forget the things of the world. Cooperating with life is a blessed work.

She repeated these words several times, and Marina woke up listening to this sentence. The day had begun to dawn. She sat up in bed, feeling a pleasant sensation in her chest. She remembered.

She remembered perfectly the woman's face, her last words. Where did she know her from?

She tried hard to remember the conversation they had had, but she couldn't. That dream was not like the others. Perhaps it was an answer to her prayers.

Suddenly, she remembered the nap she had taken in Dr. Mauro's waiting room. She had dreamed about the same woman.

This discovery moved her. Apparently, she wanted Marina to accept Adele's proposal. Wouldn't that be nonsense?

To turn maternity, sex, into a business at the service of a family's ambition?

- Forget the things of the world. Cooperating with life is blessed work.

Perhaps she was wrong. God could not be in favour of a business like that. Marina felt confused, unsure. She was still not sure of anything.

Hours later, as agreed, she entered Adele's office. The businesswoman hugged her, made her sit down on a sofa beside her and asked:

- And then? Are you going to do what I asked you?

- I was ready to refuse, however, some things happened.

- You are willing to accept!

- I would like to know a few more details.

- You will have to dedicate yourself totally to the enterprise. No one will be able to know where you are during the process. For now, that is all I can say. I have been assured that you will have our full support. Our project will be a success! So, you accept?

- Yes. I accept.

- I'm sure you won't regret it.

Adele hugged her happily and continued:

- From now on, you'll be under my care. I'll take care of everything personally. Let's formalize our agreement.

She left and then returned, handing her some papers.

- Here is the contract. Read and sign it.

Marina read it, and there was no mention of the type of service she was to provide. It was a simple employment contract in which she committed to work full time for one year, get a new car and during this time have all expenses paid. At the end of the term, she would have a prize in national currency equivalent to one million dollars.

Marina's hand trembled a little as she signed. Adele picked up the contract, handed her back a copy and considered:

- You have until tomorrow to quit your job and say goodbye to your family. A sudden business trip, no further details. The day after tomorrow, at ten o'clock, I'll come to your house to pick you up.

- One day is not enough time to prepare everything.

- It's more than enough.

She went to her desk, opened a drawer, picked up an envelope and handed it to her:

- Spend what you need. I'll pick you up tomorrow at ten.

Marina left the office wondering how to solve everything in such a short time. But it was done. Now there was no turning back. She still didn't know if she had made the right decision. Time would show her.

CHAPTER 3

Marina looked around excitedly. It was a few minutes to ten o'clock and she already had everything ready.

The day before, she had been in Dr. Olavo's office to receive what was due to her, which was easy, since she had no work contract nor was a duly registered employee. Dr. Olavo's look of surprise gave her a sense of pleasure. He told her that he had received a very advantageous job offer and would have to travel immediately. He asked who the offer had come from, and she gave him a fictitious name.

With the owner of the flat, Marina had to negotiate the breach of contract. Finally, she sent her furniture to a storage room, paying a year's rent in advance. The money Adele had given her for these expenses was more than enough.

As a last measure, the young woman called her mother and told her that she was going abroad to work, but that she would send money every month and would always call.

The telephone rang. It was Adele:

- Marina, I'll be there in five minutes. Wait at the door.

The girl went down, handed the key to the doorman and waited. The car stopped, and she saw that Adele was driving. The businesswoman pressed a button and the boot opened. Marina put her luggage in it and sat down beside Adele.

Her heart was beating fast. A thousand questions crossed her mind, but she only asked:

- Where are we going?

- To a nice, comfortable place where you'll stay all the time.

Adele didn't want to give any details. Secrecy was part of the game. For Marina, however, the place didn't matter, nor the people with whom she would associate. When it was all over, she would like to forget this unusual and uncomfortable episode.

The pleasant side was thinking about the comfort she could give her family. The rest didn't matter.

They travelled a few hours and stopped for lunch. They were in the countryside of São Paulo. Adele was a pleasant company. They talked about several subjects, and Marina gradually felt more at ease.

After lunch, they drove for another hour, and Adele left the highway and took a side road. Finally, they stopped in front of a huge wooden gate. Adele got down and Marina, seeing that she was about to open it, helped her and waited for her to pass the car to close it.

They got back into the car and drove for about three kilometres, until the car stopped in front of a graceful cottage, surrounded by leafy trees and flowerbeds. A woman appeared at the door and, seeing them, immediately hurried to greet them.

- Marina, this is Celia, someone I trust. She will look after you while you stay here.

She was a woman of about fifty, mulatto, with her hair pulled back in a bun at the nape of her neck, round face, thick lips and lively eyes. Her impeccable clothes revealed caprice and efficiency. Marina liked her. She greeted her kindly.

They went inside and Marina loved what she saw. It was a spacious house, furnished with taste and comfort. There were fresh flowers in the vases, an office with a good library, three luxurious suites, two living rooms and a dining room and other dependencies.

- This house is part of a farm belonging to my family, Adele explained. - I want you to check everything and tell me if you need anything else.

- It's better than I expected.

- I'm going to settle into the main house, which is behind the park on the other side of the lake.

- I'd like to talk to you, find out more details about how everything will go.

Adele smiled.

- Let's rest for a while. We'll talk tonight. Don't worry, you'll be well guided.

She left and Marina looked around. The place was cozy and beautiful. Celia appeared in the room and said:

- You must be tired. I have prepared you a bath with soothing herbs. Would you like something to eat or drink first?

- Thank you, Celia. I'm not hungry.

- I want you to tell me how you like me to pack your things. I've arranged a menu: nutritious, healthy food. It's in the library on the desk. It's just a starting point. Whatever you don't approve, we will change.

Marina noticed that she had opened her suitcases, sorted her clothes and put them on the bed. Celia suggested where she thought it would be best to store each item, and Marina readily agreed.

Then the young woman picked up a light robe and went to the bathroom. The bathtub was full and there was a delicate wild perfume in the air. On a console beside the tub were several jars, which Marina examined with delight.

She immediately undressed, got into the tub and stretched out with delight. She noticed that there were several little bags in the water. She picked one up and smelled it. It was from them that the perfume came. She noticed that they were delicately tied so that the herbs didn't spread.

As she surrendered to the pleasure of the moment, Marina wondered how everything was going to happen. She shuddered at the thought that she would have to give herself to a man she didn't know and who belonged to another woman.

This thought made her concerned and worried. What would he think about her? If he had agreed to the project, it wouldn't be fair for him to criticise her for agreeing to it. But, deep down, he would certainly imagine that she was a gold-digger, that she had done everything for money.

In fact, that money represented her financial independence. Even more than that: the possibility of Cicero studying and her mother stopping working. It was not for the money itself, but for the happiness that it would bring to her family.

She concluded that it did not matter what Adele's son-in-law or her daughter thought of her. After all, she had no intention of ever seeing them again. She would erase this phase of her life. After all, a year would go by quickly. Meanwhile, she would try to study hard, because she intended to continue her career, this time on her own.

After the bath, she would go to the library to check the books and ask for the ones she wanted to read. That way she would make more use of the time.

After her bath, she got dressed and went to the library. Her tiredness had disappeared, and she was too excited to try to sleep. On the table, besides the folder with the menu, there was an index indicating the books that were capriciously arranged on the bookshelf that took up two whole walls of the room.

Marina was fascinated. There were books on several subjects, and she became so interested that she didn't even notice that the day was getting dark.

Celia came in with a tray, saying:

- I brought you a papaya juice with orange and some bread. It's very hot and you haven't had anything to drink.

- Thank you.

Marina picked up the glass that Celia offered her and drank it with pleasure. It was delicious.

- Have some bread, it's fresh.

The young woman tasted it with satisfaction.

- I came to find out what you want for dinner.

- After this snack, I won't want any dinner.

- Not at all! You must eat well. I'll prepare a light and nutritious meal.

Celia left and Marina smiled happily. After all, everything was going better than she had imagined. She was going to get used to it and miss it when it was over.

After dinner, Marina went back to the library. She settled down to read, but the door opened and Adele appeared. She approached, saying:

- We need to talk. I'm leaving early tomorrow morning. We have to work out the details.

- Go ahead.

Adele sat down in an armchair and continued:

- Tomorrow morning a doctor will come to examine you. He lives in the nearest town and, although he's from the countryside, he's an excellent obstetrician. I told him that you are my niece, your husband works in Sao Paulo and will soon have to do an internship abroad. That is why you are under my care. You really want a child, but after five years of marriage you haven't had one.

Seeing that Marina was listening carefully, Adele continued:

- On my recommendation, he was chosen to examine you. Before going abroad, your husband will come here to see you. I would like him to have a diagnosis by then.

- That's fine. What will happen then?

- Dr. Gilberto will examine you and tell you what your fertile days are. We'll schedule my son-in-law's visit at the right time.

Marina sighed uneasily and Adele returned:

- Don't worry or be embarrassed. On that day, me, my daughter and my son-in-law will come to the farm. We'll do everything in such a way that you won't have to face them. I assure you that Henrique is a healthy, pleasant man and he will treat you with extreme politeness.

- I won't deny that I am nervous, but I will know how to control myself.

- I don't know if we'll make it immediately. But we will try.

Adele got up.

- I am going to bed, as I plan to get up early. You have my phone numbers; you can call me whenever you need me. Apart from the three of us, only Celia knows the truth. You can trust her. She's a good person and will do anything to make your life more pleasant.

After she left, Marina tried to read, but she couldn't. At the thought that she would have this meeting soon, she felt uneasy. She had never allowed any man to enter her intimacy. Now she would have to allow a stranger to do so.

She wished time would pass quickly, and she would soon be free of any commitments and go back to minding her own business. She tried to calm herself down. She felt that if she got too anxious it would be worse.

That night, she had trouble sleeping. Adele's words kept running through her mind. When she fell asleep, she dreamt again about the same woman who had asked her to accept the job.

Marina was walking along a road when she appeared, hugged her and said sweetly:

- Calm down. Calm down. You're not doing anything wrong. One day you will know the whole truth and you will feel happy for having accepted this commitment. I bless you for this and promise to always help you. Don't forget that I love you very much.

All Marina's concerns disappeared. A pleasant emotion welled up in her heart and she was overcome with joy. She stirred in bed and fell into a restful sleep.

She awoke the next morning rested and content. While she was having breakfast, Celia warned her:

- Dr. Gilberto will come to examine you today at ten o'clock.

- I'll be waiting.

- Mrs. Adele asked me to tell you that she will send your car in two or three days. It will be under your name, with all the papers in order.

- Thank you.

After breakfast, Marina went out for a walk. The day was beautiful, and she breathed with pleasure the pure and pleasant air.

She remembered that Adele had told her that she would give her a car, but had asked her not to go beyond the nearest town while the contract was in place, to avoid meeting someone she knew.

She walked for half an hour admiring the beauty of the place. As she was entering the house, a car stopped in front of the gate and a tall, middle-aged man carrying a suitcase got out.

Marina realized that it was the doctor. He opened the gate and, seeing her standing on the porch, he smiled. He was light brown, with brown eyes and hair, tall and elegant.

He approached her and spread a smile on his face.

- You must be Adele's niece.

- I am. And you must be Dr. Gilberto.

- That's right.

Marina invited him in. She liked his simple manner, his honest look and friendly smile.

He examined her, filled out a form with her data and Marina took the opportunity to ask for the information Adele wanted. She wrote everything down. At the end, he said:

- You look very healthy to me. Married for five years. You've never been pregnant?

- No.

- Has your husband had the necessary tests to find out if he is fertile?

- Yes. There's nothing wrong with him or me. We just haven't been able to have a child yet.

- At first glance, I don't notice anything on you. I would like you to come to my office tomorrow for a closer examination. We'll do a touch test to see if everything is in order.

Marina shifted in her chair. The medical examination would ruin the whole plan, since she had never had sex. She tried to buy herself some time:

- Tomorrow won't be possible. Some friends were supposed to pick me up for a little trip. But as soon as I get home, I'll look for you to make the appointment.

After he left, Marina ran towards Celia.

- I need to talk to Adele. Is she in her office?

- I think so. Is something wrong?

- The doctor wants to examine me at the office. I can't have that examination.

- Why not?

- Because he'll realize, I've never had sex.

Celia looked at her surprised.

- In that case, I really should talk to her.

Marina called and soon Adele answered. When she heard the situation, she wanted to know when her fertile period would be. Marina informed her and she answered again:

- There are ten days left. Keep in touch during this time. You said April 2nd to the 4th. We will be there on the 2nd. Then we'll talk about the details.

Marina's heart quickened its beats and she struggled to control herself.

- Don't worry, Marina. We'll work something out. He won't find out.

From that moment on, Marina counted the days, wondering how Adele was going to plan such a delicate matter. She felt anxious, but at the same time, she wanted everything to happen as soon as possible so that she could be rid of all that worry.

On April 2nd, Marina was having lunch when Celia said:

- Adele arrived an hour ago. Soon she will come to see you.

Marina held Celia's hand as if asking for protection.

- I feels distressed.

Celia ran her hand through her hair gently.

- I know. But soon you'll see there's nothing to be afraid of. I assure you that everything will be done discreetly and gently.

Marina sighed and Celia continued:

- When the time comes, I'll prepare some refreshments. Remember, you need to stay calm.

- Do you think once will be enough?

- Maybe not. What I can say is that you are dealing with classy, gentle and kind people. There's nothing to be afraid of.

It was after two when Adele arrived and they went to the office to talk. Noticing Marina's nervousness, she said calmly:

- This is the most delicate part of the process. Maria Eugenia and Henrique came with me.

- Did she come too? Won't it be too difficult for her?

- No. She is prepared. She knows it's necessary and that you're a stranger to Henrique. Let's go to the details. Pay attention. Tonight, at nine o'clock, go to bed. Leave the room dark, but don't lock the door. Try to rest; you can sleep if you want. But at a certain hour, Henrique will come in, do his part and go away. You don't have to say anything. Tomorrow and the day after he will see you again in the same condition. I think three times will be enough.

Marina sighed and wriggled in her chair. Adele continued:

- Don't worry about Maria Eugenia. Both she and Henrique are very grateful for your participation. If everything goes as we hope, he will not come to see you again.

- I hope all this isn't in vain.

- It won't be. You're a healthy woman. We just have to hope it's a boy.

- I admire your courage in taking risks.

- When you want something badly enough, you have to dare and exhaust every resource. Our agreement is the last step, and I am sure that we will win.

After she left, Marina tried to calm her anxiety. After all, this was a business deal that would enable her to improve her life and that of her family.

That day was hard to pass, but finally it got dark. At eight thirty, Celia went to look for her.

- It's almost time. I've come to help you get ready. To begin with, a bath with relaxing flowers.

Inside the bathtub, feeling the delicate scent of flowers, Marina began to relax. When she came out, Celia put her on a stretcher and massaged her body with perfumed oil.

Marina felt light-headed and all her nervousness disappeared. Celia dressed her in a silk nightgown and held out a glass of juice.

- Drink up. You will feel fine. Lie down and don't worry about anything. Get some sleep. He will come later.

Marina snuggled into the soft bed. She was peaceful. Celia turned off the lamp and went out, closing the door.

Marina felt sleepy and felt a soft warmth in her body. She soon fell asleep.

She woke up feeling a pleasant perfume and a hand caressing her body. She shivered and murmured:

- What is it?

- I'm sorry. I thought you were awake.

Marina remembered everything and didn't answer. Slowly he began to caress her. She closed her eyes, didn't answer. Her heart quickened its beats and intimately she wished it would all end quickly.

Slowly she went from indifference to pleasure. As he kissed and caressed her, Marina reciprocated by pressing him against her body, wanting to extend the thrill.

When he finished, he stretched out beside her in silence. She could still feel the force of the emotions running through her mind. Minutes later, he began to caress her again and again, Marina could not control her emotion.

When he finished, Henrique held her hand, gently brought it to his lips and said:

- Thank you.

He stood up, quickly dressed and left. Marina stood there, still absorbed in the memory of moments before, perplexed by her own reaction. Her body was sore, but she felt relaxed, calm, and soon fell asleep.

The next morning, Celia served her coffee in silence. It was as if nothing had happened. Marina tried to forget, but those moments kept coming back and she wondered. She couldn't be so libidinous as to feel pleasure in a relationship with a stranger.

It was just a business appointment, and she couldn't let herself get involved like that. She tried to react. She picked up a book and started reading, but she couldn't pay attention to the text.

The day went quietly. Adele didn't show up and Marina appreciated her discretion. She didn't feel like talking about that experience, especially with Adele.

After dinner, Celia came to her:

- 'It's time to get ready. He will come again tonight.

Marina looked at her seriously and asked:

- Do you think it's necessary?

- That was the arrangement. Time is precious and we can't waste it. You can't go back now.

- I will keep to the contract to the letter. Don't worry.

After the preparations, Marina went to bed, but she couldn't sleep. She felt restless. She had always been a controlled person, used to planning her projects, disciplined.

She had gotten involved in this commitment because of the money that would improve her life and her family's conditions. As Adele had insisted, it was a business like any other.

So why had she become so emotionally involved? Why, even though she was feeling fragile, did those moments never faded from her mind? She didn't like to get out of control.

She preferred that he didn't come back, but at the same time, thinking that soon he would be caressing her, something disturbed her, making her shiver.

When he arrived, Marina pretended to be asleep. But as soon as he lay on her side and held her in his arms, she silently surrendered.

After he was gone, Marina felt relaxed and decided not to think about anything else. There was no use in torturing herself. Soon everything would be over and they would never see each other again. Everything would go on as it had always been. She turned to the side and soon fell asleep.

The following night, when Henrique entered the room, she was calmer. Her moments with him did not leave her memory, but she had decided not to torment herself for it. On the contrary: it had been better than she had expected, which had made it less difficult to fulfil the deal.

So, when he embraced her, she responded with pleasure. When he left, Marina felt she would never forget that night's encounter.

The next day, when she woke up, she found a velvet box on the bedside table and an envelope. She opened it and found a beautiful emerald ring.

With trembling hands, she took a card from the envelope and read:

I will never forget the moments we lived. Thank you. I wish you happiness.

It was not signed.

Marina tried the ring thoughtfully. If everything turned out as they wished, they would never have to meet again.

At the coffee table, Celia said:

- They went back to São Paulo early this morning. Adele asked me to let you know.

- Thank you.

Marina felt a certain sadness. Suddenly, she had the feeling that time was running out.

- You seem to be sad. Is everything alright?

- Yes. I was just thinking that time is going to be hard to pass.

Celia laughed cheerfully.

- Not at all! A pregnancy is a wonderful adventure. Every day is special. You'll see.

- Do you think I'm pregnant already?

- It's too soon to tell. But that's what you came for, isn't it?

- Of course, it is.

- Afterwards, you don't have to stay locked up here. The city's not far and your car's in the garage.

- I'd better not. I don't know anyone. Besides, I don't want strangers snooping around our lives.

- Not at all. Don't forget you're Adele's niece, whose husband is abroad on an important course, and she's undertaken to look after you until he returns. I know some very nice, discreet, polite people who will be very happy to enjoy your friendship.

- I don't know...

- For your child to be healthy and happy, during your pregnancy you have to take care of yourself, lead a happy life.

- That's right. It will be as you wish. I don't know if I am good enough to play that role.

Celia smiled:

- You will tell your story so many times that you will end up believing it and being very creative. I'm sure you will.

Marina smiled. Looking at it this way, maybe everything would be more pleasant. Her job was to collaborate so that the plan would work. They believed so much in this possibility that she no longer felt she had the right to doubt.

CHAPTER 4

During the following month, Adele did not return to the farm, but called for news and recommendations. As planned, two days after her arrival, Marina wrote a letter to her mother, saying she had a good trip and sending her the London address Adele had given her. Then she gave the letter to Adele, who would put it in another envelope and send it to a person she trusted in the country. This person would post the letter as if Marina was living there. When she got a reply, the same person would send it to Adele.

Marina would get up early. After breakfast, she would go for a walk in the neighbourhood. Sometimes she would sit on the grass to rest, listening to the birds twittering, looking at the blue sky, almost cloudless, inhaling the pleasant, light air and letting herself be absorbed in contemplating the beauty of the landscape.

When she returned home, Celia was already waiting for her with a fruit juice and she went to sit in the library, pleasantly immersed in reading.

The days went by calmly and, if it was not for the memories of the nights that Henrique had visited her, she would have forgotten what she was doing there.

One afternoon, while Marina was lying on the sofa reading, Adele entered the library. The young woman stood up happily:

- Adele! How nice of you to come!

Adele hugged her affectionately and after the greetings said:

- I couldn't bear the anxiety. I came to find out how you are.

-Well.

- It's almost two months since he came to see you. So, what's up? Celia told me you might be pregnant.

Marina blushed a little and answered:

- Well... I don't know. I don't know, I don't feel anything. But my period didn't come.

Adele hugged her happily.

- Let's take the test. I brought everything we need.

She called Celia, they went to the room and did the test.

- The result will take a while. Let's go to the pantry. I prepared a snack, so the time will pass faster.

Both Adele and Marina didn't want to eat anything. They just had their juice.

- I brought you a letter, said Adele, taking an envelope from her bag and handing it to Marina. - It arrived yesterday.

- That's great! I was eager for news. I've never gone so long without hearing from them.

- Make yourself at home. While you read, I'll sort some things out with Celia.

Marina, overcome with emotion, read the letter in which her mother spoke of how much they missed her and how proud they both were that she was abroad, earning so well. She thanked them for the money she had sent them. She said she wouldn't spend it all.

Marina smiled, but felt a twinge of remorse for deceiving them. She had never lied to them, but she had promised them secrecy and would keep her vow. The matter was very serious, and she could not jeopardize the success of the enterprise.

She put the letter away. Hearing Adele's voice talking to Celia in the next room, Marina returned to the library to continue reading. Although the book was interesting, she couldn't pay attention to what she was reading.

Many things depended on that test, and she couldn't think of anything else. If she wasn't pregnant, Henrique would visit her again. As she thought about it, she felt her heart beat faster. She would prefer him not to come back. The less intimacy with him, the better.

Adele entered the room and Marina could not contain herself:

- 'So?

- We did it. The test was positive!

Marina couldn't control her emotion:

- Does that mean I'm pregnant?

- Yes. Now all we can do is hope it's a boy.

Marina put her hand to her chest worriedly.

- And if it isn't?

-I'll keep our contract. I'll register the baby as Maria Eugenia 's daughter. She'll raise her with all her affection.

- In that case, you won't get what you want.

- The fact that Maria Eugenia has a daughter shows that she can still have a boy. Maybe I can make a deal with my brother-in-law. But for now, I don't want to think about it. I'm sure it will be a boy. You'll have to take care of yourself. You'll have to see Dr. Gilberto.

- I will.

- You will go to him and tell him that your husband stayed a few days here before going abroad. If he asks, tell him it was between 2nd and 4th April. That way he will have all the elements he needs to take care of you. It will just be routine, both you and Henrique are healthy. I believe your pregnancy will go smoothly.

- That's ok. I'll do as you ask.

- It will be good if Celia goes along to hear all the recommendations and take good care of you both. I'm thrilled. My grandson will be a beautiful boy and he will have all our love!

- I'm thrilled too. I never thought I would be a mother!

- Even though you are giving birth to a son, you must react and not feel like a mother, since you will have to be separated from him at the time of his birth. Remember that the child will be Henri and Maria Eugenia's. I don't want you to suffer for having to be separated from him. Get used to the idea that he doesn't belong to you.

- Of course. I know perfectly well what to do and I will fulfil all the clauses of our contract. Don't worry.

After she left, Marina thought about her words and understood that Adele was right. She couldn't get attached to the baby. He wouldn't be hers. He would have other parents, who would raise him, love him, give him everything. He would be rich and happy.

She felt a touch of sadness, but she reacted. It was a business that would give her financial independence and the conditions to improve her family's life. From then on, she would do everything to forget that she was expecting a child.

Although she had decided to do so, it was not as easy as she had thought. In the days that followed, she went with Celia to the doctor, who was happy to tell her that she had finally managed to get pregnant.

He asked her for the usual tests and established a healthy routine, which Marina tried to follow to the letter. As much as she wanted to forget about the baby, it was the subject of every moment, whether it was during her periodic visits to the doctor or the walks she had to take every day to keep in shape.

Celia introduced her to some people, but, although they were nice, Marina did not feel like becoming closer friends.

However, when she met Isaura, it was different. Tall, dark, with a high forehead, bright eyes, wavy brown hair, she had two dimples on her cheeks when she smiled. She had been widowed for five years and was about forty. Her husband had been mayor of Bauru and died in a car accident.

Isaura was much loved in the city for her social work when her husband was mayor. After his death, even without holding any office, she continued working tirelessly for the community. They did not have any children, and this was the way she found to keep herself busy.

Marina liked her at first sight. However, at first, she did not try to strengthen their friendship. One day Celia said:

- I invited Isaura to have lunch with us today. I know you like her.

- In fact, I like her. But I'm not sure it was a good idea.

- Why? You need to distract yourself. You haven't accepted any of our friends' invitations.

- I'm in a special moment. People are going to ask me about my life. I won't be able to talk. I'll have to make up a story. That doesn't seem right. I'd rather go on like this. Time will go by and soon everything will be over and my life will go back to normal.

- In any case, Isaura will come and you will tell her the same story you told Dr. Gilberto, if necessary. She is a discreet and delicate person. She won't ask you anything.

Isaura arrived punctually at noon and Marina received her with affection. The conversation flowed naturally. The visitor was a cultured person, with a charisma that made her visit very pleasant. She didn't ask any personal questions.

Celia treated her with deference, and the three of them went through the gardens around the house, as well as the orchard. Celia made a point of showing her the herb beds and the small room next to the house, where she did her phytotherapy studies.

It was a small laboratory that Marina had never seen before and that Isaura knew very well. Celia showed her several of her notes and experiments, and Isaura guided her in a safe manner, revealing a wide knowledge of the subject.

It was after four o'clock when Isaura said goodbye, inviting Marina to a tea party at her house on Saturday.

After she left, Celia said:

- How nice that she came and approved my tests!

- She seems to know a lot about the subject.

- She has a degree in Psychology and Biology and she's also a physiotherapist. You must get to know the work she has been doing. Dr. Gilberto has been helping her. Together they have been able to assist the settlers in the surroundings, distributing medications. Besides the fact that people are poor and cannot afford expensive medications, the medical care in these farms is precarious. When she was First Lady, Isaura felt the need to do this work. It was so successful that she never stopped. People come from far away in search of treatment. Dr Gilberto treats, prescribes prescriptions and she provides the medications.

- She is an extraordinary woman. I felt it from the moment I saw her.

- That's right. I have always been attracted to herbal treatment. Nature is so rich and perfect; I believe that through it there is cure for all diseases. What is lacking is for scientists to dedicate themselves to this study.

- As far as I know, there are several of them studying.

- Only a few.

- If there are so many results, why don't they intensify their research?

- I discovered that to work with herbs one has to take care of the emotional part of the patient, go beyond the physical problems, and then gather the necessary herbs for their cure. The countryside people, intuitively, know about that.

- My grandmother understood a lot about herbs. When someone in the family didn't feel well, she always had a special tea, which, if it didn't cure immediately, relieved a lot.

- Maybe she prayed while preparing it.

- What do you mean?

- It's an old tradition of those who live in the countryside. Besides the care with which they prepare the tea, making the patient feel that they are loved, they pray over it to add healing energies.

- Do you think it works?

- Sometimes it does. I am still not sure why. I have seen many things in this world. I truly believe that life has laws that take care of everything and everyone in their own way. Whoever manages to know these laws and apply them in his life will be able to live better.

- I would like to know more. I think I will accept the invitation for tea at Isaura's house.

On Saturday, at the agreed time, Marina went with Celia to visit her friend. She lived in an old house, surrounded by a well-kept garden. Isaura received them with joy.

Tea was served in the garden bower and the conversation flowed pleasantly. Marina showed interest in her work, and Isaura took them to the place where she planted her herbs, talking about some of them and their uses.

Then she took them to the laboratory where she produced the medicines. A couple was working among the bottles and infusions. In the next room there were shelves full of bottles ready to be dispensed.

Isaura explained how the service worked. Besides the couple, who took care of the preparation of the medications, a girl attended to the prescriptions.

- Today she has already left - said Isaura. - The service is until one. I assist people, talk to them. Depending on the case, I make an appointment with Dr. Gilberto. It is not always necessary. There are chronic or simple cases that I give the medication myself. He assists them on the basis of a form that I send to his office with what I have observed.

- Are you getting good results?

- Yes, there are surprising cures. This encourages us to continue. It's gratifying to be able to do something for others.

- Is it all free?

- No. We think that the poor should have the dignity of paying. But the price is symbolic. Those who have nothing, when they get better, come or send someone from the family to give a few hours of work. This way, everyone cooperates joyfully.

Marina was moved. There was a helping community, of respect for the needy, which enchanted her.

- I would like to give a few hours of work to help - she said. - Do you think there is anything I could do?

- Sure.

- I don't understand anything about herbs, but I will do any work they ask me to do.

- I'd be happy to have you.

- When can I start?

- Monday, at two in the afternoon.

Marina felt happy. This would be a way to pass the time. Despite the comforts at home and at the library, she didn't like to be idle. Celia wouldn't let her do any housework.

- I will come for sure.

From that day on, Marina started going every afternoon to Isaura's house, who put her as her assistant.

- I want you to stay at my side, watching the conversation carefully. Then you will tell me what you noticed.

At first, when Isaura asked her opinion at the end of the service, Marina kept quiet. But little by little, as she became more familiar with the simple manner of the people attending, she noticed some peculiarities, took notes of them and at the end of the session presented them to Isaura.

- I knew you had a well-developed sixth sense.

- Sixth sense? What do you mean?

- Intuition, sensitivity. You perfectly understood Mrs Augusta's personality, you understood that her problem is more emotional than physical.

- But you still sent her back in a week. But João, who has a kidney problem, will only return in a fortnight.

- That's right. The tea I gave Augusta is a stimulant that will keep her active and treat her depression. However, she needs guidance to understand how she is attracting so many problems into her life. The way she sees everyday facts is the cause of everything. Until she changes, she will not feel well.

- Do you go to therapy?

- No. In conversation, I try to pass on some knowledge about life. Her mistaken beliefs are throwing her off balance.

- I've always thought that our emotions get out of control under pressure of events.

- That only happens in very painful moments when the suffering is real. But most of the time, what you give importance to, what you believe in, has the same effect on your nervous system, even if it is an illusion.

- I have observed people who are nervous, who are afraid of everything, who get out of control for no reason.

- You are wrong. They have a reason: the beliefs they have learned, incorporated into their way of being, which they consider to be right, but which are not always so.

- What do you mean?

- Someone said something, and the person believed it without trying to find out if it was true. The most absurd beliefs torment people, limiting them, preventing them from having peace. Many end up prisoners of their fears.

- Perhaps it's a lack of education. Here come very poor people.

- You are wrong. There are very well-educated people suffering from the same illness. The doctors' surgeries are full of them. The chronically ill. Realizing this, modern medicine has focused on the study of behaviour.

Marina was thoughtful for a few moments, then said:

- It's hard to know what's right or wrong.

- It's not about that. Life has perfect laws that determine the balance of the universe. It created man with the destiny of happiness, but determined that this conquest should be made through self-effort, so that man would value his victories.

- People don't value anything that comes for free.

- That's right. It is necessary to learn how much each conquest costs so that it can be maintained. That is why God created man simple and ignorant, but placed within his spirit like a seed, everything he needs to develop his consciousness, evolve and achieve happiness.

- We are far from that.

- Not so far. Even if things seem bad in the world where the wickedness of many dominates, there has been much progress in all sectors, alleviating human suffering, making life easier, allowing man more comfort.

- In fact, looking at it this way...

- Everything in life depends on the way you look at it. Every situation has several sides. It is your beliefs that will determine how you will deal with them. Though, the cosmic laws are perfect and will act with truth, regardless of your illusions.

- Does this mean that if I act wrongly, it will punish me?

- Life never punishes. It teaches in its own way. It signals in various ways, it tries to warn people by provoking situations in which they can perceive the truth, but for those who are resistant, who settle and do not want to change, it allows them to reap the results of their mistakes so that they learn what they are already mature enough to know.

- I have never heard anything about this. I would like to know more.

- It is necessary to observe, to pay attention to the surrounding facts.

It is amazing how everything is interlinked when we are open to this reality.

- Knowing these laws must be fundamental.

- Knowing and applying them means going by intelligence and suffering less. Whoever notices the first warnings of life and rectifies their path, lives better.

- Is it following the Ten Commandments?

- Yes, but besides that, in the Ten Commandments contain the general rules, but each person interprets them according to his or her beliefs. That is why there are so many religions, and many make mistakes through them, falling into fanaticism. The universal laws are wise and perfect. They aim at the balance of the universe and the progress of mankind. They act with love and wisdom.

- Where can I find this information?

- As I said, by observing life. It speaks to us by signs, and we learn by experiencing it. One must be attentive. An accident, an unpleasant fact, can be a warning. A disappointment is a visit from the truth trying to restore equilibrium.

- And what about misery, where everything is lacking?

- You have already said: it is valuing the lack instead of being grateful for what you already have. It is to live relating what is missing. Then there is always a passivity, in which the person believes that they don't deserve something better or aren't capable of progressing. Poverty has various aspects and acts on each person according to their needs.

- How so?

- For the complacent, the depressed, those who think they are less, and even for those who believe that to be poor is to win heaven, life goes on tightening the noose, making the situation more and more difficult, to provoke a reaction that forces them to review their beliefs and seek new paths.

- I have always thought that the cause of poverty is the lack of education and opportunity.

- Many people think this, but it is necessary to look beyond that. There are educated people, with good schooling, who can't even support themselves, while others, with none of this, have a better life. Of course, education is important, but it's not everything. The most important thing is to know how to take advantage of opportunities. If you observe the life of a person who has been successful in all aspects, you will realise that they've never missed a good opportunity. They've never been afraid to dare, to change and to try to learn.

Marina was thoughtful. She was there, taking advantage of an opportunity Adele had offered her. How to find out if this was a good opportunity?

- With the desire to progress financially, a person can do the wrong things. How to assess that?

- It is easy. When analysing a situation, we should ask: is this attitude going to benefit everyone involved? If the answer is yes, you can accept it without fear. Otherwise, and if it harms anyone, don't accept it.

Marina breathed a sigh of relief. By accepting this proposal, everyone would benefit.

It was with pleasure that Marina went to Isaura's house every afternoon, and every day she admired her work, her lucidness, and the assurance with which she assisted everyone.

At the end, she presented her notes and felt happy when she could identify people's problems. But the greatest joy was with the results. The improvement of some people was visible, while others did not have the same success. Marina became impatient:

- Why hasn't Maria improved? Mrs. Odete's case was similar, but much worse. However, she is almost fine. She doesn't even look like the same person.

- In this job we need to be patient. People are not the same. Then, our function here is to clarify, to offer conditions for improvement. Those who want to, will take advantage of it.

- Do you mean that Maria is not taking advantage of this opportunity?

-I would say she is taking less advantage of it than Odete. But that doesn't depend on us. There are other factors that interfere. The rhythm of each one, the will, how much they can perceive. Even the fear of regaining health.

- I don't believe it! If she comes, it's because she wants to heal and get well.

Isaura smiled, and there was a mischievous glint in her eyes when she replied:

- And not be able to manipulate others anymore? To no longer have to take on any work? Not to be pampered anymore?

Marina burst out laughing.

- I hadn't thought of that!

- Did you know that Maria has a kind husband who, when he comes back from the fields, does the cooking, and takes care of the children?

- So, that's it! She doesn't want to get better...

- It's not just that. What she does not want is to lose his support, his affection. It's an almost unconscious manifestation. But if I tell her that, she won't believe me.

- In that case, how to act?

- As always, by doing the best we can. We don't claim to save anyone. Life, when the time is right, will take care of it. And, believe me, it will do it much better than we will.

Marina was delighted. Talking to Isaura was stimulating. She almost always returned home thinking about the subjects she had discussed and admiring her wisdom.

Time was passing quickly. She was four months pregnant and had only a little more time to spend with Isaura. Thinking about this she sometimes felt sad.

One afternoon Isaura asked:

- You are sad. Has something happened?

Caught by surprise, Marina startled and answered:

- No. Everything is fine. What saddens me is that in a while I will have to leave. I'm really enjoying working here with you.

- When you leave, I will miss you. But I hope you will come and visit us from time to time.

- I would love to, but it won't be possible.

Isaura looked at her thoughtfully, then said

- Does your husband intend to take up residence outside Brazil?

Fearing she had said too much, Marina tried to make amends:

- It's one of the possibilities.

- I hope the best for you. If we have to work together, life will bring us together again.

Marina smiled and nodded, but inwardly she didn't believe in this possibility.

She knew that she could never go back to that place. That had been one of the clauses of the contract: she would never try to get close to the family or the people she had been with during her pregnancy.

Once she had fulfilled the contract, she would map out her life plan from then on. She had some ideas in mind. She would open her own company, buy a nice house and go and get her family.

- Anyway, Isaura, I intend to make the most of this opportunity. I have learned a lot from you. I will never forget these moments together.

Isaura smiled, and her eyes had an indefinable glow when she said:

- Me too. Our affinity goes back a long way, perhaps to other lives.

- Do you think we have had other lives?

- I certainly do. Reincarnation is a fact.

- To me it sounds like something fanciful.

- On the contrary. It alone explains social inequality and so many other things we see in the world. Have you never studied the subject?

- No. To be honest, I've never been interested in religion. I have a very free way of thinking.

- Reincarnation is a natural occurrence of life. It has nothing to do with religion, although some accept it and talk about them. Nobody can study life, understand it, without paying attention to this reality.

- You have a different way of seeing things.

- Although I have great faith in the absolute power of God, and respect the religiosity of each person, I allow myself to think on my own. I am an independent spiritualist.

- Why is that?

- Because I like to think, question, learn from life, understand its language. Religions are the interpretations that men have made of spiritual revelations at all times. So, when you study them, despite the positive aspects you find, there are others that you cannot accept.

- Aren't you afraid of being wrong?

- No. The majority opinion is not always absolutely right. If I make a mistake, I prefer it to be it because of my own mind. Then, making mistakes is natural in those who experiment, and I have learned a lot from my mistakes. They teach, they leave their mark forever.

Marina shook her head smiling.

- I understand. I also like to think, to have the freedom to experiment. From early on I tried to manage my life the way I thought best. Although I appreciate a good opinion, I never let myself be manipulated by anyone.

- That's why we get along well. We have the same way of thinking.

The conversation continued pleasantly. When Marina arrived home, after dinner, she went to the library, took the folder with the index of books and looked for something about reincarnation.

Isaura had spoken with such certainty that her curiosity was piqued. She found nothing. When Celia came in to tell her that dinner was served, Marina asked if there was any book on the subject.

- There is. The Spirits' Book.

- Does it talk about reincarnation? Isn't it a religious book?

- Yes, and it's not religious. It's by a great French educator who did research with mediums. Read it, it's interesting. Now let's have dinner.

Marina accompanied her, determined to read the book after dinner.

CHAPTER 5

Sitting in an armchair, Maria Eugenia held the book without reading, lost in her intimate thoughts. They had been in Paris for two months, and despite Henrique's attentions and the beauty of the city, she did not feel happy.

Why had she agreed to her mother's plan? Why had she entered into that false situation, acting against her temperament?

She had never known how to resist her mother's wishes. Adele, an intelligent, charismatic person, used to success and the reverence of all, imposed herself on her daughter, who obeyed her without questioning.

Henrique was her first boyfriend. As soon as Adele noticed her interest, she had the boy's life investigated. Although he was not rich, he belonged to a respected middle-class family. He had just graduated in Business Administration. Adele offered him a job in one of her companies and he accepted. She observed him for some time. Henrique was hard-working and responsible.

Adele's greatest desire was to marry off her daughter, since she needed a grandson to perpetuate her presidency of the family business. To marry off Maria Eugenia was her goal. She was pleased to note that the two were attracted to each other.

A year later, the wedding took place. Maria Eugenia loved her husband and they were happy. However, time went by and the desired heir did not appear.

After many attempts and medical tests, it was determined that Maria Eugenia was sterile. She would never be able to have children.

From that day on, Maria Eugenia changed. She wanted to be a mother. The certainty of her incapacity saddened her, making her feel handicapped.

Although Henrique swore that he loved her and that nothing had changed between them, Maria Eugenia could not keep her former joy.

Thinking of helping her, Henrique suggested adoption. But Adele did not agree. Until one afternoon she called them into her office and told them of her plans.

Henrique was embarrassed and Maria Eugenia refused. But Adele managed to convince them. It was the last attempt.

Henrique, alone with Adele, tried to convince her to give up. He felt that this situation would worsen Maria Eugenia's sadness and make her feel even more helpless.

However, Adele did not agree. She was determined. She had everything planned, she had found the ideal girl, and she didn't want to lose the opportunity.

Maria Eugenia sighed sadly. The memory of those days kept running through her mind and she regretted not having said "no".

Henrique had told her that he only accepted because he owed many favours to Adele, who in all those years had not only taught him how to face the business world but had also helped all the members of his family financially.

She was for his relatives the good angel that appeared in their lives, giving them the opportunity to produce and maintain a better life.

- Nobody can stand up to my mother! - replied Maria Eugenia, convinced.

When Adele called them, the three of them went to the farm. Maria Eugenia's heart was beating fast. She resisted the urge to run away, to say that she didn't want any part of it, that her husband couldn't have sex with another woman.

But she did nothing. She endured everything, trying hard to control her jealousy and her anger. Henrique, noticing his wife's nervousness, felt embarrassed, tense. Only Adele was calm and talked to them, affirming that all this was natural.

- Go, Henrique. Remember that you are collaborating so that we continue to own our property. Think that if our business were to pass into Renato's hands, he would soon depredate everything. You know him and you know I'm telling the truth. By doing this, he will also be protected: he will continue to receive the company's profits, as always.

Henrique left and Adele remained talking to her daughter. She knew that it was difficult for her to think that her husband was sleeping with another woman, even if it was a stranger.

- Men are different from us women. For them, a sexual relationship means nothing. He loves you. He is doing it for us, for our family. He doesn't even know her. I've arranged it with Celia, and they won't meet, talk. So, try not to take it seriously. It's just business, nothing more.

- I can't take it as business. It's about my husband.

- This is about our family. Henrique is sacrificing himself for our well-being. We should be grateful to him.

- What if it's no good? What if after all that sacrifice a girl is born?

- You will raise her as your daughter. It's in the contract. Children were not in her plan. Marina doesn't even want to get married.

- Then everything will have been useless.

- Maybe not. I might try a postponement. After all, you did have a daughter. You might have a male.

- Oh, no. I'll never do that again.

- Well, I will try my best. If necessary, I'll share our fortune with Renato so he'll give up the presidency. After all, he really doesn't like to work.

- Why didn't you do that already? It would have been better.

- I've discovered that he's been losing heavily in the casinos. Giving him money will be an extreme resort. Then, who can guarantee us that later he won't come back to claim his rights? Our plan is final. If a boy is born, everything will be settled. He will not be able to do anything.

When they returned to São Paulo, Maria Eugenia felt like asking her husband how his encounter with the other woman had gone. But he did not mention the subject, and she did not have the courage to ask.

Adele, noticing her curiosity, had told her:

- Don't ask him anything. Forget the affair. Don't make it more important than it is. It was a passing circumstance.

- And if he have to do it again?

- We'll do it again, Adele answered firmly.

Maria Eugenia felt relieved to hear that Marina had become pregnant. But, at the same time, this pregnancy gave her the certainty that they had really had an intercourse, and this aroused her jealousy.

Maria Eugenia reflected, trying to calm herself, thinking that he would never see her again. But the idea that he was in the arms of another woman tormented her.

Adele had prepared everything for her daughter's trip with her husband, and in her luggage, there was a false belly that she would wear even abroad. Her friends used to go to Europe, and Adele did not wish to take any risks.

Also, she wanted Maria Eugenia to get used to the idea of motherhood. When the child arrived, she would need to be prepared.

Adele was happy to tell her relatives and friends that Maria Eugenia was pregnant. She started preparing the layette and the room to receive the baby.

Maria Eugenia looked at the preparations trying to conceal her displeasure. It was hard for her to pretend. Wearing a fake belly was embarrassing. But Adele was on her guard, and as soon as she reached the end of the fourth month of her pregnancy, she was forced to wear it.

It was with relief that Maria Eugenia embarked for Europe with her husband. Even if she had to continue wearing the disguise, she wouldn't have to pretend. No one knew her.

Even though they were out of Brazil, Henrique was still working, since the company had an office in Paris, through which they had a relationship with all of Europe, exporting their products.

Maria Eugenia spent the whole day alone. Reading was her favourite pastime.

She closed the book she was holding and sat down again.

They had agreed that when the baby was born Celia would let them know. They would go immediately to the farm where they would pick up the child. It was there that Maria Eugenia would say that her son had been born.

They would return home, where there would be a nanny waiting for them. Adele planned to baptize the boy next, inviting relatives and friends and having a big party.

Maria Eugenia preferred a discreet ceremony, but Adele did not agree:

- No way! Everyone needs to know that you've had a child. That way no one will suspect a thing.

She knew it would be like this. Adele always did as she wished. Maria Eugenia didn't dare object.

Henrique came in, approached her, and kissed her on the cheek.

- How did you spend the day?

- Fine.

He noticed that she was pale and considered:

- Why didn't you go for a walk, do some shopping? You always liked to do that here in Paris.

- I stayed and read. The book was interesting; I didn't even think of going out.

Henrique said nothing. He noticed that Maria Eugenia was sad. He suspected that Adele's plan was making her unhappy.

He regretted having agreed to it. Maria Eugenia could not accept that she was sterile. Adele's plan made her even sadder.

He hoped that in time she would change. But to him, Maria Eugenia seemed worse. She had lost the pleasure of living, of going out, of talking. Little by little she was becoming a dull, insecure woman, very different from when he had first met her.

When he explained her fears to Adele, fearing that her plan would make her even sadder, his mother-in-law replied that, after the child was born, Maria Eugenia would forget everything.

Trying to cheer up his wife, he said:

- Get ready. Tonight, we're having dinner at a lovely place. There's a famous piano-bar where good singers perform. A friend recommended it to me.

- I would rather stay at home.

- Not at all. Let's have some fun. Maybe dance a little. Go get ready.

She got up. She didn't want him to notice her sadness. She went into the bedroom to get ready.

He sat down on the sofa, thoughtful. Even though he loved his wife, even though he had gone into the adventure unwillingly, even though he had gone on those dates out of obligation, they had been very pleasant.

Instructed by the doctor on how to motivate his wife to get pregnant, Henrique went to meet Marina intending to use everything he had learned so that his task would be accomplished as soon as possible, and he would not have to return more often.

When he entered the darkened room, he lay down next to Marina, smelled her pleasant perfume and, willing to fulfil his role, began to caress her. She responded in such a way that he forgot all about her.

She had soft lips, delicate skin, and a soft touch. And, as far as he could tell, a perfect body. When he noticed that she had never had sex, Henrique was thrilled. Adele had not told him this detail.

Touched, he proceeded with delicacy and affection. When he returned the next evening, he was eager to ask her a few questions. But he restrained himself. He had promised Adele that he would avoid further contact with her.

That night, on his way home, he found Maria Eugenia lying down and noticed that she was pretending to sleep. She certainly hadn't managed to fall asleep. He knew that this was difficult for her to accept. She lay down trying not to make any noise.

It was better this way. He was afraid that she would ask him details that he was not willing to tell her in order not to increase her dissatisfaction.

Although time had passed, he had never talked to Marina and did not know what she really was like, Henrique was surprised when he remembered the moments of those nights.

Whether it was the mystery of the adventure, or curiosity, or the fact that it had been his first, he would very much like to see her, even from afar. But Adele was categorical: she did not want them to meet. She thought she could avoid a possible interest that might arise between them.

She had promised Maria Eugenia that she would do everything she could to ensure that they never met face to face after those moments when they had fulfilled their contractual obligations.

Although he had never mentioned it, Henrique felt that Maria Eugenia thought about him constantly. There were moments when she became restless, in her eyes there was curiosity, but she did not ask any questions.

He would try to distract her by talking about pleasant matters, redoubling his attentions to show her that she need not worry because he really loved her.

Adele called the office to see how her daughter was doing. When Henrique confided that Maria Eugenia was sad, depressed, despite his efforts to cheer her up, Adele invariably answered:

- Be patient, Henrique. Do not worry. When she has the child in her arms, everything will pass. I know what I'm saying.

- She seems to have changed a lot. She's lost her joy; she looks like someone else.

- You're impressed. You must forget what you've been through. You're expecting your son! As for her, I'm sure she'll surrender when she sees the child. A child is exciting and exhilarating. Try to enjoy these moments together. You'll see that I'm right.

He felt more encouraged. A child! He was thrilled at the thought. But what about Maria Eugenia? Adele was right: they had to snap out of it.

Maria Eugenia got ready with great care. She did not want Henrique to notice her sadness. Once at the restaurant, she tried to appear enthusiastic.

The place was elegant and pleasant, and the pianist was playing romantic music. A few couples were dancing. Henrique was particularly happy. He had closed a big contract and wanted to celebrate.

He chose the wine and the dinner. While they were waiting, he asked:

- Did you like the place?

- Very much.

- I was told the food is divine.

The waiter brought the wine. Henrique tried it and poured it.

- Let's toast to our success!

- To the success of the company, you mean!

He wondered:

- I am referring to our success. To our happiness. We are here together, in this wonderful place. We have everything. Life has been kind to us.

Maria Eugenia sighed, but tried to hide her sadness:

- It's true! We have everything. All we lack is....

He placed his hand on hers affectionately.

- We don't lack anything. For me, having you is enough. I don't need anyone else.

- I wish I could be sure that's true.

- Of course, it is.

- Then why did you accept mom's plan?

- Because you agreed, and I thought you wanted to have this child.

- It's what I wanted most in the world. But I wasn't good enough for it.

- Nature does these things from time to time. It's not your fault. You're no less for it. Let's forget that story. We came here to have fun. Let's dance.

- You're right. Let's dance.

Once in his arms, Maria Eugenia tried to snap out of the situation. Despite the strange adventure, Henrique loved her, they were married. She had no reason to feel sad. That night she wanted to forget her problems.

She resolved not to think any more about the baby that would come when they returned. While they were in Paris, away from Adele and the company's affairs, she would use this time of freedom to be happy. When the time to return came, she would think of them again.

From that night on, Maria Eugenia's attitude changed. She became cheerful, well disposed.

When her husband left for work, after getting dressed up to the nines, she went off to discover the places of fashion, going to beauty salons and fashion designers, buying everything she liked and, at the same time, finding out about shows, clubs and restaurants. The only drawback was the uncomfortable fake belly that she had to wear, but, as she was willing not to think about it anymore, she pretended not to see it.

When Henrique returned in the late afternoon, he found her very well dressed, smiling and with a list of places they could go in the evening.

The first few days Henrique felt relieved. After all, Maria Eugenia had stopped worrying about the baby. But after a month of living this life, he felt exhausted. Sleeping late and waking early, he longed to rest on the weekends, but Maria Eugenia would not give him the chance.

One Saturday, when she showed him two tickets to the theatre, Henrique said:

- Tonight, I'd like to stay at home. We'll go another day.

- But I already have the tickets and made a reservation at the club. Also, I arranged for us to have dinner with Jamille and her husband. They are very kind; we can't miss it. It will be disrespectful and unforgivable.

Henrique felt irritated. He had had an exhausting day at the company where he had learned of some problems that he wanted to get around and find a solution to. He wanted to spend a quiet weekend to reflect. Then he was not in the mood to make room for a couple he had only seen once.

Maria Eugenia and Henrique met Jamille and Pierre at a fashion show. During the event, the two women had talked and become friends. As they were leaving the show, Maria Eugenia proposed that the couples have dinner together in a few days.

Maria Eugenia had waited anxiously for this meeting. For this reason, Henrique's unexpected refusal at the last minute had left her feeling uncomfortable:

- I would so like to go to this meeting... Why don't you want to go? Don't you like them?

In fact, Henrique felt uncomfortable around Pierre. Although he admitted that the Frenchman was a cultured and sophisticated man, he was deeply bored by his formal conversation.

- Since you ask. She seemed nicer to me than him, who looks down on people from the heights of his wisdom, has rules for everything.

- He is an intellectual. In fact, I know important people who would very much like to enjoy his friendship.

- I'm surprised. You never valued these things!

- But now I do. After all, we're in Paris, the capital of the world. This is the headquarters of everything. It would be unforgivable to miss this meeting! We must go.

Henrique got angry.

- Call and tell them we won't be there.

- What will I tell them?

- Make something up. Say I'm ill, that I suddenly got sick. I don't have the patience to tolerate them.

Maria Eugenia stood up, annoyed.

- Tolerate them? Is that what you said? They need patience to receive us. Last time, you barely spoke to him, you behaved like a moron.

- He was talking endlessly on a range of subjects that don't interest me in the least. I'm sure I wasn't rude. On the contrary: I treated him with respect, listening to him display his qualities.

- Are you jealous of his success?

Henrique looked at Maria Eugenia as if he were seeing her for the first time.

- Jealous of him? Have you thought about what you are saying?

- Well... You didn't have the education he has. He's a famous man in the best society. In intellectual circles, everyone consults his opinions.

- Well, I don't think so. And I'm definitely not going to that dinner. Better to call right away and tell them.

- I'm shocked! I can't do that!

- In that case, go alone. I'm staying at home.

Her eyes filled with tears.

- You can't do this to me!

- You can't make me do something I don't like.

-I've bought a special outfit, prepared myself... I really want to see the play.

- Well, go ahead. Tell them I couldn't make it and enjoy your evening. As for me, I'll stay home. I need to rest. I want some quiet to resolve some matters of the company that are worrying me.

- I never thought you were capable of doing this to me!

- Well, you saw I am. Then I wouldn't be good company today. Go, have fun, and next time don't make appointments with people without asking if I want to go.

Maria Eugenia, nervous, went to her room thinking whether she should go or not. She had never gone out for a walk without her husband. She liked to walk arm in arm with him and notice how the women looked at him with admiration.

Henrique was a handsome man, charming, elegant. She sighed thoughtfully. But, between the desire to take the walk she had programmed and stay at home, she decided to go. That way she would teach her husband a lesson. He needed to know that she would not give up something that gave her pleasure just because he did not want to go.

She got ready, did her best and before leaving went to meet him, who was reading in his study. She felt beautiful, elegant, perfumed. She would have her night of joy. He was the one who was losing out by refusing to go with her.

- How do I look?

Henrique stared at her and answered:

- Very beautiful.

- Are you sure you don't want to go?

- I am. I'm tired. I need some time to reflect.

- Reflect. May I ask on what? After all, we're here to have fun while my mother plots in Brazil. Is that what you're thinking about?

- What an idea! Of course not. I have to solve some problems at the company. That's what I'm thinking about.

Maria Eugenia came up to him, arms outstretched, and said ironically:

- Do you think that woman is prettier than me?

- What woman are you referring to?

- The one who sold herself for Adele's millions.

Henrique looked at her startled. Maria Eugenia had never referred to the case like that.

- I thought you had forgotten that incident.

- Yes, I've been trying. I really had forgotten. Your attitude reminded me.

- You better go soon, so as not to spoil your evening. After all, you've prepared so well for it.

- That's right. That's what I'll do.

- Have a good time.

She left, leaving a wave of perfume in the air. Henrique sighed thoughtfully. Maybe he didn't do the right thing by agreeing to participate in Adele's plan. Maria Eugenia, who had seemed to agree willingly, was showing that she felt hurt, humiliated and jealous. She no longer seemed the docile, delicate girl she had known. She had dived into social life, made friends with shallow people, changed her way of being, talked like them.

Her unexpected words earlier showed that she had become bitter, cruel. What would happen when they returned to Brazil and held the child in their arms?

Their child! Henrique shuddered. A feeling of love welled up in his chest thinking of the child he would soon hold in his arms.

Despite his struggle with Maria Eugenia, there was the fact that Adele's plan had given him the opportunity to have a child and bring him up as he had always wanted.

He remembered the furtive encounters with Marina, the softness of her skin, the pleasurable moments they had enjoyed. Although they were there fulfilling a contract, she was never indifferent. Even though she had never had a relationship with anyone, she had responded to his affection, making him forget the circumstances of that meeting.

Adele had told him that Marina did not intend to get married. She preferred to dedicate herself to her professional career. An ambitious woman. She had accepted the contract for money.

Henrique sighed sadly. What would make an educated young woman, as lively as she seemed to be, accept such a proposal? Adele had not told him. In fact, when it came to the subject, she would tell the essential.

In a way, her mother-in-law was also an ambitious woman. She couldn't accept losing the presidency of the company. She was a very rich woman. Even if Renato ended up with the company, she could still live very well with the resources she had.

What was at stake was power. Adele had no desire to give it up. If Renato became the president, she would be subordinate to him. That was what irritated her.

Henrique liked to be rich, to enjoy everything that money could buy. But he married Maria Eugenia because he loved her. Of course, his financial situation pleased him, but if he had not felt attracted to her, he would never have married her.

Henrique's parents lived in the city of Ribeirao Preto, where he was born and raised. He was the second son of Americo and Estela: he, a well-known doctor in the city; she, a primary school teacher. Jorge, his older brother, had followed his father's career. At the age of eighteen, Jorge had come to São Paulo and managed to get into the Escola Paulista of Medicine. Two years later, Henrique came to try the same thing. However, as he did not succeed, he stayed to take a course and prepare himself better.

It was during this period that he met Maria Eugenia, who was studying at the same school and preparing for Business Administration. She soon became interested in him. They began to study together and he came to her house.

Maria Eugenia was not very interested in her studies. She didn't have the same interest as her mother. He soon realized that it was Adele who had chosen this career for her.

It was Adele who made him change his mind about his career. She spoke with such enthusiasm about administration, the pleasure of planning and executing projects, that he became interested and ended up liking it.

His brother graduated as a doctor and returned to Ribeirao Preto to dedicate himself to the profession at his father's side. Henrique attended college and when he graduated, he was already engaged to Maria Eugenia and working in Adele's company.

She had accompanied his studies and taught him things that only practice would give him. Besides the job, she had given him her daughter in marriage. He was very grateful to her for all this.

Maria Eugenia had entered college, but dropped out in the first year. Adele realized that there was no point in insisting. She'd never make a good administrator. She had no drive. Henrique, on the other hand, was her pride. Intelligent, hardworking, handsome. He had become her right arm.

Henrique looked at his watch: it was past one o'clock. Maria Eugenia still had not returned. He decided to lie down. He felt pleasure in being able to be silent in the comfort of his flat.

He went into the kitchen and made a cup of coffee to drink with milk, just like when he had lived at his parents' house. He thought of them with nostalgia. It was a long time since he had seen them. The next day he would write a letter.

He looked in the cupboard for something to eat. He found a packet of biscuits. He sat down, and it was very pleasant to drink his cup of coffee with milk, eat biscuits, remember his life in the interior.

Then he went to his room, got ready for bed. He lay down and soon fell asleep.

It was after four when Maria Eugenia arrived with her couple friends. Jamille stayed in the car and Pierre went up to the flat with Maria Eugenia. She opened the door, turned and held out her hand to bid him farewell.

- Thank you for everything. It's been a wonderful evening.

- I've enjoyed it! - he replied, taking her hand and bringing it to his lips. - It's been a long time since I've had so much fun.

- Me too.

- I hope your husband has got better. But I couldn't help noticing that you're another person without him, cheerful, witty. I had the impression that, in a certain way, you hold back in front of him.

- Why do you say that? Henrique respects my freedom. It was him who insisted that I go out, even though he could not go.

Still holding her hand, he said:

- 'I still think that you are happier, looser without him.

She withdrew her hand and smiled:

- Thank you. Jamille is waiting in the car. I'd better go.

- Yes. Promise we'll go out again soon.

- I promise. Now go.

He went away, and Maria Eugenia sighed happily. Pierre's eyes sparkled as they fixed on her. She felt beautiful, courted. She was dazzled. She had never felt that before.

Henrique had been her first boyfriend. She had never had the opportunity to experience male admiration as she had that night.

She closed the door and went to her room. Henrique was sleeping peacefully. She was annoyed. Apparently, he hadn't missed her at all. But that wouldn't spoil her good mood.

She went to the bathroom, removed her makeup and got ready for bed. She was happy. If Henrique wanted to stay at home another few times, she wouldn't stop herself. She would make friends, go out, enjoy life as she had never done before.

She was sure that soon she would return to Brazil and would have to play the role of the obedient daughter, put up with that child and Adele's impositions.

She didn't want to think about that now. She went to bed and, thinking of the happy moments she had enjoyed that night, soon fell asleep.

CHAPTER 6

Henrique got up, washed himself and went to the pantry to drink coffee. It was Saturday, past ten o'clock and Maria Eugenia was still sleeping. She was probably late again.

He sighed annoyed. Maria Eugenia had changed. She was no longer that discreet, shy, sweet girl he liked. Since he had refused to go with her to that dinner with Jamille and Pierre four months ago, she had never stopped at home. She lived surrounded by friends, with whom she always had somewhere to go.

At first, she invited him, but as he invariably didn't go, after some time she stopped doing so. When he came home in the late afternoon, he would find her busy preparing for the evening outing.

She almost always went out with Jamille, her husband and another couple. Henrique did not like them. He thought they were pedantic and shallow. But Maria Eugenia had become so involved that she could do nothing without them. Henrique had tried several times to convince her that she was exaggerating, to which Maria Eugenia had replied:

- For the first time I am free to do what I like. Why can't I? Soon we will have to go back, then I will live as a prisoner again.

He asked her to tone it down a bit, but it was no use. Maria Eugenia would not stay at home overnight.

In an attempt to convince her, he had accompanied her a few times, and what he saw worried him even more. He noticed that she always had a glass of wine in her hands, sipping, and her companions made sure that it was always full. At such moments Maria Eugenia became witty, malicious.

Once, when they arrived home, he had told her:

- I don't know how you put up with these friends of yours. They only know how to speak ill of others.

- Well, I find them amusing. I love talking to them. I didn't know you were moralist...

- It's not moralism. I don't like parlor frivolities and gossip. That's what you do.

- You're just saying that because you can't have fun like the rest of us. For you, work is more important than anything. Well, I'm not like that. I'm young, I like to have fun. I am enjoying my stay here very much.

Henrique poured himself some coffee. While he was drinking it, he thought that he would soon be back. He regretted having agreed to this experience. Although she obeyed her mother, Maria Eugenia had no structure to accept the facts. She had changed radically and that was not good.

Maria Eugenia came into the room looking sleepy:

- I don't know what's happening in the street today. The noise is infernal; it didn't let me sleep.

- Good morning.

- Good morning. I woke up so annoyed I forgot to say it.

He didn't answer immediately, and continued drinking his coffee. After a few moments, he said seriously:

- You forgot to put your false belly in. In fact, I've noticed that you're not doing it properly, it should be much bigger. It's almost time to be born.

- I don't like this story. It's inelegant to have to go out carrying this thing. I don't think I would need to wear this disguise here. My friends don't know anything about what goes on in Brazil. They have never shown any desire to go there. Why should I wear this horrible belly?

- I don't like any of it either, but once we got into this, we have to do it right. We're making an effort to help Adele preserve the future of the company and we can't risk ruining everything. Have you ever thought if you meet any acquaintances from Brazil?

- A few times this happened, but nobody asked anything.

- Of course, they wouldn't ask.

- But I was careful to mention my pregnancy by talking about the symptoms. Nobody got suspicious.

- Your friends might find it strange that your belly isn't getting big enough.

- Don't be a nag. They never mention it.

- By my count, the baby's almost due.

- Don't even say that! I don't even want to think about going back. If I could, I'd stay here forever. I don't know why we have to worry about the company. We have enough money to live well. Afterwards, if a girl is born, this sacrifice will have been useless.

- If you think that, you shouldn't have agreed with Adele.

- You did too. In fact, you got the best part.

Henrique stared at her irritated.

- I don't understand your remark. I did what was asked of me. Put that into your head.

- But you will have a child, which I will never have.

- That child will be your child too. Although he has been engendered in another body, he will come into your arms, he will need your affection, your motherly love. One of the arguments that convinced me to agree was that this would be the only way for us to have a child.

- Let us change the subject. While we are here, I want to forget this fact. We almost have to go back home.

Henrique finished his coffee and went to the window. Despite the cold, the day was beautiful and there were many people on the street. He turned to Maria Eugenia and said:

- The day is beautiful. Let's go for a walk.

- At this time in the morning? I haven't slept enough. I'm tired. I want to sleep some more, rest. Tonight, we're going to the theatre.

- You're abusing yourself, drinking too much, coming home late every night. If you want to rest, you should stay home, sleep early, at least a few nights a week.

- I'm running out of time. We'll have to leave soon. I can't waste a minute.

Henrique looked at her seriously. He was about to retort, but changed his mind. He went to the bathroom, brushed his teeth, combed his hair, put on his jacket, returned to the living room and said:

- I'm going for a walk. Don't wait for me for lunch.

He turned around and left. Maria Eugenia didn't mind. Recently Henrique was becoming boring. He was not amused by anything and looked at her disapprovingly. He gave her the impression that he was watching her.

She felt happier when she was not beside him. She went to her room and lay down again, trying to sleep.

Once on the street, Henrique began to walk among the people who passed by elegantly, chatting animatedly among themselves. But they were strangers to him. Suddenly, in spite of being surrounded by people, he felt alone.

He remembered his parents, the comfortable farm where he spent his holidays twice a year, amidst his cousins and playing, without worrying about the future, which he believed would be as it had been until then, cheerful and happy.

He missed it and wanted to go back. Once home, Maria Eugenia would be forced to take on her duties as a mother.

This thought comforted him a little, but not enough to motivate him about the future. He felt disappointed, sad.

When he reached a place in the plaza, he sat down on a discreet bench, away from the noises of the children playing happily. He felt the need to meditate, to rethink his life.

Maria Eugenia was proving to be a different woman from what she had imagined. The naivety, the modesty she had always shown were weaknesses that Adele's iron hand concealed.

In front of her mother Maria Eugenia was discreet, polite, spoke little and her opinions, when expressed, always reflected Adele's good sense, never having disagreed with her in anything.

Henrique sighed sadly. Discovering his wife's weaknesses bothered him. He had sought in her a sufficiently mature companion with whom he could share ideas and affection in a harmonious partnership.

Now he recognized that this would not be possible. Distant from her mother's inquisitive eyes, Maria Eugenia hadn't taken the trouble to dissimulate, externalizing her childish, insecure, weak side.

Discovering this had been disappointing. Henrique felt that even after they returned to Brazil and she resumed her old posture, he would only be dissimulating his true feelings.

From now on he would have to take charge of the family decisions, since he didn't trust Maria Eugenia to have the maturity to help him choose the best.

That was not what he wanted. Adele knew her daughter's weaknesses and, perhaps that was why she adopted such firm attitudes, deciding the direction she should take in life.

Or was it Adele's attitude what had made Maria Eugenia so immature? By adopting this attitude too, wasn't he also contributing to her remaining so childish?

Henrique ran his hand through his hair, worried. Perhaps he was overreacting and Maria Eugenia was only playing, like a reclusive child who, for a while, attains freedom.

He needed to think it over. He wanted to talk to her, to open his heart and tell her how he was feeling. But lately she had become distant, never exchanging ideas or opinions.

He needed to cool his head. He got up and walked through the streets, trying to take an interest in the shop windows. Feeling nostalgic for his family, he decided to buy presents for them.

This entertained him, making him remember everyone's preferences, which made him forget his worries.

It was getting dark when he returned to the flat carrying the bags with the presents.

Maria Eugenia, lying on a canapé, was chatting animatedly on the telephone. Seeing him come in, she sat down and said she had to hang up. She put the phone on the small table and looked at it curiously:

- You've been shopping. Can I see them?

- They're presents and they're packed. I don't want to unpack them.

- Any company secretary?

- No. Where did you get that idea? They are some souvenirs for my parents and Jorge.

- Don't you think it's a little early for that?

- Not too soon. It's not long before we get back. I don't want to leave it to the last minute. Why don't you do the same?

- I'm not taking anything for anyone.

- Not even Adele?

- She has everything, and I wouldn't know what to give her.

- Something nice, a treat, that's all.

- Yeah. Maybe. But it's early. I don't want to think about going back.

Henrique put the bags in his office, came back and sat down next to her.

- You should get out a little, walk the streets on a Saturday like this. There were many beautiful, happy people. The shops were busy.

- I don't like to go out in the afternoon. I prefer the evening.

- In that case, we could go out to dinner somewhere nice.

- I have an appointment for tonight. We're going to an exclusive club. I'm excited. Jamille says it's wonderful.

- Leave it for another day. Tonight, we'll go out just the two of us. We can dance a bit.

- I'm sorry, but I can't give up. It was hard to get invitations to this club. Pierre had to use all his prestige. I can't afford to be rude.

- Do you have an invitation for me?

- I didn't know you'd want to go. You don't like to go out with my friends. Unfortunately, invitations are individual and not transferable. I'm sorry.

Henrique looked at her seriously. The situation was worse than he would have liked.

- In that case, I'd rather you didn't go. It's been a while since we've been out together, just the two of us.

- We'll go out another day. We'll have plenty of time when we get back to Brazil. I can't miss the party tonight. I've wanted to see this place for a long time. All the social columnists speak wonders of it. Then, the harder it is, the more valuable it is. You can't imagine what it's like.

- Are you willing to go, even though I'd like you to stay with me?

- I'm sorry, but it was you who advised me to go out alone with friends. Now that I'm going to get something I want so much, I don't think it's fair to give it up.

- You really want to go...

- I'm going.

Henrique felt like imposing his will, arguing, calling her to order, making her see that she was exaggerating. But he preferred to keep quiet. He hated arguments.

- Do as you like.

He went into the study, picked up a book at random and sat down on the sofa. That situation could no longer continue. The next day he would have a serious talk with her. He would put his position and forbid her to go out with those friends.

Henrique hated having to impose his opinion. In all circumstances he preferred dialogue, open and sincere conversation. But at that moment he felt that he could not tolerate the situation.

Maria Eugenia was abusing his patience and he needed to put things back in their proper places.

It was almost nine o'clock when Henrique looked for Maria Eugenia who was getting ready to leave.

- I'm hungry, and I'm going to order something for dinner. Do you want some?

- No. We'll have dinner at the club.

He picked up the phone and ordered a snack. While he waited, he observed his wife and noticed how much she had changed: thinner, restless, with heavy make-up and more showy jewellery.

Feeling watched, Maria Eugenia asked:

- What is it? Do you think I'm pretty?

He didn't answer immediately, remaining pensive. Then he said:

- You look different.

- Don't you think I'm much better?

- No. I preferred you as you were.

- You're obviously not up to date with current fashions.

Maria Eugenia put on some perfume and looked at herself in the mirror, satisfied. The doorbell rang and Henrique went to open it. Pierre, elegantly dressed, stood before him. Henrique tried hard to conceal his displeasure.

He had opened it thinking it was the food he had ordered. Overcoming Pierre's instinctive repulsion, he greeted him politely, inviting him in.

- Thank you, but Jamille is waiting in the car. We've come to get Maria Eugenia.

She came in a moment later, saying happily:

- I'm ready. We can go. See you later, dear.

Henrique didn't even have time to answer. She left, Pierre nodded slightly and they left. Henrique closed the door, struggling to overcome the unpleasant feeling.

He felt the urge to go after them and bring his wife back. Pierre, with his hair streaked with gel, averting his eyes when he spoke, did not inspire confidence.

He restrained himself at cost. If he did as he wished, Maria Eugenia would make a scene, and he was unwilling to cause a scandal. He needed to calm down and talk to her the next day. Of one thing he was sure: he would no longer allow her to go out with those friends.

Meanwhile, Maria Eugenia and Pierre arrived at the car and there was no one there.

- Jamille didn't come? - she asked, surprised.

- She had run out of patience to wait. She went with Jean to the club.

He opened the door; she settled in and he sat down beside her. He started the car and drove off slowly.

- You look beautiful!

She smiled contently and asked:

- Why are you going so slowly?

- I want to admire you longer. At the club it's going to rain admirers and I'm going to be dying of jealousy.

Seeing that she smiled and remained silent, he continued saying:

- For my own sake, I would never take you to that club.

He stopped the car and looked at her with passion. He held her hands, kissing them effusively.

- You know I love you! I can no longer hold this passion that is consuming me. I want you for myself.

He hugged her tightly, kissing her lips fiercely. Maria Eugenia trembled with emotion. She had noticed long ago that

Pierre was attracted to her. It was exciting to see that she was an attractive woman, that men other than her husband desired her.

Henrique had been her first boyfriend. She had never had the opportunity to meet other boys, to experience the game of seduction. She had fallen in love with Henrique and had been happy to marry him.

But now he was different, distant, she was in Paris, living a love affair. A different experience.

He kept kissing her, murmuring passionate words. Maria Eugenia surrendered to this emotion with pleasure.

- My darling I need you. Let's not go to that club. Let's go somewhere where we can be alone with our love. I feel that you want me too.

She shuddered in fright. The joke was going too far. She had no desire to betray her husband. Pierre insisted, kissing her on the lips, the neck and the cheek.

- Let's live our moment of love! Soon you will be gone, back to your country and perhaps we will never meet again.

Maria Eugenia shivered with pleasure at his kisses. She recognized that Pierre was right. She would soon have to go back to Brazil, bear that child she hated because he was Henrique's child with another woman, and do everything just as Adele wanted.

Henrique had his extramarital relationship; she could do the same. Then they would be even. Adele and Henrique would never know. She could consider herself revenged for having had that child thrust upon her that she didn't want.

- Let's go, she said, trembling with desire.

He started the car and soon they were in a luxury building she didn't know.

- It's a flat I have when I want to be alone, to think.

They went inside. He closed the door and led her into the bedroom. Slowly Pierre began to undress her.

Suddenly she remembered her fake belly. She excused herself, went to the bathroom and removed the uncomfortable disguise. She went back to the room naked. Pierre, looking at her with a mixture of surprise and lust, embraced her and kissed her ardently, and together they rolled over in bed.

When they had calmed down Pierre lit a cigarette, staring at her curiously.

- Tonight, you've made me the happiest man in the world!

- I'm thinking of Jamille. She's waiting for us at the club.

- Don't worry, Jean will make her forget all about us.

- What do you mean?

- He and she already had an affair. I don't think they'll waste time waiting for us.

Maria Eugenia wasn't shocked. Although she had never done it, she knew that in some groups it was fashionable to swap couples.

Pierre kissed her again, saying cheerfully:

- I was glad to hear you weren't pregnant. Why are you wearing that fake belly?

Maria Eugenia felt a shiver of fear. She had forgotten that detail.

- I would like to have a child. Since I can't, I pretend I'm pregnant.

- Just like that, for no special reason?

- Yes, I like it.

- In that case, the person who spoke is no longer here. Taste is taste.

- That's my secret. I'd rather you forget about it and never tell anyone.

- I won't. I'm a tomb.

Suddenly, Maria Eugenia felt she'd gone too far. There was a different gleam in his eyes that made her want to leave immediately.

- I think we'd better go.

- Are we going to the club?

- No. I'd rather go home.

- In that case, let's stay here a little longer and enjoy our loving moments.

Pierre caressed her and her fear went away. He was in love. He would keep her secret. Then she would soon be gone and never see him again. It was better to enjoy it anyway.

- All right, she murmured, responding ardently to the kiss he gave her next.

She wanted to forget the world, the conventions, her husband and the life full of rules Adele had imposed on her. If she could, she would never return to Brazil. But that was an impossible dream.

Thinking that way, she surrendered to the emotions of the moment with euphoria.

It was dawn when she finally managed to convince Pierre to take her home.

- I have to go, Henrique's up early. I don't want him to see me coming.

- Don't worry, he won't suspect a thing. But I'll never forget this night.

She thought for a few seconds, then answered:

- When I am in Brazil, at home, I will also remember these moments.

- You don't seem happy to be back. Why?

-In fact. There I will have to take on my family responsibilities. I won't be able to do anything like I did here.

- With the husband you have, you must lead a dull life.

She didn't like the comment. He noticed and didn't give her time to answer:

-I'm sorry, I didn't mean to offend. It's just that I can't understand how a woman like you, young, beautiful, full of life, can be satisfied living with someone who doesn't like anything and thinks only of business.

- Henrique is a good man and very competent. After my mother, he is the one who takes care of all the company's business.

- I heard that your company is doing very well. He must be very competent.

- He is. But it's my mother who runs everything. She always gets what she wants. She's firm and sure in her actions.

- I wonder what your life will be like between the husband and the mother you have. I begin to understand why you don't feel like going home.

- It's not because of them. I like them both. It's that here I'm a stranger, I can act freely. There's a society there, I'm well-known, people talk. There's a family name to uphold. Do you understand?

Pierre hugged her, smiling:

- Of course, I understand. You must enjoy your freedom while you are here. I will help you have more and more fun. Let's live this time and enjoy life.

- That's what I want.

- Do you have any idea how much time we have left?

- Less than a month. I'm not sure.

- In that case, we can't waste any time. I'll take care of it tomorrow.

Maria Eugenia got up and said:

- Let's get going. It's late.

This time he didn't stop her. They got dressed and he drove her home. It was a few minutes to four when she entered the house, trying not to make any noise.

She was feeling guilty and feared finding her husband. It seemed to her that, seeing her, he would know what she had done.

She took off her shoes, cautiously entered the bedroom and went straight to the bathroom. She closed the door carefully, took off her clothes and went into the shower. She felt dirty, and the water falling on her body was as if it was washing away some of her guilt.

She stayed there for a while. Then she dried herself, put on her nightgown and went to sleep. Henrique was sleeping and she lay down trying not to touch him so as not to wake him up.

Seeing that nothing had happened and that everything was calm, Maria Eugenia sighed with relief. Then she could think about the adventure, relive the moments of passion.

She knew that the attraction she felt for Pierre was not love. But the pleasure of those moments, the new experience, the certainty that she was a woman desired, beautiful, appreciated, dazzled her.

Maria Eugenia had always been a dull person in the face of Adele's charismatic radiance. While her mother was revered wherever she appeared, she always remained in the background.

But this time her mother wasn't there to dim her brightness, and she felt alive, strong, sought after. She even thought that maybe it was time to react to Adele's wishes, to start confronting her, not allowing her to continue to decide her life.

In her fantasies, Maria Eugenia already saw herself returning home, saying no to her mother's impositions. As for Henrique, he would be easier to handle. He was always busy and would not be an obstacle to her desire for freedom.

Lulled by this dream, Maria Eugenia finally fell asleep.

CHAPTER 7

Marina stood up with some difficulty. Her body felt heavy. In the last few days, every now and then a sharp pain came over her, as if the baby was pushing down.

She felt tired and wished to end the wait. At the same time, when she thought that she would have to give up her child, she felt a tightness in her chest and a sense of guilt. Then she thought of the benefits that child would bring not only to Adele to consolidate her family's assets, but also to herself, who could give her mother and brother a better life.

Nevertheless, she was very curious to see her son's little face, to look for the features of her family in him.

She went to the kitchen to drink coffee. Celia, seeing her, asked:

- How are you feeling?

Marina sighed and answered:

- Tired.

- According to our calculations, the baby will be born in the next few days. Adele arrived last night. She's at the big house. Later she will come to see you.

- She'll stay until the baby's born?

- Yes. She came prepared. She brought all the trousseau.

Marina had coffee with milk and a bread with cheese. Then she said thoughtfully:

- I hope all this isn't in vain.

- I hope so too.

Marina was getting up from the table when Adele arrived and hugged her affectionately.

- So, how are you feeling?

- Tired.

- Not for long now. Let's talk in the living room.

After they settled down on the sofa, Adele continued:

- Maria Eugenia and Henrique arrive from Europe tomorrow. They need to be here when the baby is born.

Marina didn't answer. If she could, she would like to sleep and only wake up when everything is over. Sometimes she thought she was paying too high a price to be financially independent. But what was done was done, and she couldn't go back. Even if it hurt, she would carry the project through to the end.

- Another letter arrived from her mother.

- How nice! I miss her so much.

- Soon she will be able to see them. I had some presents sent from London to give them.

- You didn't have to do that.

- I want everything to be as natural as possible. Bringing them presents is what you'd do if you were just coming from there.

- You're right.

They talked about other matters, and Adele stood up saying:

- You must be anxious to read the letter. If you feel anything different, let me know.

After she left, Marina opened the letter. The news was good. Cicero was finishing high school. That would be great, because next year Marina was planning to bring them to live with her.

Then, it was time to move on and forget this difficult experience.

At night, Adele came to keep her company. Her pleasant conversation charmed Marina, who admired her very much, not only for her brilliant intelligence, but also for the clear way she explained her ideas.

During those months, occasionally she appeared at the farm to stay for a weekend. Marina thought it was a privilege to be in her company and tried to talk about her interests and learn what she could.

She talked about her professional projects, exposing her ideas. Adele had a special way of seeing, making her see other sides of the subject, which delighted her.

That night was no different. At the end, Adele commented:

- I'm sure you'll be very successful professionally.

- You're not just saying that to cheer me up?

- Absolutely not. On a subject like this, I don't usually joke. You have a drive, you know what you want, you study, you work to be better and better. And there's one thing that's essential to me.

- What's that?

- You don't cultivate the "dream of love".

- It may not seem like it, but I am a loving person. I love my family. What I don't want is to get married, to have a person bossing me around, wanting to stop me from doing what I like. If one day I come to like someone, I will only get into a relationship if they respect my privacy.

Adele clapped her hands, smiling:

- That's right! I have seen women who have been successful in everything, including professionally, but when they fell in love it was a disaster. In a short time, they became passive, without any will of their own, erased and insignificant. You are an honourable exception.

- Perhaps it's because I saw the suffering of my mother, who married for love to a man very different from her. She was delicate, kind, cheerful; he was rude, chauvinistic, quarrelsome. When I saw her sad because of his rudeness, she would ask us to leave. But she was scandalized, saying that a woman must obey her husband. And she became more and more passive and sadder each day. Until, when she was pregnant with my brother, my father ended up leaving us because of our neighbour's daughter.

- How old were you?

- Thirteen to fourteen. But despite her despair, I felt great relief.

- How did you manage financially?

- It made no difference. My father spent the little he earned as a salesman on the street. My mother always supported the household by sewing for others.

- That's why you don't want to get married.

- Part of it is. Because I could never take what my mother took. I would have left him at the very beginning. I always wanted to be in charge of my own life. That's why I studied hard from an early age because I believe that to achieve that I need to be financially independent.

- That's why you accepted my proposal.

- Even without it, I am sure I would achieve my purpose. But your offer shortened the path and made it possible for my family to have better living conditions, especially my brother, who is young and needs support.

- And your father? What became of him?

- I never heard from him again. He disappeared completely. My mother was very ashamed of what he did. The neighbour, who was her friend, started harassing us and we moved to the other side of town. We haven't heard from him since.

- You never missed him?

- No. We didn't have any affinity. We didn't even talk.

- And your brother? He never asked about his father?

- One day, I was already attending college in São Paulo and I went to visit them. Cicero was eight years old and asked about his father. So, I did what my mother never had the courage to do: I told him the truth in every detail.

- How did he react?

- Very well. He didn't mention it anymore and became more friendly with mom.

They talked more, and then Adele left.

The next morning, still on the plane, sitting next to Maria Eugenia, Henrique said:

- We are arriving. We'll soon be home. Haven't you forgotten the recommendations?

- No. I did everything mom asked, as always.

- You don't seem happy about our return.

- And I'm not. Leaving a delightful life in Paris to take part in this farce... Instead of the pleasure of going out with friends, an unknown child to cry in our ears.

Henrique put his hand on her arm, saying seriously:

- You shouldn't say that about our son.

- Your son, you mean.

Henrique frowned, trying to contain his irritation.

- If you think so, why did you accept this project? No one forced you into anything. In fact, I was hoping you would say no.

- My mother is very convincing.

- No one forced you. You agreed because you wanted to. Now you have to do everything right. This is a very serious case, which, if not handled well, could cause us serious problems. As far as I'm concerned, I'll do everything as agreed. And you must do the same.

- I know that. That's why I agreed to come back. I wanted to stay in Paris.

- You know that's impossible.

The plane landed soon after, and when they were released, they left. Adele's secretary was waiting for them, and after the greetings, she said:

- Mrs. Adele couldn't come. She went to the farm to prepare everything for the baby's birth. - Turning to Maria Eugenia, she continued: - How are you feeling? Tired?

- Yes, she answered. - I can't wait to get rid of this weight.

- That's how it is. The last month is the worst. I remember very well when my son was born. But it was worth it. The joy of being a mother makes up for everything.

Maria Eugenia smiled, trying to look cheerful. Once home, Marcia made a point of showing her the baby's room and some of the clothes.

- You should see the ones Mrs. Adele brought for the baby's birth. They're wonderful.

Maria Eugenia couldn't wait for Adele's secretary to leave, but she, enthusiastic, continued:

- I want to know if everything is to your taste. I helped with the decorating, of course, under Mrs Adele's guidance. But if there is anything you don't like and want to change, let me know. I want everything to be to your liking.

- Thank you, Marcia, for your dedication. It's beautiful. In fact, like everything you do. You have very good taste.

Henrique, noticing that Maria Eugenia was trying to cover up her irritation, said:

- Thank you for your interest. Everything looks wonderful. But Maria Eugenia needs to rest. She didn't do very well during the flight. Her health comes first. Then, more rested, you'll come and examine everything in detail.

- Of course, Dr. Henrique, of course. You're right. I'm sorry, sir. I figured she'd want to see everything. After all, it's her first child. But it was a long trip. I'm going to get going. If you need anything, just give me a call. What time should I send the driver to pick you up to go to the farm?

- That won't be necessary. I'll drive myself.

- Whatever you say. See you later.

She left and Maria Eugenia went to her room. Henrique went with her. The maid had already opened her suitcases and was unpacking.

- You may go, Dalva, said Henrique. - We want to rest.

After she left, Maria Eugenia stretched out on the bed, saying nervously:

- I'm glad you noticed. I couldn't stand that conversation any longer. I can't wait to rip out this ridiculous belly.

- You can't do that yet. Not here. Oh, well. It's close. Tomorrow we'll go to the farm. A few more days and everything will be solved. Now I'm going to take a bath. I want to go to the company to see how things are going.

- What exaggeration! You'd better rest, since tomorrow you intend to drive to the farm.

- I won't be long. Get some rest.

After he left, Maria Eugenia stretched her legs and closed her eyes. She remembered the friends she had left behind in Paris, the moments she had spent with Pierre, and smiled.

It had been a delightful farewell. She intended to return as soon as possible. She was ready to find some excuse to go to Paris to meet him.

That was how she thought to make up for the sacrifice she was making for Adele's interests. She felt no guilt for betraying Henrique. After all, he was on Adele's side. He did everything she wanted. He deserved to be punished for that.

When they arrived at the farm the next afternoon, Adele received them with joy. She had everything planned. After the greetings, they went to the bedroom, where she explained:

- The baby is due to be born at any moment. Celia will take care of everything.

- And what about the farm workers? Won't they get suspicious? - Henrique asked.

- I know what to do. You will go around the house, walking around, so that everyone can see you. After the baby is born, even if it is during the day, Celia will wait for the night, when the employees have already gone home. Then she will bring everything that is needed and we will prepare the scene. In the morning, when they come back, you'll be in bed with the baby by your side.

- And what about her? - asked Maria Eugenia.

- She'll stay a few more days, until she can drive, and then she'll leave without anyone seeing. The next day, Celia will tell people she knows that her husband came to pick her up to have their baby in the city.

So began for them a time of waiting. Maria Eugenia and Henrique did everything as Adele had determined.

Two days later, Celia called to warn Adele that the contractions had started. She went to Henrique and told him:

- It's time. I'm on my way there. I'll let you know as soon as he's born.

Henrique sat in an armchair, excited. His son was being born. He felt like going there, to follow everything, to know how he was.

But he held back. He couldn't. And Marina, how would she be, having a child that would never be hers? Wouldn't that be too cruel?

A thousand questions crossed his mind. She had accepted the conditions. She had chosen freely. What kind of woman was she that gave birth to a son in exchange for money?

At the same time, wasn't he also cheating, putting at risk even his relationship with Maria Eugenia, to maintain his financial position?

Nevertheless, it was gratifying to be able to have a child. Even though it was achieved through a business deal, no one could deny the fact that the baby was his son. He would never know how it was conceived, but the important thing was to love it, to raise it, to make it a happy person. This, for sure, he would do.

Adele arrived at the house where Marina was staying and went straight to her room.

- How are you?

- Fine. I think it won't be long. The contractions are very often.

Adele approached Marina and stroked her hair, saying:

- Everything's going to be fine. You'll see.

Marina wriggled nervously on the bed:

- I don't know. What if it's a girl?

- Let's not worry about that now, said Celia.

- Everything will be just as we agreed. Don't be afraid, Adele said.

The contractions returned and Marina sighed in distress.

- Calm down, pleaded Celia. - Come on, let's go.

While Celia looked after Marina, Adele took a step back. She was not a religious person. But at decisive moments in her life, she always used to think about the power of God.

She felt that there was a superior force that took care of everything. She respected this force in such a way that she maintained a personal ethic, believing that, as long as she did her best and remained good, she would be supported by it.

Despite the circumstances of that project, Adele was certain that its realization was not harming anyone. On the contrary.

That boy would have a family, be loved, study and become a rich man. He would benefit greatly. On the other hand, Marina was an honest woman who intended to use that money to work, to improve the conditions of her family. As for her, Adele, she would be preserving the health of her company, whose greatest asset was its thousands of employees.

She was certain that if her brother-in-law Renato took over the presidency of the company, he would lose all the progress that had been so hard won, not only because of his lack of administrative capacity, but also because of his irresponsible conduct throughout his life.

In addition, Adele was giving Maria Eugenia the opportunity to be a mother and Henrique the opportunity to be a father. Thus, she felt at ease to ask for divine protection and at peace to await the outcome of this project.

When she returned to the room, Celia helped Marina by asking:

- Come on, push, it's almost coming out.

A greater effort, a contraction, and behold, the child was born.

- God bless us, cried Celia, overcome with emotion. - It's a boy!

Adele wept uncontainably, while Marina relaxed with relief. A loud cry filled the room, and tears rolled down their cheeks.

- Please! I want to see him at least once, Marina asked in a voice choked with emotion.

- Of course, agreed Adele. - You have every right.

Celia took care of the boy, wrapped him in a towel and took him to Marina, who looked at him with great emotion.

- He's a beautiful boy, Adele commented. - Strong and healthy. Thank you, Marina. I'll never forget the good you're doing us.

She bent down and kissed him on the forehead with affection. She motioned to Celia, who left and took the baby with her. Marina's face twitched and she pressed her lips together trying not to cry.

- I know what you must be feeling. I know that you will keep our agreement and never try to get close to him.

- I am a person of my word. As much as it pains me, I will keep our agreement.

- I'm sure of it. But if one day you need anything, I'll be there for you. The good you've done for us is priceless. I'll be grateful to you for the rest of my life.

Celia returned without the baby that she had left sleeping in another room. The afternoon was ending, but they wanted to wait to take the baby away without anyone seeing.

- Now I will take care of you, she said, smiling.

- I was fine until now, but I am feeling pain again.

- It's natural. You still have to expel the placenta. Then you will take this tea and sleep. You need to regain your strength.

Adele sat down in the armchair beside the bed and only got up after Marina was well settled and asleep.

She and Celia went to check on the baby, who was sleeping peacefully. Adele approached him and gently caressed his rosy cheek.

- It's a beautiful boy! - she exclaimed happily.

- Beautiful and strong. Thank God everything went well. Your problems are over.

Adele sighed satisfied:

- Now I'm going home, to tell them the news. As soon as I know there's no danger, I'll call you, so you take him.

- That's fine.

- You will have to teach Maria Eugenia to take good care of him. I want her to do that from day one.

- All right. I've already prepared a routine for her. But feeding is the most delicate part. I've organized everything for the first few days. We'll see how she reacts. She'll need an experienced nanny.

- I've already chosen one that I think is great. She'll start the day before they go home. But I want Maria Eugenia to stay here for a few more days and look after him herself. She has to learn to love him as if he was really her own son.

- That's a good idea. On the other hand, she'll have to rest so as not to arouse suspicion.

When Adele arrived home, Henrique was waiting anxiously for her. As soon as he saw her, he asked:

- So?

- It's born, Enrique. It's a beautiful boy. Congratulations, dad!

He hugged her with emotion. Maria Eugenia appeared in the room and, seeing her, Henrique ran to embrace her, saying:

- It's born, Maria Eugenia! We have a boy!

- You have a boy! - she corrected.

Adele intervened:

- Don't ever say that again. You have a boy. Later, when he comes home, we'll celebrate. We won! Aren't you happy, my dear?

- Yes, answered Maria Eugenia, trying to feign joy.

The maid came into the room and asked if she could serve dinner. Adele agreed. After she left, Adele said:

- After the servants leave, Celia will bring the boy. Then we will celebrate.

It was past midnight when Adele called Celia:

- You can come now. It's quiet now. Don't forget what we agreed. Bring everything as if the birth had happened here. Don't forget anything.

A few minutes later, Celia's car pulled up outside the house. Adele, accompanied by the couple, went to meet her. Maria Eugenia tried to control her anger. That boy was an intruder, the fruit of her husband's intimate affair with another woman and proof that she wasn't good enough to be a mother.

She felt diminished, irritated, nervous, but she tried hard not to let anyone notice.

When Celia got out of the car, she picked up the basket in which the boy was sleeping. Adele approached and picked up the baby, showing him to the couple.

Looking at the little rosy face, Henrique felt strong emotion. It was his son! Adele wanted to place him in Maria Eugenia's lap, but she said, scared:

- He's so small! I'm afraid to hold him.

- He's yours. Take him. There's no danger.

Adele put him in her daughter's arms. Maria Eugenia's hands trembled, and she said nervously:

- Not now. I need to calm down.

Henrique came closer and asked

- Let me hold him.

Maria Eugenia handed him over, relieved. He entered the house with the boy in his arms, looking at him expectantly. He sat down in the living room. He couldn't get enough of looking at his face, trying to find the family traces.

Noticing the little pink fingers that appeared on the sleeve of the blue woollen jacket, he put his finger to examine them. Even in his sleep, the baby held his father's finger firmly. Henrique felt his eyes water and, overcome by emotion, he said softly:

- I will take care of you. I will do everything to make you happy.

Meanwhile, the women had gone to the couple's bedroom, where there was already a crib and a chest of drawers that Adele had filled with a trousseau for the first days.

- Now you will put on a nightgown, lie down. You've just given birth and you'll have to rest.

While Maria Eugenia changed, Celia set the scene. She had brought the bedclothes that Marina had used, towels and everything else to make it look like the birth had taken place there.

Adele watched with satisfaction. When Celia finished, she went to call Henrique, who was still holding the boy.

- Come, let's go. Let's put him in the crib.

Henrique obeyed. He looked around and said:

- It looks like this is where the baby was born.

- Now let's celebrate our victory, Adele smiled.

On the table was a tray with glasses and a bottle of champagne. Henrique opened it, poured it and Adele said happily:

- Today we begin a new cycle. The way we got here is in the past. We will never speak of it again. Life has approved our projects, since it granted our request. Let us be grateful for this gift and welcome this child with all our love and affection. We toast to our happiness and to the future.

They touched their glasses and drank with satisfaction. Maria Eugenia smiled to cover up her annoyance. She was not happy. But she didn't dare show her true feelings.

Then Celia took the baby and approached Maria Eugenia.

- He must be wet. You need to change the diaper.

- Me? I don't know how to do that.

- I'll teach you.

She put the baby on the bed and said:

- Come on. See how I do it.

She changed the diaper, then asked:

- Now it's your turn.

- There's no need. You've already changed him.

- I did it to show you. I want to see if you've learned.

- I don't have to do that. We're getting a babysitter.

Adele came over:

- You're the mother. You'll have to do that, at least while you're here. When we go back home, we'll have a nanny.

Adele spoke firmly and Maria Eugenia thought it best to obey. She knew from experience that when Adele wanted something, she wouldn't give up until she got it.

With trembling hands, she changed the diaper. The boy began to cry. She looked frightened at the two of them.

- Every healthy baby cries a lot. It's the only form of expression he has to complain when something bothers him, Adele said.

- He must be hungry, said Celia. - I brought a bottle ready. I think it's still warm. Take him and sit in the armchair.

The boy was crying loudly. Maria Eugenia took him in her arms and did as she was told. Celia put the bottle in the boy's mouth and he immediately began to suckle.

- Hold it like this, half-tilt, explained Celia.

Maria Eugenia obeyed, pleased that he had stopped crying.

Henrique, in a corner of the room, watched contentedly. For the first time he felt pleasure that they had accepted Adele's plan. It was one more of the many favours he owed her.

Meanwhile, Celia showed Adele the script she had made for Maria Eugenia.

- I don't think he wants it anymore, said Maria Eugenia. - I put it in his mouth and he doesn't suck.

Celia moved closer:

- He sucked well. Now hold him upright against your breast. He has to burp.

Maria Eugenia was feeling sick. She didn't know if it was the smell of the milk or the nervousness of having to take care of the baby. Fortunately, he burped soon and she could put him back in his crib, to her relief.

- And then, how are you feeling? How are you feeling? - asked Celia, smiling.

- Terrified. I hope you won't leave me alone with him while we are here.

- I'll be around, but you're the one who has to take care of him. You always wanted a child so much. Now you do.

Maria Eugenia didn't answer. She wanted a child, yes, but one of her own. This was a stranger, the son of an unknown woman. To bear his presence, to take care of him, would be a sacrifice she would have to make for the rest of her life.

The next day, everything went as predicted. Nobody suspected anything. Three days later, Adele had everything prepared for their return to the city. On the eve of their departure, she went to see Marina, who, as agreed, was getting ready to leave.

She took her the receipt for the deposit of the equivalent of one million dollars that he had deposited in the bank in her name.

- Thank you for accepting my request. I will always be grateful to you. But our relationship ends here. Let's forget everything, pretend we never met.

- I understand. Don't worry. I'll stick to the deal.

- I left all the instructions with Celia. Tomorrow we'll leave before seven. As for you, as soon as you're able to drive, you can go back to Sao Paulo. What are you planning to do?

- First, I'm going to see my mother and brother and tell them about my plans.

- I wish you all the happiness in the world.

- Thank you. I want you to know how grateful I am for the way you took care of such a delicate matter. Despite everything, at no time did I feel uncomfortable. On the contrary. Celia is a wonderful woman. If I could, I would live my life beside her. During my stay here I have learned a lot. I met Isaura, a wonderful woman, who taught me how to be better. I feel I have to leave without being able to say goodbye to her. But I recognize that it is necessary. Besides all this, I took advantage of your library, I studied a lot, which will help me in my professional career.

Adele hugged her affectionately.

- Goodbye, Marina. I will take care of our boy with all my love. We will make him a good and happy man. I know you'll achieve everything you want. You are an intelligent, strong and capable woman.

- Goodbye, Adele. Thank you for everything.

After she left, Marina sat down thoughtfully. She was free to go back and take care of her life. She felt good, she was sure that her son's life was in good hands.

She went to her room, looked around and, remembering the day she had arrived there, smiled. She felt like a different person, she had matured, she had learned.

She went to Celia's room. She had not yet arrived from the farm. On a chair, he spotted a woollen coat that the baby had worn the day he was born. In a quick gesture, she picked it up, went to her room and put it in her bag, under everything.

Deeply moved, she thought that at least she would have this souvenir of the little being she had helped to come into the world, but which could not be hers.

CHAPTER 8

It was getting dark when Adele, Henrique and Maria Eugenia, carrying the boy, arrived at the house. Henrique helped his wife downstairs while Adele went inside.

The butler was waiting in the hall with a woman in her thirties, tall, thin, with brown hair tied up in a bun at the nape of her neck, dressed in white.

Adele greeted her and said:

- Ariovaldo, pick up the bags.

Seeing that Maria Eugenia was entering with the baby, assigning the girl said:

- This is Elvira, the nanny.

She came closer:

- Pleased to meet you, ma'am.

- Thank you, Elvira.

- Take him and look after him.

Elvira held the baby and asked:

- What time did he suckle?

- When we left the farm, said Maria Eugenia.

Adele intervened:

- It's been over two hours. In his bag you'll find the milk he's taking and how to prepare it.

- Yes, ma'am.

She took the boy away and Maria Eugenia said relieved:

- I'm going to rest a bit. I haven't slept a wink tonight. He cried several times and I was worried.

- Let's talk in your room, Adele suggested.

- We have some things to settle.

Turning to the butler, who was passing by carrying some suitcases, Adele said:

- Tell Henrique that we are waiting for him in the room.

Shortly afterwards, Henrique went to them.

- We have thought of several names; we have to decide. Tomorrow you, Henrique, will have to register him.

- I thought of Dionisio. It was my grandfather's name. What do you think?

- It's fine with me, answered Maria Eugenia.

- It's a beautiful name.

- Then it's chosen. I'll go early tomorrow morning.

Adele approached Maria Eugenia and said firmly:

- Everything has worked out so far. I don't need to recommend what you as a mother need to do.

- I'm not a mother and I don't know what a mother does, she said nervously.

- You weren't, but now you are. This is your son. He is your responsibility. He needs your care, your affection, your love. That's what a mother gives, Adele returned. - I chose Elvira very carefully. She's an excellent person and a skilled nanny. She will know how to look after the boy very well. But I don't want you to leave him exclusively with her because of that. I want him to be with you a few hours a day. He needs to feel the love of his parents.

- He's very small. He doesn't know anything yet.

- Your mistake, my child. Doctors say they feel emotions when they're still in their mother's womb. They feel rejected when their parents don't love them, which can cause traumas that will accompany them for the rest of their lives. I want my grandson to be a happy child, physically and mentally healthy. So, I demand that you make an effort to give him all the love. After all, he is giving you the chance to be a mother. Be grateful for that and do your part.

Maria Eugenia tried to cover up her annoyance. Besides tolerating the presence of that intruder, she would still have to pretend the love she felt. She bowed her head and said:

- I will do what I can.

Henrique came up to her, hugged her and kissed her gently on the cheek.

- Forget how this child came into the world. You are now his real mother. I am sure that such a small being, so in need of love, will awaken that feeling in your heart.

- I have to go, Adele said. - I want to rest. Tomorrow, we have to announce Dionisio' birth to relatives and friends and make the usual celebrations.

Meanwhile, Marina, driving her own car, carrying the presents that Adele had bought, arrived at her mother's house in Sorocaba. It was getting dark and, as soon as she stopped the car, she saw Cicero at the gate, looking curiously.

Her heart beat faster, anticipating the joy of their return and the pleasure of being able to tell them that they would never be apart again.

She got out of the car and Cicero ran to her, holding out his arms. Marina pressed him to her chest, kissing him on the cheek.

- You really came! - he exclaimed, elated. - When mom told me, I couldn't believe it. I missed you so much.

- I missed you too. Let me see you.

She pushed him away a little and continued saying:

- How you've changed! You're taller than me.

- I am already fifteen years old.

- You're a man, and still as handsome as ever.

Cicero smiled proudly.

- I look just like you.

In fact, the same green eyes, dark skin and golden-brown hair.

- Did you rent a car?

- No. I bought one.

- Wow, you must have made a lot of money!

- A little. Help me with the bags.

Cicero rang the bell, and soon Ofelia appeared on the veranda. Seeing them, she ran to hug her daughter. Cicero couldn't contain himself:

- Mom, she bought that car. Look how beautiful it is!

- Are you all right? - asked Ofelia as soon as she could control her emotion. - You, so far away! I was so worried. I'm glad you're back.

- I missed you terribly, said Marina. - But I had to, to get what I wanted. We have a lot to talk about. Let's go inside.

- Go ahead, I'll take everything inside, said Cicero.

They went in hugging. Marina looked around and, after having lived in one of Adele's houses, found the small room smaller and poorer. As always, everything was rigorously clean, there were flowers in the vase, but she felt happy to be able to offer them a more comfortable and better life.

Once in the room, Ofelia asked;

- So? Did you like living in England?

Marina preferred not to talk about it, but Ofelia's curiosity was natural and she had to answer. She described the city a little, the customs and ended up saying:

- It's all very beautiful, but I couldn't wait to go back. I prefer to live in Brazil.

- And do you think it was worth it to stay so long away!

- Very much. From now on, we're all going to live together in Sao Paulo.

- Life is very expensive there. Do you think it will be enough for all this?

- Yes. I'll set up my own firm and you won't have to sew outside anymore. I want Cicero to continue his studies.

- He finished high school last year. But I couldn't enroll him in preparatory school. We couldn't get a place for him and I couldn't afford a private school.

- It's OK. It's the beginning of the year. When I get to São Paulo, I'll take care of it.

- You must be hungry. I'll check on dinner.

- You don't have to. Let's have a snack; I bought some things on the way. Let's open the bags. I brought some souvenirs for you.

Cicero had placed the suitcases on the sofa and approached contentedly:

- I knew you wouldn't forget me.

Marina separated the packages, handing them out happily. Adele had not saved money. She had bought several gifts for each one, based on the information she had given her.

It was a success. There were clothes, games for Cicero, novelties for the kitchen that thrilled Ofelia, all in very good taste.

- You must have spent a fortune, Ofelia remarked, worried.

- Not that much. I earned very well. I'm glad you liked it.

- Feel that perfume, Marina! How delicious! I'll be ashamed to wear it.

- Not at all! You'll wear everything and more. I want you to live well, in comfort. In that time, I learned that beauty is very important in our lives. There, I lived in a beautiful house, full of beautiful things, and that did me a lot of good. Beauty touches our soul and makes us want to be better.

Ofelia looked at her in admiration.

- You have come back different.

- Yes, today I'm a different person. I know what I want in life. But I also know how to get what I want. Tomorrow we'll make arrangements to move to São Paulo.

- Like this? Wouldn't it be better if you first settled there, see if it works out, and then we can come to you?

- Not at all. We'll go as soon as possible. It's only a matter of time before we hand over this house and dispose of the furniture.

- We're not taking our things?

- Only personal objects and family mementos.

Cicero rubbed his hands together happily:

- Yay! I always wanted to live in the capital.

- I still think it's better that you go first. Where are we going to stay until you get a house?

- In a hotel, of course.

- I've never stayed in a hotel, said Cicero.

- You'll like it. Don't worry, mom. I've already made the reservations for the day after tomorrow.

- So fast! Do you think there'll be time to arrange everything?

- Yes, it will. We just have to talk to Mr. Joel and give him the key. As far as I know, you don't have a lease.

- I never had to. I've always been a woman of word. I've never been late on rent.

- Let's eat and then we'll go to his house and talk.

- Okay. I'll go to the kitchen. I'm going to the kitchen to make coffee.

Marina took the two bags of food and said:

- Come, Cicero, let's set the table.

Cicero's agile eyes shone with pleasure at each package they opened and placed on the table. Marina smiled happily. It was to give them a better life that she had accepted Adele's proposal.

She didn't worry about the future. During the months she had spent on the farm, she had time to plan step by step what she would do.

As soon as they arrived in São Paulo, she would look for a comfortable house to rent and buy the essentials they needed to settle in. Then she would open her law firm, rent a suitable place and set up her office.

It had to be a nice, cozy place. She would hire a secretary and dedicate herself entirely to the work. She knew some important businessmen with whom she had made contact when she worked for Dr. Olavo.

She would visit them, present her company and make herself available to them. She was sure that she would be successful. It was just a matter of time.

After lunch, they went to talk to the owner of the house, who was more a friend of the family than a landlord. Although he felt the loss of his friends, he was happy to know that they were improving their lives.

When Marina said that they would hand over the key the next day, he said:

- So soon? You have just arrived. Why don't you stay a few more days? Our city has progressed a lot.

- I know, Sir Joel, but I've been out of the country for almost a year and I want to start work soon.

- Have you arranged the truck for the move? My nephew, Juca, has a truck and he's good at it.

- We're not taking the furniture, said Ofelia.

-No?

- No, Marina confirmed. - I have everything in São Paulo. We'll leave it at home. If you don't want to keep it, you can give it to whoever needs it.

- That's very generous. Thank you.

All agreed, in the afternoon of the next day, with the bags already in the car, they handed over the keys and said goodbye.

Cicero was overjoyed, Ofelia a little scared. She had never been to São Paulo. Marina smiled observing her worried look, which she tried hard not to show.

As they got into the car, Marina held her arm and, looking into her eyes, said in a firm voice:

- Everything will be fine, mom. Don't worry, we're turning over a new page in our lives. Be happy. We are going to be very happy.

Marina's firmness and courage had always impressed Ofelia. She was a winner. She had managed to graduate, to go abroad, to build a career. She certainly knew what she was doing.

Ofelia smiled and answered:

- I know daughter. Just the fact that we can all live together is already a happiness. Let's go.

- Yes, mom. Let's leave without looking back. Our life is starting today.

All settled, Marina started the car. At that moment, the past was behind her.

As soon as they were settled in the hotel, Marina asked for the newspaper and began to look for a place to live. Ofelia didn't want to go to a flat. She liked to have a yard, to plant. Marina agreed. She wanted her to settle in soon and, most of all, to feel happy.

A week later they had rented a house in Vila Mariana. It was a good house, with three bedrooms, two bathrooms upstairs, two living rooms, kitchen, garage and small yard.

To Ofelia and Cicero, it looked like a palace. Marina wished for something better, but thought it would only be for a short time. As soon as she was earning well, she intended to buy a nice house. Then she would do everything to her liking.

Then they went shopping. Marina chose everything of good quality; Ofelia was worried. In a few days the house was furnished with everything they needed to move in.

As soon as they were settled in the house, Marina prepared the paperwork to open her law office. In less than a month she had rented three rooms in a building downtown, enrolled Cicero in a good school and was taking care of the decoration of her office.

While waiting for the documents to start working, Marina made a list of the companies she had had contact with when she worked for Dr. Olavo and scheduled visits with the directors to present her firm and make herself available to them. She was very well received by most of them, who remembered how efficient and capable she was.

She presented herself elegantly dressed, showing security and firmness. She noticed the looks of admiration she aroused, she was aware that she was more beautiful and better prepared.

She had gone to the bank where Adele had deposited the money under her name. She had left a part for the first expenses and saved the rest.

When everything was ready, she hired a receptionist and a young man for external services.

Already on the second day the phone began to ring and the first contracts began to be studied.

Marina dedicated herself entirely to the work. Two months later, she already needed to hire a secretary.

Marina felt happy. Her mother had settled into her new life. At first, she didn't want someone to do the housework.

- There is no need. I can take care of everything.

- I know, but I want you to have some free time to take care of other things.

- You didn't let me bring the sewing machine. I'm an active person. I can't sit around and do nothing.

- You'll have to take care of the house. I want you to teach Rosa to do things the way only you know how. I'll be very busy and you'll have to do the house shopping.

- Of course, of course. You can be sure I'll enjoy every penny of it.

I want to cook. I'm not going to let someone else take care of my children's food.

- If you want it that way, do it. But I'd like you to get some friends, go for a walk. There are many beautiful things to see in this city.

When Marina hired Rosa to work at the house, she put as a main condition her dedication to Ofelia. After listing the working conditions, she concluded:

\- Try to please mom. She has always lived in the countryside. I want her to get used to it and be happy here.

\- Don't worry, Mrs. Marina. I know how to do this.

Rosa was a twenty-five-year-old mulatto girl, bright eyes, big smile, generous breasts and a well-made body.

\- If you really know how, you won't regret it. I know how to be generous when the person deserves it.

\- I'll take care of it. With me Mrs. Ofelia will never be sad.

In fact, Rosa had a special way of dealing with Ofelia. She noticed right away that she resented Marina for having chosen someone else to work in the house. So, right from the start she tried to do things the way Ofelia liked them.

Very cheerful, always cheerful, in a short time she won Ofelia's good will and Cicero's friendship, telling them about the customs of the city, talking about the most beautiful places, offering to accompany them when they wanted to go for a walk.

She went shopping with Ofelia at the market, at the supermarket, always cheerful and happy, helping her with all her help.

Marina had reason to feel happy. The first customers were showing up, the money was rolling in and she was confident that she would get everything she had planned.

In the midst of so many activities, she had almost forgotten her business with Adele. Then one afternoon, sitting in her office, she opened a magazine and her heart leapt.

There was a photo of Adele, Maria Eugenia and Henrique, the latter carrying his son in his arms. Her avid and curious eyes fixed on the boy. She recognized that he was beautiful. He must have been six months old. She never got tired of looking at him. There were other photos of Maria Eugenia and Henrique. She was seeing them for the first time.

She felt a different sensation. He had been in her bed; they had met intimately. But he was a stranger. She remembered the emotions she had felt in those moments.

Her legs were shaking and her hands trembling. She stood up and took a glass of water. She needed to wake up. Those people had passed in her life, but they were gone forever. She couldn't give in to emotion like that.

It had only been a business deal, a contract that had been good for both parties. She was happy, she had got what she wanted. So were they. She needed to face the situation as she had always done with serenity and calm.

She needed to prepare herself. They lived in the same city. It could happen that they would meet somewhere at some point. If it did, she could not show any emotion. Officially, they were strangers who had never been part of her life.

At this thought, Marina felt a little sad. She admired Adele and would like to keep in touch with her. But it was impossible. Despite the deep bond that united them in the person of that child, it was this same bond that had separated them forever.

She looked at her watch. It was five o'clock. There was still a case she needed to read, but she was not in the mood and left it for the next day. She decided to end her workday, go out, walk a little.

She picked up his bag, gave her secretary some recommendations and left. Once on the street, she went for a walk, looking at the shop windows, trying to distract herself. When she passed a bookstore, she decided to go in.

In the past few years, she had read almost exclusively books about her profession. It would be good to look for a more pleasant reading.

She picked out two that she thought were good. She leafed through them indecisively.

- You can take this one. It's very good.

She turned around and saw a tall, dark, strong, well-dressed boy who was looking at her, smiling slightly.

- Have you read it?

- I've read both. I liked this one better. Although it is a light, unpretentious book, it is true and touches our spirit.

- Do you work here?

He smiled, flashing his neatly bared teeth.

- No. I'm just a regular reader. Reading is my favourite pastime. I came to pick up two books I had ordered.

- Ah, in that case, I'll take it.

Marina held the book and went to the check-out. She was paying when she saw the same boy behind her. She went to pick up the package and soon he was also by her side.

- What books did you buy? - she asked, noticing that his package was bulky.

- Professional books. I am a doctor. Allow me to introduce myself.

Then he took a card from his pocket and handed it to Marina, who took it and read it:

DR. RAFAEL VILARDI - PSYCHIATRIST

- You chose a difficult profession, she said, smiling. - My name is Marina Siqueira, lawyer.

- It's a pleasure to meet you. Would you like to have coffee with me?

Marina had picked up the package. She stared at his face and thought:

"Why not?"

It had been a long time since she had had anyone to talk to. A handsome, intelligent man was just what she needed to distract herself. She smiled and replied:

- All right.

They left the bookshop together and chatted as they walked. They stopped at a teahouse and he said:

- I like it here. Is it good for you?

- Yes.

They went in, sat down and at first talked about their professions, comparing the points they considered similar. He spoke easily, his voice was pleasant and Marina felt at ease.

She told him that she had recently lived in the city, opened her office and brought her mother and brother to live with her.

- You are a hard-working, courageous woman who knows what she wants. I haven't met many like that.

- I don't conform, I go after what I want. My father left us and my mother fought hard to bring us up. Seeing her efforts, I promised myself to study, to progress, to give her and my brother a better life. I am succeeding.

- Most girls put all their hopes in marriage. To fulfil a dream of love is all they wish for. You never thought about it?

- No. Marriage was never on my mind.

- You're very beautiful. That can't have been easy. How did you manage to scare off the suitors?

- Simply by not dating.

He looked at her in disbelief.

- You mean you've never had a boyfriend?

- Never. I went out with some boys, I made some attempts, but they soon wanted to take possession of me, to rule my life, and I had other plans.

He looked her in the eyes and asked:

- Don't you like men?

Marina blushed and answered:

- I'm not homosexual, if that's what you want to know.

- Sorry, I didn't mean to be intrusive. It's hard to believe that a beautiful young woman like you doesn't think about getting married and having children. Even if you're a more lucid person, that's a woman's job.

- I've never been in love. Maybe that's why.

- Will you face marriage if you ever fall in love?

Marina laughed:

- Maybe. It depends. But so far, we have talked about me. It would be good to talk about you.

- There's not much to say. My parents live in Rio de Janeiro, I have a married sister who also lives there, two beautiful nephews. I have lived in São Paulo for many years. I came to study medicine. After graduating, I did a specialization course in the United States. After I finished, I worked there for three years. When I missed Brazil, I came back and decided to live in São Paulo.

- You didn't want to live in Rio?

- No. I left some friends from my student days here. I love this city. I bought a flat, set up my practice here. When I miss it, I visit the family.

- As for marriage...

- I've escaped as much as you have, and I can assure you it hasn't been easy. When they have a crush on someone, they don't give up, they want to get married anyway. To be honest, that idea doesn't excite me. It's hard to live together with the mind that most people have. It's hard before, during... And after the separation it gets worse.

Marina laughed pleasantly.

- If you think so, we can be friends. We don't run any risk.

She held out her hand, which he shook happily.

- Finding a woman like you deserves a celebration.

- Why do you say that?

- I would like to be friends with you. I don't like to take risks either. Would you agree to have dinner with me one evening?

She laughed good-humouredly:

- Maybe. I need to make friends.

Marina looked at her watch and continued:

- It's time to go.

- Shall I drive you home?

- No, that's okay. My car is in the car park nearby.

She stood up. So is he.

- It was nice to meet you. Thanks for the coffee.

- My pleasure. Aren't you going to give me your phone number?

She took a card and handed it to him. After the handshake, Marina left.

Rafael sat down again, took the card she had given him and looked at it thoughtfully.

She was an intelligent, beautiful, pleasant with a great mindset woman. It would be interesting to know her better, to know if she was really all that.

He believed that women like to play roles, fantasise, manipulate, to get what they want. Perhaps appearing disinterested was just a clever tactic to get hold of a husband. In his experience, he had seen all this and much more.

She looked him in the eye as she spoke, and that revealed sincerity. But he had to find out if there wasn't some intention behind it.

Rafael was a profound student of human behaviour. He liked to question, look at all sides of a situation, understand what motivated people to choose this or that attitude.

Marina would be a good element for his studies. He didn't know any others with that kind of common sense. He kept the card in his pocket, planning to call her in the next few days.

CHAPTER 9

Marina arrived home a little later than usual. The work at the office was growing. She had hired an intern in addition to her secretary. She had lawyered up for two important clients, reached advantageous agreements, and this had brought her new clients.

Upon entering the house, she noticed a cheerful atmosphere. There were flowers on the dining table, which had been arranged with great care. A delicious smell came from the kitchen, and she went to see what it was.

- Hum! What a good smell! I can see that dinner is going to be special.

Ofelia smiled as she stirred a pot and replied:

- Today marks six months since we came to São Paulo. We have to celebrate.

- I noticed the whimsy of the table. Did you set it yourself?

- Of course. I've been taking that course for a month now.

- From what I've seen, you're really enjoying it. Did you do the flower arrangement too?

- Yes. Do you like it?

- It's beautiful. Is Cicero here yet?

- Yes. He's in his room.

- I've had so much work that I haven't been able to give him the attention he needs. How is he doing in his studies?

- Fine. He is studious, you know. Dinner's ready. May I serve it?

- I'll go upstairs, wash up a bit. Five minutes and I'll be down.

- Tell Cicero.

Marina nodded and went to her room. She put on a soft slipper and washed herself. As she went downstairs, she passed by her brother's room and knocked.

- Cicero, dinner is ready.

- I don't want any dinner. I'm not hungry.

Marina was surprised. He had a good appetite. He was always the first to sit down to eat. Was he ill?

She opened the door and went inside. The light was off and Marina turned it on.

- Don't turn it on, he complained.

- I have a headache.

She came closer, put her hand on his forehead. It wasn't hot.

- You don't have a fever. I'll ask mom for some medicine for your headache.

- You don't need it. I'll just stay in the dark and rest and it will go away soon.

- Mom made a special dinner to celebrate our coming here. She'll be sad if you don't come down.

- I don't want her to be sad.

- Then let's go downstairs. Maybe if you eat a little, you'll feel better.

- All right, then. You can go. I'll wash my face and go downstairs.

Marina went downstairs and told Ofelia:

- Cicero doesn't want to have dinner. He has a headache.

- Again?

- What do you mean?

- The last few days he hasn't been well. He comes home from school, closes himself in his room, doesn't talk, and when I ask, he says he has a headache.

- In that case, I'll make an appointment for a doctor's appointment.

- Sure. But I think he has some problem and doesn't want to tell me. Talk to Cicero; maybe he will open up to you.

A little later, the young man came down and joined them at the table for dinner. Marina noticed that he was pale and had dark circles under his eyes, but said nothing.

The food was tasty and the dinner went merrily. Cicero ate everything that his mother put on his plate. But immediately after dessert he went back to his room.

Shortly after, Marina made a slight sign to her mother and went to him. She found him lying in the dark. She went in and didn't turn on the light. She sat on the side of the bed, smoothed his head and inquired:

- Well? Has your headache improved?

- Not yet.

Marina continued rubbing his head in silence for a few moments. Then she leaned over and kissed him on the forehead.

- I love you. I want you to be happy. I feel that you are not feeling well. Has something happened?

He burst into sobs and Marina continued rubbing his hair gently, hoping that the pain would pass. When he calmed down, she asked:

- So you won't tell me what's bothering you? Don't you trust me?

- It's just that you and mom do everything to make me happy, but I'm not reciprocating.

- Don't say that.

- I'm doing badly at school and you pay a lot of money for me to study. It's just that everything here is different from the countryside.

- It's natural that you find change strange.

- I don't like that school. I'd like to go back to the countryside.

- Do you think the teaching is more demanding here?

- Yes. They don't explain the subjects well. They speak in a different way. I don't like them, and the classmates even less.

- What do you mean?

- They make fun of me, imitating my way of speaking. I don't want to go to that school anymore.

- You've always been brave. You won't run away now. You will stay and face the situation.

- But the girls laugh at me when I talk.

- It's the country accent. When I came to study in São Paulo, I went through the same thing.

Cicero sat on the bed:

- You don't speak like me and mum.

- Because I learned to speak like the people here. That's what you're going to do.

- I don't know how. I talk without realizing. When my classmates get close to me they imitate my way of speaking and laugh.

- And your grades, how are they?

- Low. I just don't understand what some teachers say.

- I was told that this school is very good. But I think their curriculum is more advanced than the school you were at. Why didn't you tell me this before?

- After everything you did for me, the clothes you gave me, the house, everything, I was ashamed that I didn't live up to your expectations.

Marina smoothed his head again and answered:

- I hope you'll be happy. That's all. And whenever you don't like something, I want to know. Be honest, talk to me, tell me what's bothering you. We'll work it out together.

- It's just that I don't know if I'm going to make it through the year.

- Don't worry about that. If you don't pass, you'll do it all over again. You have changed your life and are adapting to the new moment. What you can't do is get discouraged.

- Maybe I should change schools.

- Not at all. You're going to face your classmates, your teachers, turn things around. I'm going to help you do that.

- How's that?

- I'm going to hire a private tutor to help you with your studies and help you beat that accent.

- Are you sure this is going to work?

- Yes, I'm sure. Tomorrow I will go with you to the school to find out about the curriculum and the books used in the course. With a good teacher, you will soon have won this battle. You're intelligent, strong, capable.

- You really think so?

- I'm sure of it. Now, get out of bed and let's go downstairs and watch television with mom. There's a good movie playing tonight.

Marina turned on the light and Cicero jumped out of bed. His face was flushed and his eyes were bright. They hugged each other and went downstairs to the living room.

The next afternoon, Marina went to Cicero's school to talk to the headmistress. She learned that he wasn't doing well in his studies, he couldn't keep up with his classes and, considering the grades he brought from his previous school, the headmaster believed that the school he had attended was very poor.

Marina explained that her brother was having difficulties adapting, even because of his accent, which was made fun of by his classmates.

- They don't do that out of spite. They like to play, she explained.

- These jokes hurt, especially at Cicero's age. He even wanted to leave school.

- If he does that this time of year, he'll repeat the year.

- No, he won't. My brother is a studious and intelligent boy. I will look for a private teacher to help him with his studies, but I would like you to make your students aware that they should respect their classmates and not demoralize them just because they have a different accent. In my opinion, the school has the duty to educate its pupils by teaching them to respect each other's differences.

- I will talk to the teachers and see what we can do.

Marina thanked her and left. It was class break and in the corridor she found Cicero talking to a lady.

Seeing her, he called out to her:

- Come, Marina. I want you to meet Mrs. Rute, my Portuguese teacher.

Marina greeted her and Cicero continued:

- Mrs. Rute is the best teacher I have. When I have a hot head, she talks to me and calms me down.

Rute was a woman of about 40 years old, tall, thin, bright and cheerful eyes, brown hair. Marina liked her.

- Has he been giving you a lot of trouble? - she teased.

The teacher smiled and answered:

- No. Cicero is a good boy.

- He is having trouble adapting. The change was big. He had never left the countryside and is finding the city customs strange. Only now I discovered that this school's curriculum is much completer and more advanced than the one he used to attend.

- Indeed. The courses in our school are hard, which is very good, since it prepares you better. Many of our students, when they finish high school, don't even take a course: they go straight to university.

- I am looking to hire a private tutor to help him. But I don't know of any. I've been working abroad, and we've been in São Paulo for six months now. Could you recommend someone?

- I am a widow with a teenage daughter. I give private lessons to help with expenses.

Cicero intervened:

- Could the lady do that for me?

- If your sister wants, I'll do it with pleasure.

- Of course, I accept.

- How nice, Mrs. Rute! I'm sure I'll really learn.

They agreed to start the next morning and Marina said goodbye happily. She noticed that Cicero liked that teacher. For her, this would help him a lot in his improvement.

A fortnight later, when Marina arrived from the office, Cicero had already returned from school.

- So, what's up? - she asked. - How is it going?

- Better. Today I had a maths class and didn't understand much. But tomorrow morning Ms. Rute will explain everything to me.

- But you have to pay attention in class.

- I do. But the other teachers talk fast, they don't like to repeat anything and I'm embarrassed to ask what I don't understand. The other day a teacher called a student stupid because he didn't understand what she taught. Then the others, when we left for the playground, started to call him a donkey, making big ears and neighing. I felt sorry for him.

- A teacher should not call a pupil a donkey. She is being paid to teach him. If he knew the lesson, he wouldn't need her.

- Mrs. Rute is different. She explains again, gives examples, makes us repeat what we understood. Sometimes she tells a funny story, and it's easy to remember the lesson.

- I'm glad you hired her, Ofelia intervened. - She's a very special woman.

- By the looks of things, she's already won you over too.

- It's true. Sometimes we talk a bit after class. She lost her husband in an accident when their daughter was two. They loved each other very much. You must see how her eyes sparkle when she talks about him.

- In a way, you've been there too. You raised the kids on your own.

- It is different. Her husband died; mine left me. She can think of him with love; I can't.

- Do you still remember him?

- From time to time. But when it happens, I don't feel nostalgia, but anger, revolt.

- You have to forget. What's past is past.

The phone rang and Rosa answered. Then she called Marina:

- It's for you.

- Who is it?

- Dr. Rafael Vilardi.

Marina answered immediately.

- How are you, Marina? Remember me?

- Of course! I'm fine. How are you?

- Fine. Would you like to have dinner with me tonight?

- I just got back from the office. I've had a rough day.

- So have I. It's more reason to indulge in dinner together, have some good wine, catch up. How about that?

Marina thought about it for a while and decided:

- Okay. I really need to clear my head a bit. What time?

- Eight o'clock, okay?

Marina checked her watch. It was seven o'clock. That would give her time to take a shower and get ready.

- Yes, that's fine.

- I'll come by your place at eight. What's the address?

She remembered that she had given him her business card, which only had the phone numbers and office address on it. She said so and he wrote it down. Then he hung up the phone.

Ofelia, curious, asked:

- Is he an admirer?

- No. A friend. We met the other day in a bookshop, talked, had a coffee together. We're going out to dinner.

Ofelia looked at her and smiled.

- It's time you got yourself a boyfriend. All you do is work and study. At your age that's not right.

- Don't fantasize about it. Dr. Rafael seemed like a nice guy, and I'm looking to make friends, have some company to go out with, hang out a bit. I don't intend to get involved in a relationship. You know, I don't want to lose my freedom. Marriage is not on my mind.

She went upstairs to get ready. Ofelia, seeing herself alone with Rosa, said:

- Marina is different from all the other girls. Why does she run away from marriage? I would like her to find a good man, get married and have children. That is a woman's destiny.

- Maybe she got this way because of what her father did.

- Could be. That's one more fault of that bastard.

- Don't worry, Mrs. Ofelia. She says that because she hasn't found a man who interests her. When love appears, we forget everything. When I separated from my husband, I swore I'd never attach myself to any man again. But when Nelsino came along, it was as if everything changed. I fell for him.

- But you didn't want to move in with him.

- I really don't do that. What I want to do is date. Go every Saturday to the club with him, dance until dawn. Then I go back home, he goes to his place. There are no fights, argues, problems, and that's it.

- Wouldn't you like to have children?

- I had two that died before they were born. Now I won't try any more. I'm very well here.

At eight o'clock sharp the doorbell rang and Rosa went to answer it. Rafael introduced himself. She asked him to come in and led him into the living room where Ofelia, seeing him, stood up and went to greet him.

- I am Rafael Vilardi, Marina's friend.

- It's nice to meet you. Please sit down. My daughter won't take long.

He settled on the sofa and she said:

- Would you like a coffee, a water, a drink?

- No, thank you.

Ofelia turned to Rosa and asked:

- Tell Marina that Mr. Rafael has arrived.

She obeyed. Ofelia sat down in the armchair next to Rosa and continued:

- I am glad that Marina has agreed to leave for a while. That girl studies and works too much. She doesn't go out to have fun. At her age that's not right.

- Yes, it is. I too sometimes overdo it at work.

Marina went down the stairs and entered the living room. She looked beautiful in her elegant dark red dress, her golden hair neatly combed. He stood up. She walked towards him:

- I'm sorry I'm a few minutes late. I like to be punctual. But I didn't have much time to get ready-she said, holding out her hand to greet him.

- I didn't notice. I waited in excellent company.

- I see you didn't waste any time, answered Marina, smiling.

- He's being kind, my dear. We haven't even had time to talk.

- Today we are going out, but I promise I will come back one day to talk to you. You remind me a lot of an aunt I like a lot and haven't seen for ages. You make me miss my family.

- We can go whenever you like, said Marina.

- Then let's go now.

He said goodbye to Ofelia and they left. Rosa appeared and warned them:

- Dinner is ready. Can I serve it?

- Yes, I'll call Cicero.

- Handsome boy, isn't he? Did you see the way he looked at her when she entered the room?

- Yes. Marina looked beautiful.

- She should always look like that. He was dazzled.

- She assures that it is just friendship.

Rosa shook her head and answered:

- For now it might be. But that could change.

- I don't know if it is good or bad. Love can bring many changes. Serve dinner. I'll tell Cicero.

On the way to the restaurant, the conversation between Marina and Rafael flowed pleasantly.

- Your mother deserves the affection you feel for her.

- That's true. She has always been very devoted to me and Cicero.

- You can tell by the shine in her eyes when she talks about you two. She's a trustworthy person.

- You must be very good at your profession.

- You analyze people accurately.

- Not always. Your mother is a sincere, simple, practical person, without psychological games. Others, on the other hand, are closed, afraid to show themselves as they are, play roles all the time and it takes time and effort to really get to know them.

- The way you talk, you don't seem to trust human beings very much.

He smiled and replied:

- Experience has shown me that it is better not to prejudge. To trust or not to trust depends on the circumstances.

- What do you mean?

- People act according to what they believe and often underestimate their own qualities. They prefer to pretend, assuming to be what they are not, thinking of winning the admiration of others. Sooner or later they will discover that, whatever their motivation, the best thing is to be true.

Marina did not answer immediately. Maybe it was not good to deepen that friendship. Rafael was intelligent, observant. But she didn't like people penetrating her intimacy.

The car stopped in front of the restaurant, they got out and went in. The place was very nice, with live music. Rafael had reserved a table.

Once settled in, he tried to talk about current affairs. He had noticed that Marina didn't like to talk about behaviour. Why? It was as if she wanted to impose a distance. He, realizing this, decided to temporize.

Soon she felt at ease again and dinner went pleasantly. Some couples were dancing, and Rafael invited her to the dance floor.

- I don't know how to dance - she shied away.

- I don't think so. You don't want to dance with me.

- That's not the point. It's just that I never allowed myself to go to dances. I didn't have time. I worked and studied hard. So, I never learned.

- You deprived yourself of the most enjoyable thing in life.

- That much?

- But there's still time. Come, I'll teach you. This slow music is easy.

She shook her head negatively, but Rafael stood up, took her hand and pulled her.

- Let's go. You'll love it.

The musicians were playing a well-known blues and Marina decided to give it a try. On the small dance floor, Rafael wrapped his arms around her and she let herself be led to the rhythm of the sound. She knew and appreciated that music, so she had no difficulty.

When the band stopped, Rafael said smiling:

- You glided very well. You have rhythm, you are malleable, you have all the qualities of a great dancer.

- No kidding. It was the first time I dared to dance.

- I can hardly believe it.

The musicians began to play a samba. Without saying anything, he wrapped her arms around her and they began to dance. At first, she fumbled a little, but soon she got the step right and from then on everything worked out.

- You were born to dance. Didn't I tell you?

- I must admit I liked it. Dancing is very good. I really like music, and dancing is integrating body and soul to it.

- That's what it is. You have defined it very well.

They returned to the table as dinner was being served.

After dessert, they danced again. Marina forgot everything, letting herself be led by him in the various rhythms.

Rafael danced very well. He was light and led her safely. Marina, her face flushed from the exercise, was happy.

It was after two o'clock when Rafael left her at her house's door.

- It was a very pleasant evening, she said, holding out her hand to say goodbye. - Thank you.

- If you really liked it, we can do it again. It was so good that I didn't even see the time pass.

- Did you see what time it is? I think we overdid it.

- Not at all. Happy moments should be multiplied. I know very nice places, beautiful places, with good food, good music. I want to take you to all of them. I'll call and arrange it.

- Thank you. Good night.

- Good night.

She went inside and heard the sound of his car driving away. Marina was lighter, happier than she had felt for a long time. She tried not to make any noise and went up to her room.

Happy, humming one of the songs she had heard, she took a quick shower and went to bed. Soon she fell asleep.

Rafael went home thinking about Marina. She was a wonderful woman. While they were dancing, he felt the urge to squeeze her in his arms and kiss her. He restrained himself with an effort. He knew that if she noticed what he was feeling, she would never meet him again.

She seemed to be different from the women he had met. There was something about her that imposed distance. Maybe the fact that she didn't want to fall in love or get married was the reason. But, on the other hand, why did a woman who vibrated to the rhythm of the dance, showing such a thirst for life, such inner fire, decide to close her heart? Fear of her father's betrayal and abandonment? Or had she had some unpleasant experience that had made her nurture this desire?

She was healthy, that didn't seem natural to her. It would be exciting to try to find out what was hiding in that heart. She was intelligent, perceptive. To achieve his goal, he would have to be patient, go slowly, win her trust little by little.

But he was willing to achieve that. If you think about it, this task was not difficult, since he had had so much fun that night.

Arriving home, he went to bed, but it took him a while to fall asleep. In his head, the memory of those moments reappeared and he smiled satisfied.

He began to make plans to take her to fashionable places and decided to start choosing the next outings as early as the next day.

Having settled that, he felt calmer and was soon able to fall asleep.

CHAPTER 10

The sun was hiding, colouring the sky with orange hues, when Maria Eugenia entered the house in a hurry, without noticing the beauty of the afternoon or the delicate perfume of the flowers that perfumed the garden.

She headed anxiously towards Dionisio' room.

- How is he? - asked Elvira.

- He's fine. He no longer has fever.

She approached the crib where the boy was sleeping and placed her hand on his forehead.

- Yes, he seems to have relapsed. Did he take the whole bottle?

- Only half. His throat must still be irritated.

- It should be gone by now. He's been on his meds for over a day. Since he was born, almost two years ago, it's never taken this long to heal.

- That's the way it is, Mrs Maria Eugenia. He's already better, it's just a matter of time.

The boy woke up and, seeing her leaning over the crib, smiled and said:

- Mummy...

Immediately Mary Eugenia took him in her arms and kissed him gently on the cheek. The boy passed his hand around her neck, pressing it against her breast, and Maria Eugenia kissed him again.

Then she sat down on the sofa with him on her lap, stroking his curly hair.

Henrique entered the room and looked at them satisfied.

- I see he's better now, he said, coming closer.

- Yes. But he's still not eating properly. Stay with him. I'll go to the kitchen and find something for him to eat. He only took half of his bottle and during lunch he didn't eat anything.

Henrique held the boy, but he stretched out his arms saying:

- I want mummy.

- She will be right back. Daddy will play with you.

Henrique picked up some toys and sat down on the floor with the boy. While Dionisio entertained himself, he watched him with satisfaction.

Soon the boy would have his second birthday and he was getting more handsome every day. He had learned to talk very early, revealing a sense of observation and above-average intelligence.

Henrique was impressed by the attachment he showed Maria Eugenia from the very first days. Obliged by Adele to take care of the boy, at first, he had seen that she did so unwillingly.

Observing her attitudes, Henrique noticed that she rejected Dionisio, which worried him a lot. Although she wanted to keep him as little as possible, the boy cried when she moved away and calmed down only when she put him in her arms.

As he grew older, it was clear to see how attached he was to her. When they were together, she would run his little hand over her face and say in his childish language:

- Beautiful mummy!

He showed such affection that Maria Eugenia was truly moved. He was so tiny, so dependent on her care, his face would light up when he saw her, and she could not resist.

She forgot his origin, the moments of sadness she had gone through because of his existence, and surrendered to the love that blossomed in her heart.

Each day this love took over her life. She changed her attitudes radically. The social life she had enjoyed in Paris was completely forgotten.

Adele watched with satisfaction. She had achieved everything she wanted. Even Maria Eugenia's manner of treating her had changed. She had become more confident and, if she agreed with everything her mother said about the company, when it came to Dionisio she reacted by saying that she was enough to look after him.

Maria Eugenia returned carrying a tray.

- Look what mom's brought for you.

He shook his head negatively:

- Don't want it

She put the tray on the small table, picked him up and said:

- It's the porridge you love. It's very tasty.

- If he doesn't want it, I'll eat it, said Henrique.

- No, dad. I made this for Dionisio. He's going to eat it all, so he can get big and healthy.

- Take it boo-boo.

- I know. But you need to eat so it'll go away soon. Let's go.

She began to talk and play, and the boy slowly ate. Henrique looked on in amazement.

After making sure that he didn't really want to eat any more, Maria Eugenia handed him over to Elvira to wash his hands and change his clothes.

Seeing her walking away, Dionisio complained:

- Mom!

- I'm going to take a bath and I'll be right back, she said.

This attachment of Dionisio made her feel loved, desired. She loved Henrique and he treated her with love, affection and respect, but she often questioned in her heart whether he would have married her if she had not been Adele's daughter and heir to her fortune.

He was a handsome, intelligent man, and she noticed how women looked at him with admiration. She did not see herself as an attractive woman. Since her adolescence, this fear had haunted her. She had noticed how people changed with her when they found out her last name.

This thought had made her suffer during the period when they were waiting for Dionisio. For this reason, the love of the boy became very important to her, making her affective side, blocked by the fear of being used, blossom.

The purity of a child unafraid to show her feelings removed all her doubts.

She took a shower, dressed herself and went to Dionisio's room, who had fallen asleep. She placed her hand on his forehead and, noticing that he had no fever, went downstairs to wait for dinner.

As soon as she reached the living room, the telephone rang. The maid answered. Maria Eugenia heard her say:

- I'll see if she can answer it.

Turning to Maria Eugenia, she continued softly:

- It's for you.

- Who is it?

- It's a man, he sounds like a foreigner. He said his name is Pierre.

Maria Eugenia made a gesture of displeasure. Lately she didn't like to remember her escapades with Pierre. But she went to answer it.

- Hello.

- How are you, Maria Eugenia?

- Fine, and you? Is Jamille well?

- We're very well.

- You remembered us after so long. How's that wonderful city?

- Fine, as always. But we've just arrived in Brazil, precisely in Sao Paulo. My first thought was to call you. I couldn't stand the nostalgia any longer.

Maria Eugenia felt an unpleasant tightness in her chest. They never told her they planned to visit Brazil.

- How long do you intend to stay in São Paulo?

- I don't know. We have plenty of time. What I want is to see you today. I can't get you out of my mind.

- It won't be possible.

- How can it not? You seem evasive... You don't want to see me?

She tried to get around it:

- It's not that. My son is sick, I can't leave him at the moment.

- Finally, the boy is born! I saw the photo in the magazine.

Maria Eugenia shuddered. His tone sounded intentional.

She felt afraid. Besides Celia, Adele, Henrique and herself, Pierre was the only one who knew of her secret.

She tried to dispel the fear. She tried to give her voice a more cheerful tone and answered:

- I would like to see you both too, but my son has a fever and needs my care. I won't be able to go out.

- I know. You wouldn't be able to justify going out to your husband. I understand. I didn't go to your house because I know your husband might not like it. I'm letting you know the hotel phone number. I expect a call from you tomorrow.

She wrote down the number, then said:

- If he gets better, I'll call tomorrow.

- I won't wait long. If you don't call, I'll come to your place. I can't wait any longer.

- Fine. I'll call you anyway.

- I'll be waiting.

Maria Eugenia hung up the phone in concern. Pierre's tone struck her as inquisitive, very different from the one he'd used in Paris.

At that moment she began to think how imprudent she had been to let him discover her secret. She sincerely regretted having involved herself in that adventure.

She tried to push the fear away. She was prejudging. Pierre had never given her cause to suspect her of his friendship. She was changed, no longer that dissatisfied, nervous, useless woman.

Now her life had taken another course. There was Dionisio who had become the main reason for her life. He needed a good mother and she would never fail to fulfil this role.

The presence of Pierre and Jamille would not cause her any problems. He liked adventures, he didn't believe he loved her as he said he did.

Noticing how much she had changed, he would lose interest.

Then they would most likely leave soon and everything would go back to the way it was before.

Henrique approached:

- What is it? You seem worried. Who was that on the phone?

- Pierre. He and Jamille have just arrived in São Paulo. They want to visit us.

- You know I don't like them.

- I didn't like them being here either. I'd rather not see them. They want to go out and have fun, and now I don't want to go back to those late nights.

- I'm glad to hear that.

- But I don't think I'll be able to dodge it. At least we'll have to welcome them home a few times and go out and show them our city.

- It will be unpleasant.

- But when we were in Paris, they took me everywhere.

- Tell them that at that time you were on holiday, but that today you have commitments. That you have to wake up very early because of Dionisio.

- That is my intention. I intend to see them as little as possible.

- How long do they intend to stay?

- I don't know. He didn't say. But we'll soon find out. They're out for a walk. They certainly intend to visit other states in Brazil. I think they won't stay long.

- That would be a relief. Dinner is being served. Let's go.

He put his arm around her waist and they went into the dining room. Henrique was happy. Fortunately, Maria Eugenia was showing that she really had changed. Blessed was the time Adele had had the idea of getting them a child. Dionisio had won over Maria Eugenia, balanced their marriage and made them happy.

Meanwhile, Pierre and his wife were chatting in the luxurious rooms of the hotel where they had stayed.

Jamille paced up and down, irritated:

- I don't know if we were right to come here. You said Maria Eugenia would come running to welcome us and put us up in her house. But apparently you were wrong. She wasn't in any hurry to see us.

- She was surprised Maybe her husband was nearby. I don't believe she has forgotten us. After all, we have taken her everywhere fashionable.

Jamille sighed nervously:

- That was back when we had money. Besides, thanks to you we have nothing left.

- You don't have to remind me of that. I was earning and thought of multiplying our fortune. It was unfortunate. But I swore I'd make it right. Don't you believe me?

- Coming to this end of the world, full of uneducated people, hoping to recover what we lost, is an illusion. Who's to say she'll pay?

- If I tell them what I know, they'll lose a lot more. I guarantee they will pay whatever I ask. They don't lack money.

- Are you sure your suspicion is well-founded?

- Of course, I'm sure. She was wearing that fake belly. For what purpose?

- She might have wanted a child so badly she pretended to be pregnant.

- Not at all. I read in that magazine that the birth of this child consolidated the family fortune. There's a catch. She was wearing a fake belly. This child can't be hers.

- What if it is? She may have had this child after she returned from Paris.

- No way. There wouldn't be time. Did you see how old the boy is?

- You have to do something fast. We're spending the rest of the money we have to stay in this hotel for a few days. What do we do when it's over?

- I'm sure she'll put us up at her place. You'll see.

- And if she doesn't?

- I'll make my own arrangements.

- We could have stayed in a cheaper hotel.

- No, we couldn't. They can't know we're broke. Leave it to me and don't worry. I know what I'm doing.

Early the next morning Pierre didn't want to have breakfast in his room like Jamille. He went down to the dining room.

The waiter put the coffee and milk pots on the table and indicated the large table where tempting treats were to be found.

Before he could leave Pierre asked:

- My wife and I want to talk to someone who knows the city well and can guide us.

- You can talk to Milena. She attends to tourists. Coming out of the cafeteria, it's the first door on the right.

Pierre took his breakfast calmly and then went to look for Milena. She was a pretty brunette, very well dressed, kind smile, smart eyes, who answered him promptly.

Pierre was very kind. He said he was in Brazil for the first time and had come to Sao Paulo to meet some acquaintances, but he needed some information.

- What do you want to know? - she asked, her eyes shining with interest.

- It is about Dr. Henrique Silveira Couto.

- I know him. He is married to the daughter of the president of the Malta Organizations.

- That's right. We met two years ago in Paris and, as we are in São Paulo, I would like to get their address. She smiled slightly and answered:

- We are here to provide tourist information only, not personal information.

Pierre was already expecting this answer. He approached Milena:

- I'll be honest with you. My wife is really keen to see these acquaintances again. She says they're socialites.

- She's right. Besides projection, they have credibility. Many famous people would like to be friends with them.

Pierre fixed his gaze on hers and said dreamily:

- How beautiful you are!

She was surprised:

- What did you say?

- I'd stand here for hours looking at you.

Pierre stared at her in admiration. Milena felt appreciated that he was admiring her. A fine, rich man. She sighed, thinking:

- "Too bad he's married!"

Dealing with tourists all the time, Milena dreamed that one day one of them would fall in love with her and take her to see the world, like in a fairy tale.

- On second thought, I don't see a problem in giving you their address. Wait a moment.

She went into the adjoining room and shortly after returned handing Pierre a piece of paper:

- Here you are.

- Thank you. I'll call and arrange a visit. When we met in Paris, Mrs. Maria Eugenia was expecting a child.

- That's right. It's a beautiful boy. She really wanted to be a mother but it took a long time.

- To have a child, Pierre said, cutting her off from her thoughts, is the dream of many women.

- This child didn't represent just that. It was so much more.

- Why was it so?

- I heard that it came at a good time. If she hadn't had this child, his mother, Mrs. Adele Figueira Rocha, would have lost her position as president of the Malta Organizations.

- Is that so? And that's very important?

- You don't know their companies?

- No.

- Well, it's like I'm telling you. It was very lucky. Sometimes I wonder... Why is it that everything works out for some while for others it's just trouble? Look at the case of this Maria Eugenia. Besides being born rich, having a wonderful life, she married a handsome, charming man who lives around her all the time, and she even had a beautiful son when she needed.

- Life is like that. But a woman like you should not lose hope. One day someone will come along for you. Oh, if only I weren't married!

Milena blushed with pleasure. That conversation first thing in the morning made her think she had made her day. Pierre said goodbye, lightly kissing the hand she held out to him.

- We'll see each other again, he said, smiling.

He went back into the bedroom, where Jamille, lying on the sofa, was leafing through a magazine.

- What a long time you took! Where did you go?

- To mind our own business. I already know everything I need to know.

In a few words she told what she had heard from Milena, then finished:

- I am sure that behind this story there is a very well forged plan so that they could keep the power and the presidency of these companies as they always had.

- If this is true, they will have every interest in defending this secret.

- There's no doubt in my mind. Why would Maria Eugenia stay away from Brazil for so long, wearing a false belly? I'm sure she's sterile. What they did was a farce.

He rubbed his hands together, satisfied:

- We're done for life.

Jamille looked at him mischievously and replied:

- You never told me how you discovered her belly was unnatural.

- You also never told me how you know Jean's problems so well.

- You know I'm not curious. What are you going to do? So far she hasn't called us.

- I've got the address. I'll call and say we'll come visit this afternoon.

- She wasn't receptive.

- She must be scared. That's better. Everything will be easier that way.

Meanwhile Maria Eugenia tried to push away the worry about Pierre and Jamille's arrival. But she felt that this visit would do her no good.

She knew she should call them, be cheerful, receive them with attention, but the memory of her stay in Paris was very distant from her at that moment.

Now, having changed her life, she recognized that she had let herself be carried away by rebellion, committing acts that she deeply regretted.

Henrique surrounded her with affection and attention. With the arrival of Dionisio, he had become more accessible and more devoted, striving to return home early and enjoy their company to the full.

She absolutely did not want to lose this happiness they had earned, and the presence of Pierre and Jamille reminded her of a time she wished to forget.

All morning she felt restless. She paced from one side to the other wondering what to do. Elvira came over with Dionisio.

Maria Eugenia noticed that he was agitated and weeping. Worried, she put her hand on his forehead.

- He's not running a fever, but he doesn't look well.

- He woke up like this today.

- Maybe we should take him to the doctor.

Elvira hesitated a little, then answered:

- He's not sick. I think he has an evil eye.

- What's that?

- You know jealousy, envy.

- I don't believe in those things.

- Well, you should. Last night I had a negative dream and I also woke up restless. It feels like something bad is going to happen.

Maria Eugenia looked at her in amazement. She was feeling the same way. She tried not to take it seriously.

- Nothing is going to happen. It was just a dream.

Elvira thought for a moment, then said

- Look, Mrs. Maria Eugenia, when I feel like this, I go to Mrs. Eunice's house. She gives me a pass and all this disappears.

- Is she a witch doctor?

- No. She's a spiritualist medium. She has a centre where she treats people. My mother volunteers there. Dionisio is in a bad way, and when I'm near him I feel sick.

- We'd better take him to the doctor. In fact, you can tell he's not feeling well. His throat hasn't healed yet.

- It's much better. I feel that it is not a doctor that he needs. You could take him to Mrs. Eunice's house. She lives on this street, on the next block.

- I won't do that. Let's call Dr. Oscar.

Maria Eugenia went to the telephone and spoke to the doctor, who offered to see them in half an hour. Then, turning to Elvira, she ordered her:

- You're going with me. Get ready. I'll have the car brought in.

Maria Eugenia called one of the employees and said:

- If anyone calls, tell them I've gone to take my son to the doctor.

Once in the car, though worried about Dionisio, she felt relieved that she had left a message. If Pierre called, he would know that the boy was sick, and she would have a good excuse to avoid their company.

Before the doctor, Maria Eugenia voiced her concern. He made a careful examination, after which he said:

- You don't need to worry. He has improved a lot since yesterday. The throat infection has subsided. Everything is fine.

- But he doesn't want to eat. He says it hurts.

- The way it's progressing, he'll soon be cured.

- If you prescribe him a fortifier, perhaps he will eat better.

The doctor smiled and shook his head negatively:

- Your son is in excellent health, despite this cold. He is well nourished and, from what I know, has an enviable appetite. Rest assured: he's fine.

Once in the car, Elvira could not contain herself:

- Didn't I tell you the doctor wouldn't fix it?

- This discomfort is from the cold. Dr. Oscar said he'll be fine soon.

Elvira noticed that Dionisio was sleepy and settled him lovingly on her lap. He fell asleep, but Maria Eugenia noticed that it wasn't a peaceful sleep. His frown twitched and he stirred as if he wanted to get rid of something that was bothering him. From time to time his body would tremble and he would open his eyes, frightened.

Elvira did not give up her purpose of taking him to Mrs. Eunice. When they were passing in front of the house where she lived, Elvira asked:

- Mrs. Maria Eugenia, let's stop here and take Dionisio to Mrs. Eunice. She lives in this beautiful house.

Maria Eugenia hesitated.

- I don't like bothering others. I don't even know her.

- You'll like her. She's a very good person and she'll take good care of us.

Seeing that Maria Eugenia was undecided, she continued:

- It costs nothing. It will only take a few minutes. Please.

- Fine. I'll do what you ask.

Elvira indicated the house and the driver stopped in front of the main gate.

- You talk to her, said Maria Eugenia, embarrassed. - We'll stay in the car.

Elvira went downstairs, rang the bell and talked to a young woman, who went back inside the house. A little later, a middle-aged woman approached Elvira.

While they were talking, Maria Eugenia, from inside the car, saw a tall, elegant lady with blonde hair. She immediately noticed that she was a classy person.

Then Elvira approached the car and asked:

- Let's go inside. She's going to see us.

Maria Eugenia handed Dionisio to Elvira and went downstairs. Eunice was waiting for them inside the gate. She held out her hand as she approached.

- How are you?

- I'm fine. Sorry to bother you at home. But Elvira insisted.

- Come in, she answered simply.

They entered and were led into a living room. Eunice accommodated them gently.

It was a very beautiful house, a pleasant environment. There were natural flowers in several vases arranged with art. Maria Eugenia could not contain herself:

- What a pleasant aroma! What beautiful flowers!

Eunice smiled:

- They perfume our life and fill our eyes with beauty.

Then she went over to Elvira and placed her hand on Dionisio's forehead, who, still asleep, was stirring restlessly.

- What a beautiful boy! - she commented.

- He's not well - commented Elvira. - I've been feeling a lot of anguish when I've been near him.

Eunice continued to stroke his little head, and he opened his eyes and began to cry convulsively. Maria Eugenia, sitting next to them on the sofa, stood up, frightened.

- Don't worry, it's nothing. He'll be fine. Please, sit down and say a prayer. That's what he needs, Eunice said, looking Maria Eugenia in the eye.

She sat down again and, without taking her eyes off the boy, began to pray in silence.

- What's his name?

- Dionisio, answered Elvira.

She fixed her eyes on him and murmured a prayer in which she asked for Dionisio to be cured. Maria Eugenia noticed that her eyes were fixed and did not blink.

Eunice stretched her hands upwards and remained a few moments longer in silence. Then she began to run her hands over Dionisio gently. Little by little he calmed down, until he fell asleep again. But Maria Eugenia noticed that this time his sleep was peaceful.

Then Eunice said to Elvira:

- Go into the next room with the boy. I need to talk to your boss.

She obeyed. When they were alone, Eunice sat down next to Maria Eugenia on the sofa. She put her hand on hers and said:

- You are distressed, and you have passed this on to the boy.

- Indeed. I'm not feeling very well today. But I don't understand. How could Dionisio have been affected? I love him very much and would never do anything to hurt him.

- I know. But children are greatly influenced by their family environment. You must know that when we think, we release energies around us according to the quality of our thoughts. Your worries created a negative energetic environment that influenced the child.

- What can I do to prevent this from happening?

- Avoid feeding unpleasant thoughts.

Maria Eugenia ran her hands through her hair in concern. How could she avoid the fear that had set in since Pierre's arrival?

Eunice continued:

- Sometimes we don't understand what happens to us, we let ourselves be swept away by rebellion and end up committing acts that we regret later.

Maria Eugenia looked at her in amazement. How could she know that? Eunice continued:

- That boy has brought light into your life. You have changed for the better. However, life is bringing up some unresolved issues from the past and you need to face them with courage to overcome them.

Maria Eugenia could not stand the pressure and began to cry. She was sobbing desperately and Eunice let her vent. When she calmed down a little, Maria Eugenia said:

- I'm sorry. I'm out of control.

- You're afraid that your secret will get out.

Maria Eugenia tried to hold back a startled cry.

- How do you know? Who told you this?

- A spiritual friend who wants to help you. It was him who brought you here today.

- How can that be? No one knows. My family knows the main thing, but they don't know the mistake I made. If my husband finds out, he won't forgive me.

She sobbed again in despair. Eunice held her hand tightly and said:

- Although there are people plotting against you, I must tell you that the spiritual help protecting you is very great. You must trust. You must not lose your temper or imagine the worst.

- But I don't know what to do. How to deal with this?

- Calm down. When we are doing our best, life protects us. You are dedicating yourself to this boy with a lot of love. He was given to you as an addition of divine kindness to help you achieve a better life. For this, they needed the cooperation of many. And now that everything is going well, they will help so that the fruit of this effort will not be lost. However, I must warn you that the success of this project depends on you, on how you accept the facts and choose your attitudes.

Maria Eugenia was fascinated. Eunice's words were deep in her spirit. Looking into her eyes, she had the feeling that she knew her. Then, as if moved by a greater force, she began to talk about her life.

CHAPTER 11

While Eunice held her hand, Maria Eugenia spoke naturally, feeling safe, confident, without understanding why she was exposing her innermost feelings as she had never done with anyone.

She told Eunice how hard it had been to live with her mother, how afraid she was of not feeling able to satisfy her mother's expectations of her. About the wedding, the child that had not arrived, the possibility that her mother would no longer be the majority shareholder and would have to leave the presidency, and the plan she had used to get what she wanted. She told her everything, even the phone call from Pierre. And she finished in tears:

- Now, analysing what happened in Paris, I recognise how wrong I was. And, what is worse, I realize that Pierre is not to be trusted. When I answered the phone I felt a sense of imminent danger that I can't explain. For the time being he has done nothing to make me feel that way. I even think that I am exaggerating, but this fear doesn't let me.

- You are right: these people are not well-intentioned. He lost large sums in gambling.

- Pierre liked to gamble.

- Not only gambling, but also spending. His financial situation is very bad. He is after money.

Eunice did not use the word "blackmail" so as not to scare her even more.

- My God! He didn't appreciate our country. He once said he would never come here.

- He knows you are people of means. That's what he came for. This is an unscrupulous individual with a terrible record.

- I'm lost. My husband will find out everything, and our marriage may fall apart.

- Let's ask our spiritual friends for help. I am sure they will inspire you in your decisions. You need to stay calm.

- I don't know if I can do it. I made a mistake and I am being punished.

- God does not punish anyone. If he allows some challenges, it is for your spirit to mature.

- Help me, please. I feel that you can do this.

- Let's pray and ask for help. Try to relax, forget your worries for a few moments. Imagine we are sitting on the edge of a very blue lake, the sun surrounding us, the flowers scenting perfume, while a shaft of very bright blue light comes down from above and envelops us.

Eunice paused slightly and murmured a heartfelt prayer, asking for the assistance of the spirits of light to inspire Maria Eugenia and help her to overcome the challenges that sought her.

As she spoke, Maria Eugenia gradually calmed down, and at the same time a great peace enveloped her. When Eunice fell silent, she sighed and said:

- What a relief!

- Prayer connects us with the dimensions of light and opens up space so that the enlightened spirits can involve and help us.

- What would you advise me to do?

- Don't be afraid. This couple will look for you at home. Receive them naturally. At no time should you let them know that you are afraid. I would like you to write on this paper their names, the hotel where they are. I will keep praying on your behalf.

- What will I do if he mentions our meetings in Paris?

- Deny it. Pretend you don't remember. If he makes any reference to your false pregnancy, deny it. Say that he is mistaken, that you were pregnant and did not know it. That the child is yours and your husband's.

- And if they do not believe it?

- Imagine that this is your truth and affirm it at any chance. I'll give you my phone number. If you hear anything new, let me know.

Maria Eugenia stood up:

- I don't know how to thank you. I was in agony, now I'm calmer.

- Yes, your son is getting over a simple cold. He'll be back on his feet by tomorrow. He's a beautiful boy. His spirit is linked to you from other lives. He loves you very much. He has come to help you overcome all your challenges.

- Indeed. He's very attached to me. That's what won me over. Today I even forget that he wasn't born of me.

- It's better this way. You've been too jealous of the woman who gave him the chance to be born. Be grateful to her. One day you will know why everything had to happen this way.

- You mentioned other lives. How can that be?

- Someday we'll talk about that. I'll explain many things you need to know.

- That's ok. Now we have to go. Thank you for everything.

They went into another room and Maria Eugenia asked Elvira:

- How is he?

- Sleeping peacefully. He doesn't have those jitters any longer.

Eunice intervened:

- He'll sleep a lot now to recover. Don't wake him up even to eat. When he wakes up, he will be better and hungry.

They thanked her again and left. Maria Eugenia was much calmer. Dionisio slept serenely, which increased her sense of peace.

- See how much better he is? - said Elvira when she put Dionisio in bed and he didn't even wake up.

- I did. Thank you for taking us there. This woman is wonderful.

- She has helped me a lot. I knew you would like it.

One of the maids came over:

- This gentleman called and left this message.

Maria Eugenia took the paper, but before she could read it she knew it was from Pierre. He kept repeating the number of the hotel telephone and asking her to call.

Determined, she picked up the phone and called. Jamille answered, and Maria Eugenia tried hard to sound cheerful.

- Jamille? What a pleasure to hear from you!

- Pierre said you'd seen the doctor.

- I owe you an apology. It's just that my son is ill and I had to take him to the doctor. I'm very attached to him. When there's any trouble, I get desperate.

- I understand. I don't think we've come at a good time. But since you left us, we've remembered a lot about the times we spent together. It was wonderful! We're thinking of doing it again.

- At that time my son was not yet born. Now I have to look after him and I can't go away for a long time. But Henrique and I will be very happy to receive you at our house tonight for dinner. That way we can talk.

Jamille laughed and replied:

- 'All right. We will go. But I notice that you have changed a lot. You're more homely, a housewife.

- You are right. The birth of my son changed my life. Now my greatest pleasure is to be with him.

Jamille was silent for a few seconds, then asked:

- He must be grown up by now. When we met in Paris, you were already pregnant with his child.

- I have a confession to make. I had a hard time getting pregnant. Not that there was any impediment. It's just that I was afraid of the deformity of my body. I was terrified of getting fat. If on the one hand I wanted motherhood, on the other I didn't want to get fat.

- As I recall, you were pregnant in Paris, weren't you?

At that moment, Maria Eugenia thought:

"She knows. Pierre told her about the fake belly."

She answered, trying to give her voice a joking tone:

- I was. But I put on a girdle to disguise it and pretended I didn't. But now everything's fine. After Dionisio was born, my body went back to normal.

- That's just as well. I never wanted children because of that either.

- We'll have dinner at eight. We're waiting for you. Write down my address.

Jamille pretended she had. After she hung up the phone, she thought. Pierre could have been mistaken.

An hour later, when he came in, Jamille said immediately:

- Maria Eugenia called and invited us to dinner tonight.

Pierre gave her a victorious look.

- That's just as well. If she hadn't called, we'd have come to your place anyway. What did she say?

Jamille recounted the whole conversation and finished:

- I think we're in a ditched canoe.

- Why? When I called, she got very nervous. I could tell she was afraid.

- But today she was calm and happy. She said that when her son gets sick, she gets desperate. That could be the cause of the nervousness you noticed. Every mother gets neurotic when her son is sick.

- What a son, no way! She wore a fake belly in Paris.

- By the way, I'll remind you again, you never told me how you found that out.

- I don't need to tell you. You can imagine perfectly well.

She made a face, pretending to be jealous:

- Traitor!

- That was providential. It could become our salvation.

- What if you're wrong? She could really be wearing a girdle to hide her belly. After all, we did go out at night, to trendy places. It's understandable that she would do that.

- What I saw didn't look like a girdle to me. Afterwards, she was very embarrassed when she realised I saw it. She asked me to keep it a secret. That meant that if others knew, it could be dangerous.

Jamille shook her head negatively and replied:

- Any woman in her place would be embarrassed. Maybe she was interested in winning you over and wanted to cover up that girdle.

- I don't think so. If she was pregnant, I would have noticed. I didn't notice anything.

- I hope you're right, because we're running out of money. I don't know what will happen to us if we don't get what we want from her.

- I always get what I want. Calm down. Tonight we have to pretend we're still as rich as we used to be. You're going to that dinner with your jewels and all your attributes.

- Jewels that are as false as our ostentation.

- I don't like it when you talk like that. It's bad luck. You must believe we'll make it.

- I'm trying. But there's something not quite right about this story. Where did you go anyway?

- Out on a tour of the city. And I didn't like it. I'm making an immense sacrifice to be here. That'll make me raise the price. They will pay dearly for it.

Jamille shrugged and resumed the magazine she had been leafing through.

After she had spoken to Jamille, Maria Eugenia called Henrique to inform him that they would have guests for dinner. She explained:

- I had no choice. They were determined to come visit us. So I went ahead of them, they visit us and leave. I don't think they'll be here long.

- All right. I'll be home in time to welcome them.

Just before seven, Henrique had already returned home.

- Did you take Dionisio to the doctor?

- Yes. Dr. Oscar said it was just a cold and he will be fine soon.

- How is he?

- Sleeping peacefully. I think he's recovering.

- That's good. I was worried about him.

- So was I.

Maria Eugenia didn't said she had taken the boy to Eunice's house. She preferred not to say anything.

At eight o'clock Pierre and Jamille arrived. The maid took them into the living room where Henrique and Maria Eugenia were. They both rose to greet them. After the greetings, settled in the sitting room, Pierre took a drink:

- I am glad to see you both so well. Maria Eugenia is looking better. And what a lovely house you have!

- Indeed. We're doing very well.

- Motherhood has done Maria Eugenia good, Jamille remarked.

Even though her visitor said it so naturally, Maria Eugenia noticed a hint of irony. But she wasn't intimidated. She was ready to sweep away that unpleasant past and free herself of that friendship.

- You look great too, Maria Eugenia answered, smiling.

Henrique offered her a drink. They accepted a glass of wine. While they sipped, enjoying some snacks that the maid had placed on the table, Henrique asked:

- Is this the first time you have come to Brazil?

- Yes, Jamille answered, looking into Henrique's eyes as she thought:

"How handsome he looks! I had never noticed. This trip is starting to get interesting…"

- How long do you intend to stay in our city? - Henrique asked.

In Pierre's eyes there was an indefinable gleam when he said:

- It depends.

- On what? - inquired Maria Eugenia.

- On what we find here. We're in no hurry. We're just taking a walk.

- Our city has very beautiful places. I'm sure you'll appreciate them. I'm sorry I can't guide you as I'd like to. Unfortunately, at the moment we are engaged in a project in our company which takes up all our time.

- But Maria Eugenia will be able to show us around, said Jamille smiling.

- I'll see what I can do, she replied. - It so happens that my son is still very small, very attached to me, and is ill. To be honest, I'm not up to date with social events now. Since he was born, I have withdrawn from social life.

- That's not possible! - said Pierre. - You used to love the night life, the salons, the movement. I always thought motherhood was a prison, but I didn't expect it to do that to you, always so cheerful.

- But I'm still cheerful. Now more than before. My son has brought a new motivation into my life.

Henrique came over, put his arm around Maria Eugenia's shoulders and said:

- It's true. Dionisio has brought us a greater motivation to live. Haven't you ever thought about having children?

Jamille had a slight startle:

- God forbid! Don't even say that!

- Jamille doesn't like children. When they're small they're a lot of work; after they grow up, a lot of trouble. I agree with her. We chose not to have children. We live very well, free, without having to sacrifice our pleasures for their sake.

- You're wrong, said Maria Eugenia. We are not sacrificing ourselves for our son. On the contrary: being with him gives us great pleasure, a joy I have never found in the salons we frequent anywhere in the world.

- I see you're really in love with your son, Pierre said.

- I really am. He's very handsome and very clever.

- Who does he look like? - Jamille asked.

Maria Eugenia picked up a picture frame from one of the tables and brought it to Jamille:

- See for yourself. Who do you think he looks like?

She held the picture frame for a few seconds, then said:

- He looks just like his father.

Maria Eugenia smiled triumphantly.

- Let me show you something.

She left the room and returned with a photo album. She opened it and gave it to Jamille.

- Look at this photo.

Jamille looked at it. It was an old photo of a small boy. On the bottom of the page was written:

HENRIQUE ON HIS FIRST BIRTHDAY

Maria Eugenia brought the picture frame with the photo of Dionisio close to her and asked

- And so?

- They look like the same person, she said, surprised. - How can they be so similar?

- Because I'm his father, that's why. What are you surprised at? said Henrique and continued: - But, if you look closely, you will notice he has the same mouth and the same expression in his eyes as Maria Eugenia.

Pierre approached his wife. They both looked at the two pictures and had to agree.

The maid told them dinner was about to be served and they went into the dining room. Pierre looked at the works of art, the tasteful decor, the luxury and comfort of the mansion. His eyes sparkled with lust.

The resemblance of the photos made him somewhat uncertain as to the boy's parentage. There was no doubt that he was Henrique's son, but his resemblance to Maria Eugenia was not at all obvious.

The dinner took place in a formal manner, since both Jamille and Pierre were afraid that the plan they had devised would not work out.

Henrique was being absolutely formal, doing the honours of the house, trying to be polite to people he did not like and whom he wished would leave as soon as possible. Maria Eugenia, careful to pretend happiness and calm, not wanting them to notice how much their presence bothered her, was not communicative at all.

After dinner the couples sat in the living room to talk.

Pierre and Jamille asked questions about Brazilian customs, feigning interest and trying at the same time to find out what they could about the couple's lives.

At a certain point, Elvira discreetly approached Maria Eugenia and said softly:

- Excuse me if I am interrupting you, but Dionisio has woken up and is crying, calling for you.

- Have you seen if he has a fever?

- He's normal. He was sleeping peacefully, but suddenly he woke up screaming and calling for you.

Maria Eugenia got up:

- Excuse me, I need to see my son.

Jamille stood up immediately:

- May I accompany you? I'd very much like to meet him.

Maria Eugenia hesitated a little, but agreed:

- Come with me.

They went up to the boy's room and Jamille, though feigning indifference, observed every detail of the house. Inside her, an angry thought nagged at her. Why did they have all that, live in luxury, while she and her husband had to be left with nothing? It wasn't fair. Maria Eugenia didn't value what she had. The same applied to her husband, a prosaic family man who, despite all the power he possessed, was content to work and live a limited life without enjoying all that money could give them. It was true that they lived in luxury, they had comfort and good taste. But what was the use if they remained complacent, without taking advantage of the goods they possessed?

She and Pierre had exquisite taste, they knew how to value position, social power, everything that money could buy. They had as their most important rule that people are worth what they possess. For them, not having any more money, being poor, was the worst of punishments, and they would do anything to get back the goods they had squandered.

As soon as they entered Dionisio' room, he, still sobbing, said:

- Beautiful mother... I luv you!

Maria Eugenia ran to him and took him in her arms. Kissing his little face tenderly, she went on to say:

- I'm here, my son. Calm down.

Little by little he stopped crying. Maria Eugenia continued stroking him.

- Has he eaten? - she asked Elvira.

- I brought him the bottle, but he hasn't eaten yet. I think he had a bad dream. He was sleeping peacefully and suddenly woke up screaming and calling for you.

Maria Eugenia, remembering some phrases that Eunice had said, wondered if the boy's nervousness was being caused by the presence of those unpleasant people.

Due to the circumstances, she felt that the atmosphere in the house was a bit heavy, as it could be told that none of the four were at ease.

- He needs to eat. Let's see if I can get him to take the bottle.

She sat down in the armchair, settled the boy on her lap and offered him the bottle. He stared at her adoringly and soon began to suckle.

Jamille watched in silence. It was hard to imagine that this child was not their son. It was very likely that Pierre had made a mistake.

- I'm sorry, Jamille. That's what I told you: Dionisio is very attached to me, more than to his father. And now that he's sick, he demands more of me. That's why I told you that for the moment I cannot leave.

- I understand - she answered slowly. - But I don't think you can cancel yourself out like that. He is monopolizing you. If he's doing that now that he's little, can you imagine what he'll do when he's older?

- He has done more for me than I am doing for him. He gave me love, happiness, motivation to live. You shouldn't talk about what you don't know. I think if you had a son, maybe you wouldn't need to roam the halls looking for entertainment to pass the time. I know what I am saying. For a long time that's what I did, but when I returned home, in the solitude of my room, when the noises of the salons disappeared, I felt the weight of the loneliness, the unhappiness, the emptiness that was my life at that time.

Jamille stirred in her chair, uneasy. She had often felt an emptiness after the orgies she had been involved in, eager to find something that motivated her to live.

In fact, she had long ago come to the conclusion that life was not worth living, that everything was just an inglorious struggle in which the strongest wins, but that victory was useless because it was incapable of giving her happiness.

Suddenly she felt a touch of envy for Maria Eugenia, with her life as mother, wife, housewife, devoted to the love of her family. She didn't know what that was.

From an early age her mother, a rich woman, descendant of an important family, whose marriage had been arranged by family convenience, had taught her to value name, money, power, appearances.

Her parents were polite. She had never seen them argue or exchange affection. She met Pierre at a party and they began to go out together. His family was very rich. They went to all the fashionable places.

Until one night Pierre's father locked himself in his office and shot himself in the head. No one ever knew why. He left a brief note saying goodbye to the family.

From then on, Pierre's mother shut herself away in a villa they owned in Italy and never again frequented society. Three years after Pierre and Jamille's marriage, one cold morning they received the news that she had died of pneumonia.

Pierre, an only child, continued to live as usual, among friends, spending a lot of money on late nights and leading a frenzied life. In this way he squandered all the fortune he had inherited from his parents.

All these thoughts crossed Jamille's mind as she watched Maria Eugenia feeding her son, eyes glowing with affection, something she had never been able to feel in her life.

Her relationship with her husband was what she hoped it would be. Both of them liked to live intensely all the sensations that life could offer, without wanting anything more than that.

Suddenly Jamille felt tired of all this. The intimacy with Pierre was lukewarm, conventional, and so both of them had agreed to seek in other arms the sensations they did not feel together.

In front of their friends, they boasted of having an "open marriage", a fashion that was catching on in Europe. They accepted life as if there were nothing better than what they were getting.

The loss of money had made them get out of that comfort zone and feel afraid of the future for the first time. They had lost the only thing they valued: money. How could they bear poverty and humiliation?

Dionisio finished breastfeeding and Maria Eugenia caressed him, murmuring words of affection, wanting him to be quiet.

In the living room Henrique did his best to hold a conversation with Pierre, talking about books, theatre, customs. They had nothing in common.

Pierre, on the other hand, tried to bring the matter to Henrique's company in an attempt to find out as much as he could about it. But as he had no knowledge of the subject, which he found monotonous, he was unsuccessful.

When Maria Eugenia and Jamille came down, accompanied by Elvira carrying Dionisio, they both stood up politely.

- Is he all right? - Henrique asked.

- Yes, Maria Eugenia answered. - He has no fever, but he is still very nervous, which means he is still not feeling well.

Elvira sat down on the floor beside the boy with some toys, trying to entertain him.

- He can't take his eyes off you, Jamille commented.

- He wants to see if I'm here. When he's indisposed, he only calms down when I'm around.

- That's a question of discipline, remarked Pierre. - My parents, for instance, when I was a child never allowed me to be present when they had visitors.

- Here at home, we value the well-being of our son. I'm sure that our friends, when they visit us, understand this.

- Of course, Jamille hastened to say, smiling. - I am also in favour of a more open upbringing. When I was a child, I was very discriminated against by my parents, demanding ones, who never allowed my presence at the table at meals before the age of twelve. And, even afterwards, I was forbidden to speak, to give my opinion in adult conversations. I think that's why I hate my childhood. I only began to exist and be part of the family after the age of eighteen.

- Fortunately, customs have changed a lot, commented Maria Eugenia. - But I only do what I think is good for us. My son always comes first.

Half an hour later, the couple said goodbye, to Henrique and Maria Eugenia's relief. When they were alone, Henrique said:

- I'm glad they're gone. I didn't know what else to say.

- Indeed. They have nothing to do with us. I didn't understand how I could have strengthened this friendship so much in Paris. I guess I was out of my mind.

- They haven't said how long they will stay. I'm sure they'll come back to us.

- I don't think they will stay much longer. They have nothing to do here. Then we don't encourage them to stay.

- I hope so.

As soon as they got into the taxi that Henrique had called for them, Pierre blurted out:

- What rude people! With the cars in the garage they didn't even have the courtesy to take us to the hotel.

- You can tell they don't like us.

- I don't care about that. I don't like them either. But they will pay dearly for it.

Jamille was thoughtful for a few seconds, then said:

- You know what? I think we came to the wrong place. We've made a useless expense. They don't have any secrets. You're wrong. We won't get anything.

Pierre frowned and replied:

- You're the one who thinks. I'm not giving up.

- The child is his father's face and the boy's attachment to her makes us believe she's his real mother. Then, she has a passion for him that she certainly wouldn't have if he were her adopted son.

- Even if this boy is their legitimate son, I hold other trumps.

- Which ones?

- He strikes me as whipped and old-fashioned. What would he say if he knew his wife had cheated on him with me?

- What do you intend to do? You want to get your ass shot off? I think he would be quite capable of that.

Pierre looked at her with arched eyebrows, smiling mischievously as he replied:

- He won't need to know anything. She's the one who's going to give us what we need. Have you thought how much it's worth to her to keep the marriage going? Do you think Maria Eugenia would like her husband finding out about her escapades in Paris?

- Will it work?

- I'm sure it will. You'll see.

- It has to be fast. We're running out of money.

- I'm on it. I know how to do it.

Arriving at the hotel, Jamille went to her room and Pierre went down to the bar. As he drank his favourite wine, he wondered what he would do to get what he wanted.

CHAPTER 12

Marina arrived home in the late afternoon to find Ofelia worried.

- Has something happened? - she asked.

- Yes. Cicero came home from school feeling unwell and went to his room. I went after him, tried to talk to him, but he started crying and saying nonsense. Rute arrived for class and Rosa told her what was happening. She went to his room and asked me to leave her alone with him. They have been there for more than ten minutes.

- I will go see what is going on.

Marina went up to her brother's room and entered. Cicero was lying down and Rute, standing at the side of the bed, kept her hand on his forehead. Eyes closed, she seemed to pray.

Cicero, also with his eyes closed, trembled from time to time. Marina, surprised, understood nothing. Rute opened her eyes, gave him a slight sign to wait and closed her eyes again.

After a few minutes, Cicero opened his eyes. Rute removed her hand from his forehead and asked:

- How do you feel?

- Relieved. I don't know what it was. I felt an anguish, it seemed that I was going to die. I was short of breath, I couldn't stand still.

- It's over now. You have mediumship. Do you know what that is?

- No.

- You've been feeling these things for some time, haven't you? I guess since you were twelve or thirteen.

- That's true. But before it wasn't strong. It passed right away. Now it seems to have grown.

- Your sensitivity is opening up. You are a medium.

Marina intervened:

- Could it be? It's hard to believe. Cicero has always been a balanced boy.

- Mediumship is not a sign of unbalance.

Marina remembered the conversations she had had about this with Celia and Isaura when she was at the farm and the books she had read on the subject.

- I'm sorry. That's not what I meant. It's just that I have never noticed anything different in Cicero.

- He's very sensitive. Perhaps the change of life has hastened the development of his sensitivity. But, in any case, I can see that he has that characteristic.

- How can you know?

- Today, when I arrived here, he was being enveloped by the spirit of a very sad and weeping woman. She talked to me and I managed to calm her down. With prayers, she was rescued and taken away. Only then did Cicero return to his normal state.

Marina sat down beside the bed, not knowing what to say. She knew that these things happened, but never imagined that it would happen inside her house.

- I don't know what to say, Rute. I can see that you know the subject. What would you advise me?

- Study. There are many books about it, research, study centres where there is practical guidance on mediumship.

Marina approached Cicero, smoothed his hair and said:

- Why did you never tell me what you were feeling?

- I was afraid. I thought I was going crazy. So many strange thoughts go through my head. There are times when I am fine, together with my friends, but suddenly everything changes. It's as if I were another person: I feel sick, angry, I want to fight. I try to control it, but I don't always succeed. Please, Mrs. Rute, take this away from me. I don't want to feel these things.

- Calm down. I do not and no one has the power to prevent your sensitivity from manifesting itself. It is a natural condition for everyone, although each one has a certain time for it to appear. But being a medium is a blessing. You don't need to be afraid.

- But I am. I don't want this business of spirits.

- That's why I advise you to study the subject. It is the only way for you to learn to deal with your sensitivity and use it to your advantage. In time, you will realize that to be a medium is to penetrate the secrets of the universe. It is to discover the laws of life, to become more lucid and wiser.

Marina looked at him torn. On one hand, she knew that Rute was being sensible, advising the best. On the other hand, she did not want her brother to suffer so much conflict.

Rute put her hand on Marina's arm and said:

- He is a strong spirit and he has ways to deal with it. You must trust and help him. I am sure he has come to your side because you can do it.

Marina sighed and hugged her affectionately.

- Thank you, Rute. You have been a friend to my heart. I will follow your advice. Can you tell me some books to start with?

- Yes, I can. But I'd like to do more. I have a friend who is a very gifted medium, she has a study group. I'd like you to go to a session there for a spiritual consultation.

- What do you think Cicero? Let's go?

- I'll go if Mrs. Rute goes along.

- Okay, I will go. But first I must talk to her and find out when we can go. Now, get up from there. You don't think you are going to skip our class today.

- That's right, Marina reinforced. - Let's go downstairs. We're waiting for you there.

They left and immediately Cicero got up, went to wash and comb his hair. He felt light, happy. He didn't even remember the discomfort he had felt.

Later, alone in her room, Marina remembered the woman she had dreamed about twice and who had spoken to her about reincarnation. She was sure that it had not been an ordinary dream. That contact had been so real that she never forgot it.

The conversations with Celia and Isaura at the farm, about life after death, mediumship and reincarnation, perhaps they were not by chance, but messages that life was sending her so that she would study the subject.

The phone rang and she answered. It was Rafael inviting her to the theatre.

- I don't know if I will be able to go. Cicero did not have a good time today.

- It is a clever and very good comedy. I'll tell you what: I'll come to your house at eight, then we'll see; if you don't want to go, we'll stay and talk.

- Come indeed. Cicero loves you. In fact, you've already won over everyone here at home.

- That's just as well, because it's been an oasis for me there. I love your mother.

At eight o'clock Rafael arrived and was welcomed with joy. Rosa went to call Marina, who came down. After the greetings, they sat down in the living room and Rafael asked:

- So, how is Cicero?

The boy appeared on the threshold smiling and answered:

- I'm great. So much so that I am going for a walk.

Rafael looked at Marina surprised:

- Wasn't he sick?

Ofelia entered to greet him and Rafael got up to hug her. Since he had been in that house for the first time, more than a year ago, they had become friends.

Perhaps because he lived far from his own family, Rafael felt at ease with Ofelia's affection, Cicero's curiosity, always questioning things, and Marina's enlightened intelligence.

She was so spontaneous that in front of her he didn't need to resort to the usual behavioural analyses to know right away what she wanted to say or do. Nor did he have to guard against the usual feminine games, full of subterfuge and hidden intentions, which he hated.

Marina was direct, simple and practical, unlike him, who questioned the smallest gestures of people, wanting to discover what lay behind each of their attitudes.

Used to being highly valued by women, Rafael had been a little disappointed at first, noticing that she didn't intend to win him over, but after a while he felt relieved and at ease.

On the other hand, Marina enjoyed his company, his witty intelligence, his culture, good humour and discretion, having never gone down the path of conquest.

They often went out together and Marina enjoyed going to theatres, cinemas, concerts and restaurants with him. In addition to

Rafael being very pleasant, she felt comfortable going out at night with him.

It was Ofelia who answered:

- Cicero was terrible. He came home pale and depressed, went to his room and didn't want to see anyone. When Rute arrived for class, she went to his room to check on him. I don't know what she did, but after she and Marina went downstairs he appeared all excited, as if nothing was wrong with him. He ate very well and went for a walk, which he only does when he's in a good mood.

Rafael looked at Marina and said:

- It must have been an emotional crisis. At his age it happens a lot. In these cases, attention and a good talk usually solve it.

- This time it was more than that, Marina said. - Sit down. I want to talk about what happened.

- I'll make some fresh coffee," said Ofelia, leaving the room.

- Tell me Marina. What happened?

- We never talked about it. Do you believe there is life after death?

- Yes, I do. In my work I have come across cases that made me think about it a lot. Why do you ask?

- Because when I arrived at Cicero's room, I found Rute with her hand on his forehead, talking. He was crying in anguish. She comforted him, prayed and he got better. Then she explained that he is a medium and that the unpleasant emotions he was feeling were from a spirit.

- What about him?

- He felt relieved to hear this. Without understanding what was happening, he was afraid he was going crazy. Luckily Rute understood the subject.

- The sixth sense is a reality. We all have it. I think we need to learn more about our emotional and spirituality.

- Dreams are intriguing too. Twice I dreamt of a woman who, although I had not seen her before, seemed very familiar. We were in a beautiful garden, where the flowers, the vegetation, have very vivid and beautiful colours. We talked, but I don't remember everything we talked about. All I know is that she spoke about reincarnation. But I am sure that these were no ordinary dreams. They were so real! I still get emotional when I remember them.

- Dreams have always fascinated me. They are differentiated states of consciousness, in which many variables interfere. In my profession they are revealing. Sometimes they portray situations that the person prefers not to see. Studying them is part of my work. I have read about astral journeys and I have had some patients who have even seen their body sleeping in bed while they moved around the room, with lightness and extraordinary well-being.

- While I was away, I had occasion to get to know about this, but knowing that my brother is a medium and needs to learn to deal with his sensitivity worries me a little.

- It's something new for you. The unknown is a little frightening. On the other hand, being able to discover the secrets of life, to get proof that life continues after death, is a blessing. Having this certainty changes all our concepts and attitudes. Reincarnation is a wonderful key to understanding social inequalities, because it reveals the results of our choices in other lives. I have had many cases that made me think that all this is true. But there is still a side of me that doubts a little.

- That's what happens to me. I did not seek this path, but since it happened here, with my brother, I am willing to seek proof and learn how these things work, to help Cicero. Rute has a medium friend who runs a spiritual study group. She even does spiritualist sessions. She wants to take us for a consultation.

- In that case I want to come with you. I have many unanswered questions inside me. Cases that occurred with friends, with patients, with life in hospitals.

Ofelia returned to the living room with a tray and served coffee and cake. Then she went into the bedroom to watch TV.

- What does your mother think about this?

- She has always attended the Catholic Church. I thought she wouldn't like what happened. I took some time to tell her, but I was surprised, because when I finished, she said: "I always suspected that this boy was somehow different. Ever since he was little, he has all the signs. When I saw that he was tormented, I had to take him to a witchdoctor. She prayed over his head and he improved immediately. The next morning, he woke up feeling fine".

- Popular wisdom... Your mother is a great woman.

- She is a simple woman, she only did the first grade, but she has a kindness that I respect and admire. I am very proud to be her daughter.

- I am very interested in the case of Cicero. There are certain facts that I have witnessed that medicine does not explain and that suggest spiritual intervention. Once, when I was a resident in a hospital, a middle-aged patient who had suffered a car accident was in a coma. His wife approached him and spoke words of affection, asking him not to leave her to return to her and their children.

Marina listened with interest and he continued:

- As a doctor, I knew that a patient in a coma does not know what is happening around him. Wanting to calm her down, I asked her to leave and said that in the state he was in he could not hear anything she was saying. But she refused, saying that she would bring him back and that he would not leave. As his condition was serious and it was already early morning, I let her sit by his bedside. Later, a nurse called me saying that the patient had shown signs of improvement. I rushed to examine him, and indeed he was coming out of his coma. His first words, still stunned, were: "Alzira, you called me and I came back. Now I'm not going away anymore".

- Does that mean he heard what she had told him?

- Everything indicates that he did. She looked at me triumphantly, content, as if to say, "See, didn't I tell you?" By medicine, he could never have registered her words. I have often wondered whether we are really spirits and can therefore live outside the body while retaining all our senses.

- That would be the only explanation.

- I have seen terminally ill patients who said they were being visited by their dead relatives. One of them even knew the day he was going to die. He saw the spirit of an uncle who promised to pick him up on that date. And he really did die on the planned day.

- In that case, doctors could study these facts more easily.

- Some even do so, or at least respect those who believe in life after death, but unfortunately the prejudice is still great and many do not mention these cases, for fear of being mistaken for healers. After I specialized in psychiatry, many times, during the treatment of a patient, I saw that he transformed himself, as if he were another person: his posture, his voice. And some said intelligent things that went beyond the culture and knowledge they possessed. There was one who, during a fit of rage, began to destroy everything around him and we couldn't contain him to put on the straitjacket. One of the nurses arrived and entered the room, although we wanted to stop her. She held out her hand to him and in a firm voice told him to stop. He looked at her and she kept talking, saying that she didn't want to put the straitjacket on, but if he continued to rebel, wanting to destroy everything, she would be forced to do it and dope him.

- Brave woman!

- At the moment I was terrified. I thought he was going to attack her and I was getting ready to intervene when surprisingly he started to cry, sobbing and saying that he was going to leave because she was stronger than him. So she took his arm and led him to the bed. He sobbed for some time. Then he said that she had set him free. That it was not he who was angry, but his persecutor, who wanted to finish him off. He told her that he saw what was happening, but could not react. He said that when she entered and confronted him, very strong rays of blue light came out of her hands, which immobilized him.

- What an impressive thing!

- Indeed. For a few days I couldn't think of anything else. I went to look for her. Then I discovered that she was a practicing spiritualist. Her spiritual guide had told her to go and attend to the case and had helped her in the process.

- We have many things to learn. This time I'm not going to miss my chance.

- Neither will I. After all, it's really great to find out what will happen to us after death, since that is the path of all of us.

They continued talking about the subject. When Rafael said goodbye it was agreed that he would accompany them to the centre for spiritual studies.

The meeting was scheduled for two days later. Rute, Marina, Rafael and Cicero should be there punctually at eight o'clock in the evening. Ten minutes earlier they arrived at the place.

It was an old house in a middle-class neighbourhood. At the gate, a young man welcomed them and ushered them into the well-kept garden. They climbed the steps leading to the veranda and entered the hall, where a young woman welcomed them and led them to a room with rows of chairs and a large table at the back, surrounded by chairs. On the table, some books, pads of paper, pens. Behind, leaning against the wall, was a piece of furniture on which were a vase of flowers, a tray with jugs of water and glasses.

Cicero grabbed Rute's arm. Marina saw him and asked:

- What is it Cicero?

- I don't think I will stay. I have goose bumps. You are staying. I will wait for you in the garden.

- Not at all, said Rute. - Don't be afraid. You are protected here. Nothing bad will happen to you.

They were invited to sit down in one of the rows. Almost all the chairs were occupied. The atmosphere was warm and cheerful.

A young woman approached Rute and asked:

- Who is going to see Mrs. Eunice?

- Cicero - answered Rute. - But Marina, his sister, and Rafael would like to talk to her for an orientation.

- That is fine. The meeting will begin. I will call when it is time for you to enter.

The lights were turned off, leaving only a blue lamp lit. Soft music filled the air. A man sitting at the head of the table asked everyone to concentrate and said a short prayer requesting the presence and protection of the spiritual friends for the work of the night.

Then the lights were turned on and a young man stood up and began to speak about the need for prayer as an element of connection with the spirits of light. His voice was vibrant and emotional, his words spoken with conviction were impressive as he affirmed that spiritual help is all around us all the time, that it is we who close our hearts to it when we sink into negativity and that prayer renews our energies and provides the field for spiritual help to act in our lives.

Marina felt an inner joy, a great well-being. It seemed to her that she had already been in a place like that.

The young man sat down and soon after a girl stood up and began to tell about an experience she had had outside the body. They were very interested, but at that moment they were called to the consultation.

They followed the girl down a corridor to a small room where behind a table Eunice was sitting.

Rute was going to stay outside, but the woman asked her to come in as well. Eunice held out her hand to them, looking into each of their eyes. Then she asked them to sit in front of the table.

Cicero looked at her in admiration. She smiled:

- You are seeing a spiritual friend. He is here to help us.

- He is smiling at me. I seem to know him already.

- You are part of our group.

- But this is the first time I have come here, said Cicero, surprised.

Eunice smiled:

- That doesn't mean we haven't met before. You came here because of your sensitivity. It's time to study the cosmic laws and the phenomena of influences. You must learn to balance your energies, to choose your paths well.

- I would like to study all that too, Marina interjected.

- I know. You are ready, you just need to remember a little. As for you, you could have already developed your enormous healing potential if you had not ignored the calls life made to you.

She paused, then asked:

- Who is Olinto or Olivio?

- Olinto, my paternal grandfather, answered Rafael.

- A tall, handsome gentleman, light brown hair, square jaw, cheerful eyes.

- It's him! - exclaimed Rafael, thrilled.

- Yes.... he says that he has tried to help your father, but that he is stubborn and does not listen to the advice he gives him. He says he loves Diva because she is very patient with him.

Rafael could not stop a few tears from rolling down his cheeks. When he managed to speak, he said:

- Diva is my mother!

Marina and Cicero could not contain their emotion. At that moment they had proof that life goes on after death. Not only the presence of Rafael's grandfather, but also the words he had spoken, mentioning the name of his daughter-in-law, made a great impression on them.

Eunice looked fixedly at Marina and continued:

- There is the spirit of a girl here. She says her name is Norma. She is a friend of yours from other lives and she asks to tell you: "Everything is all right. There is no mistake. You fulfilled the promise you made to me. Count on me always. I will do all I can to make you very happy."

Marina remembered very clearly the dream she had that afternoon in Dr. Moura's waiting room, the garden where she had talked to a woman who had told her she was a friend from other lives and that when the time came, she would remember the reincarnation.

Surprised, she fell silent. Eunice asked:

- Did the message make sense to you?

- Yes, answered Marina.

Noticing that the others were looking at her curiously, she clarified:

- I once dreamed of her, who said the same words to me. I have never forgotten that dream.

- It was an astral journey, not a dream. You met in the astral while your body was asleep. I would like Cicero to enrol in our mediumship course. There he will have theoretical lessons on cosmic laws and practical classes to learn about the energies that surround us.

- All right, he agreed.

Eunice continued:

- As for you two, I will point you to some books and, if you wish, you can attend our study session once a week.

They both agreed. Eunice stood up and extended her hand to them.

- It was very nice to meet you both. If you wish, you may take a pass in the next room. Go with God.

They thanked her and left. They went to the room indicated and each one sat where they were told, while two people, one in front, the other behind, raised their hands and shortly after passed them over their bodies without touching them. Soft music filled the air and the delicate perfume of roses in the vase on the table gave them a pleasant sensation of well-being.

While Cicero had a crying fit, Rafael intimately promised himself to study spirituality with persistence, Marina felt that a pleasant breeze enveloped her and that energy was familiar to her. In a mixture of recognition and longing that she could not put into words, she allowed two tears of happiness to wash down her face, certain that she had finally found her way.

They left in silence, each immersed in their own thoughts. Once on the street, Rute could not contain herself:

- So? Did you like it?

- I felt goose bumps the whole time. How did she know everything without me saying anything? - Cicero said.

- How are you feeling now? - asked Rute.

- Light, very well - answered Cicero. - So much so that I am even hungry.

- In that case, let's eat something - invited Rafael. - There is a very good place nearby.

Once in the car, Rafael said:

- That woman has an amazing mediumship! After the proofs she has given us, there is nothing to doubt.

- Indeed, Marina interjected. - How could she know about the girl in my dream and the words we had talked about?

- You all wonder, but for Eunice, who sees the spirits and hears what they say, she can only narrate the facts - replied Rute.

- But not all mediums are like her. I have come across some who claim things that never happened and even confuse the heads of naïve people, said Rafael.

- Indeed. Eunice is a lucid, upright and very generous person, which guarantees the presence and help of enlightened spirits. Furthermore, her practical and active temperament does not allow her to get lost in the illusions and dramas of the world. A born leader, many people surrender to her charisma. However, she keeps her head on straight and has an enormous capacity for work.

- She really gives one a feeling of confidence, said Rafael. - From today onwards I shall dedicate myself to studying these phenomena. After all, dying is the fate of us all. Thinking about it, one cannot understand why most people prefer to ignore this subject.

- Perhaps fear is greater than the need, Marina commented.

- Fear - intervened Rute - when it is not provoked by a real situation of risk, can be dissipated by knowing the facts. There are countless proofs of the survival of the spirit after death. When you discover them, it becomes easier to overcome fear and look to the future with more optimism.

During all the time they were together, they commented on the events of the night.

It was past eleven when Rafael, after leaving Rute at home, took Marina and Cicero. The latter bade Rafael a quick farewell, saying cheerfully:

- Mom must be waiting for us anxiously. I'll tell her the news.

He went in quickly. Marina held out her hand to Rafael.

- Thank you for accompanying us. Your support was very important to me. Although I liked Rute, I felt a little insecure. Cicero is a sensitive boy; I was afraid he would be too impressed.

- You know how much I enjoy your company. I would go anywhere with you. But I confess that I did not expect what happened to us. I have a good feeling in my heart, which has renewed my motivation.

- You never seemed to me to be unmotivated. You have an optimistic view of everything.

- This is a job I do every day, trying to improve my living conditions. I have learned that optimism not only helps us to live better, happier lives, but also contributes to maintaining physical and mental health. It happens that, dealing with human problems, being the confidant of highly deluded, pessimistic, irresponsible people, who take pleasure in the same postures without my being able, no matter how hard I try to make them realize what they are doing with their lives and take charge of their inner world, all this has worn down my good will.

Marina put her hand on his arm, looking into his eyes.

- I never noticed that you felt this way.

- When I graduated, I was full of plans and ideals, believing that my knowledge, my love for my profession and the desire to make people happier would be enough to achieve a good performance.

- But you have succeeded. You are a respected professional, you have written books, you have helped people.

- I have tried, but the great truth is that nobody changes anybody. People come to me in search of guidance for their lives, but few really listen to my arguments and try to put them into practice. Most go to the consultation in search of some remedy that will magically rid them of all their worries. When you identify the source of the problems and suggest what to do to overcome them, they do not accept.

He paused slightly and, noticing that Marina was listening carefully, he continued:

- Out of self-indulgence, they don't want to acknowledge that it was their inadequate way of looking at things that created the problematic situations that prevent them from having a happy life.

- This should not make you sad. You are doing your best, using your knowledge for your clients. But the responsibility to do or not do what you advise is theirs. It is not up to you.

- I know that. What I want to tell you is that tonight the discovery of reincarnation as a learning possibility made me regain enthusiasm for my work. I understood that my role is only to show the various options that the person has at that moment. If they choose the best, all right. But if they continue on the same path, one day they will become aware of what I wanted to show them and will do the right thing. Tonight, I discovered that my role is only to show those who feel lost a path that is more suitable to the circumstances, without worrying about what each one has chosen.

Tonight I was certain that life takes care of each one much better than I do. Before those who seek me, I am only a chance for change that they can use if they want.

Rafael's eyes shone and Marina felt moved by his words. Usually, he did not talk about his personal feelings. It was the first time he exposed his innermost thoughts, his expectations of the work to which he had dedicated his whole life.

- You're a wonderful man, she said, rising to her feet and kissing him gently on the cheek.

He hugged her, answering with emotion:

- No. You are the one who has filled my life with joy and happiness.

Deeply moved, he kissed her on the lips. Marina felt her heartbeat faster as a sensation of pleasure invaded her.

CHAPTER 13

Maria Eugenia answered the telephone and, hearing Pierre's voice, felt a tightening in her chest.

- I need to see you urgently, alone, not at your house, he said.

- Unfortunately, as you know, I can't leave because of my son.

- Find a way. I have something very important to discuss with you. I assure you it is of your interest.

- What is it? Can't you tell me over the phone?

- Not at all. I'll expect you this afternoon at my hotel. Jamille's going on tour, and I'll be waiting. She wanted to escape.

- I can't. My husband might not like it.

- You didn't think so before. If you don't come, I'll find him and tell him everything that happened between us in Paris.

Maria Eugenia felt her legs shaking. Her heart started pounding.

- Fine, I'll go, she answered in a faint voice.

- At two o'clock. Don't be late. I'm in an emergency situation. If you don't come by 2:15, I'm going to look for your husband. I'm not joking.

- You can wait. I'll be there.

She hung up the phone and let herself fall into an armchair. More than ever, she regretted the levity of those times. But it was late. She had to face the situation.

She had no doubt that Pierre was trying to take advantage of the situation. She just didn't know how, if he wanted money or if he wanted to have fun at her expense, demanding that she give him the same attention as before.

She wouldn't accept either one of them. However, what to do if he carried through with his threats?

She in no way wanted to jeopardize her relationship with Henrique. They were living the best phase of their marriage. Maria Eugenia loved her husband and did not want to lose him.

For a moment it occurred to her that the wisest thing would be to tell him everything and put an end to Pierre's blackmail. But how would Henrique react if he knew he had been betrayed? He would certainly despise her, perhaps even leave her.

No. Henrique could never know the truth. Anxiously, Maria Eugenia showed up at Pierre's hotel at the appointed time. In the lobby she asked the concierge to notify him of her arrival and went to wait in the sitting room.

Shortly afterwards Pierre arrived, elegant as always, and greeted her seriously, his face showing sadness.

- What do you want of me? - she asked.

- What we have to talk about cannot be said here. We'd better go to my room.

- No, I prefer another place.

- In that case, let's go to the conservatory. It's empty at this hour.

Maria Eugenia accompanied him, trying to control her uneasiness. The place was very pretty, full of ornamental plants and fancy decorations. There really wasn't anyone around.

He led her to a discreet corner where they sat down in comfortable armchairs.

- And then? - she asked.

He sighed sadly, then said:

- I decided to come to Brazil to talk to you because we are going through a desperate situation. I have lost everything, I am ruined.

She didn't hide her surprise:

- You don't look like that... You are living as usual. This hotel is one of the most luxurious.

- For me, it is the lifestyle I have enjoyed all my life. When I discovered that I had lost everything, I thought of suicide. Jamille stopped me at just the right moment. For her sake, I decided to continue living, but I have no strength to live in poverty. That is why I decided to come and see you and ask for help.

- Me? As much as I would like to help you, I do not know how I could. My mother takes care of all our money.

- I found out about her companies. They have vast resources. Believe me, if it wasn't for the distressing situation we are in, I would never have dared to bother you. If you want to know, we don't even have enough money to pay for the hotel.

- I don't know what to say.

- Ask your husband.

- You know he doesn't like you very much.

- Talk to your mother.

- She's a difficult woman. I've never been able to face her.

- I'm desperate. If you can't help me, I'll go and find your husband. Even though he doesn't like me, in view of the facts he'll want to see me far away from here.

Maria Eugenia turned pale:

- What do you intend to do? Tell him all the crazy things I did in Paris?

- If I have to...

Maria Eugenia felt like slapping him but held back. He continued saying:

- I don't want to resort to scandal. I know your mother would do anything to keep me from talking about that fake belly you were wearing in Paris.

So that was it! He knew her family's secret and intended to get money out of them. Maria Eugenia felt her head cloud over and tried hard not to faint.

Pierre, noticing her pallor, was sure that his suspicions were well founded. He looked around and went over to the small table where there was a jug of water and glasses. He helped himself and went back to Maria Eugenia:

- Drink this. You'll feel calmer.

She held the glass with trembling hands and took a few sips. She was so frightened that she did not dare to dispute what he had said.

Pierre continued:

- Look, I don't want to hurt anyone, least of all you, of whom I have fond memories. But I'm desperate. If you get me some money, I'll go away and you will never hear from me again.

Maria Eugenia drank the rest of her water, trying to gain time. She didn't know what to say. When she calmed down a bit, she asked:

- How much do you want?

- You know... Because of the situation, I'm in debt. I want to pay everything off and have money to start over.

- If you continue living the life you've always had, there won't be enough money. You will always be poor.

- I intend to work, he lied. - I have the idea of going back to Paris and opening a business. Jamille will help me.

- How much?

- Five million dollars.

Maria Eugenia gave him a startled look:

- All that? It's impossible! I'll never raise the money.

- Well, that's what I need. That amount means nothing compared to the assets of your family's business.

Maria Eugenia wrung her hands in despair. Pierre continued:

- Look, I'll give you a deadline to get the money. But remember, the longer I stay at this hotel, the more I am spending. The amount could increase.

Maria Eugenia stood up. Although her legs were shaking, she wanted to get out of there as soon as possible, to stop seeing that malicious and false look from Pierre. His proximity disgusted her.

- I need to go. My son is not well yet.

- That's all right. I'll call back in two days to see if you have the money.

- It's impossible to get that much money in such a short time.

- I can't wait any longer. If you can't, I'll go find your family.

- No... I'll see what I can do. Don't do anything without talking to me.

- Okay, okay, okay. Remember, in two days, at this same time.

Maria Eugenia left without saying goodbye. As she got into the car, the driver asked:

- Are you all right? You look so pale!

- It's just a slight discomfort. Let's go home. I need to rest.

On the way home, Maria Eugenia searched desperately for a solution. But the more she thought about it, the less she believed in the possibility of getting what Pierre had demanded.

She had never had to think about money because she had always had everything and all her needs met. But despite this she knew that five million dollars was a large sum even for her family's resources.

Then, what excuse could he find to ask for such a sum? Both Henrique and Adele were intelligent and would not be easily fooled. He would have to tell them.

However, she would rather die than have to tell her husband that she had betrayed him and her mother that she had been so soft as to let Pierre know such an important secret.

Her head ached, and she could not even think straight. She came home and went straight to her room. She didn't want anyone to notice her nervousness. Once there, she threw herself on the bed and broke down in sobs.

Elvira knocked on the door and Maria Eugenia didn't open. She knocked again.

- Who is it? - asked Maria Eugenia.

- Elvira. I need to speak to you.

Maria Eugenia stood up quickly and went to open the door. In her confusion she hadn't even asked about Dionisio. Had she got worse?

Seeing her upset face, Elvira asked:

- Has something happened? Are you ill?

- No. I have a headache. Is Dionisio all right?

- He was until half an hour ago. Suddenly he woke up crying desperately, calling for you. It took a lot for him to calm down. But he's restless, he shakes now and then.

- Have you seen if the fever is back?

- He doesn't have a fever; he's just restless, nervous, irritable.

- I'll go and see him.

They went to Dionisio' room. When he saw them coming, he said in tears:

- Mamma, I want you.

Maria Eugenia took him in her arms and stroked his hair.

- I'm here, son. Don't cry. I'm here.

Tears streamed down her face and she sat up, cradling the boy lovingly. Elvira could not contain herself:

- Has something happened? You are very upset.

- Yes, it has happened, Elvira. But unfortunately, I cannot tell you what it is. And please don't tell anyone I'm in trouble. Not even Henrique.

- But he'll perceive your nervousness.

- I have to control myself. I'm going to bed, and I'm taking Dionisio with me. When Henrique arrives, tell him I have a headache, I took some medicine and I want to sleep.

- In that case, it's better that I stay with Dionisio.

- He will cry again. You know how attached he is to me.

- Then I'll stay with the lady.

- That's all right.

They went back to Maria Eugenia's room with Dionisio. She lay down with the boy and Elvira sat on the side of the bed. The dimly lit room was very calm.

Dionisio, hugging her, felt calmer, but he didn't sleep. Elvira put the little plush horse in his hands and he smiled.

- I've never seen a child so attached to his mother, commented Elvira. - The lady was not well and he felt it. That can only be it. Before the lady left, he was cheerful, in a good mood. It all started suddenly. I couldn't figure out why. But when the lady came in looking down, I immediately saw that he had sensed something.

- I'd rather he didn't feel it. I don't want him to suffer for anything in this world.

- So do I. That little angel doesn't deserve to suffer.

- If it depends on me, he will always be very happy.

Elvira remained silent for a few moments. Then, noticing that despite appearing calm, Dionisio shivered from time to time, she said:

- I think it would be good to take him to Mrs. Eunice. He's still agitated.

- Right now I'm not willing to go out. We'll see. If he doesn't improve, we'll go tomorrow.

That night Maria Eugenia didn't come down to dinner. Claiming a headache, she continued to lie in the dark, telling Henrique that it was nothing and that she would soon be fine.

He personally took care of Dionisio and spent a long time playing with him, trying to distract him so that Maria Eugenia could rest.

When Henrique went to bed, she pretended to be asleep, but she couldn't get to sleep that night. Occasionally, overcome by tiredness, she would fall asleep, but would be plagued by nightmares in which Pierre would appear demanding money from her, threatening to go to the newspapers and tell her secret. She would wake up in distress, her body covered in sweat, desperate.

In spite of this, the next morning she got up before Henrique woke up, took a shower and put on some make-up, trying to disguise her dejection.

She went to see Dionisio.

- So, Elvira, how did he spend the night?

- He slept, but his sleep was not peaceful. He would shudder now and then, and wake up crying. I took him in my arms and nursed him. When he fell asleep, I would put him back to bed. I think I did this about three times.

Maria Eugenia put her hand on his forehead. His temperature was normal. She remembered that Eunice had told her that the boy was sensitive to her emotions. She needed to control her thoughts. But how?

She tried hard to look happy. During breakfast Henrique asked her if she was better. She answered that she was very well.

After he left, Elvira said:

- The lady is not well. When you come near me, I feel a despair, an anguish that I can't explain. I think we should go and talk to Mrs. Eunice.

- Maybe later. I don't want to disturb her at this time of the morning.

- She's very nice; she won't notice. I'm speaking because of Dionisio. If he's feeling what I'm feeling, it would be good to relieve him.

- Perhaps you are right. Do you really think she won't bother?

- Yes, I do. Shall I call her and tell her what's going on?

- You do that.

Elvira left and came back a little later:

- She said she was thinking about us and hoping we'd go see her. Did you see how she is? She sensed that we are not well.

- So let's go right now.

Eunice received them with affection. After asking them to think about God, she approached each of them, laying her hands on them in prayer.

Then she asked Elvira to go into another room with the boy, because she needed to talk to Maria Eugenia.

When she was alone with her, she said:

- What I feared has happened?

- Yes, it has, and I don't know what to do. I'm desperate. He knows my secret and has asked for five million dollars not to tell. I have no way to get that money. I don't know what to do.

Eunice closed her eyes for a moment, then said:

- I see someone who can help you. She is a beautiful woman, elegant, tall, with dark hair. She has so much charisma that everyone obeys her.

- You are describing my mother.

- This woman has practical sense, is skilled and very powerful.

- She really is my mother. Her name is Adele.

- That's the one. Go find her and tell her everything.

- But she'll blame me. She'll turn against me. I won't have the strength to tell her the truth.

- It's your only way out.

Maria Eugenia was crying in despair.

- I won't have the courage. She'll be disappointed in me.

- You're suffering the consequences of your past attitudes. Talking to your mother, acknowledging your mistakes is a form of rehabilitation before your own conscience.

- My mother will not understand.

- On the contrary. Your mother loves you very much, although she has always been strict in her discipline. Wanting everything to be right is her way. Go to her immediately, open your heart to her sincerely, tell her your feelings, how much you love your husband and your son. I guarantee she will stand by you and help you sort everything out.

- I shudder to think that I will have to face her judgement.

- Leave your pride aside. It serves no purpose. Open your heart and you will see that everything will work out.

Eunice placed her hand on Maria Eugenia's head and murmured a heartfelt prayer, asking the Spirits of Light to help her find the courage to face the situation.

Then she asked:

- Are you feeling better?

- Yes, that despair has disappeared. I will do what you advise. I will go and find my mother right now.

At two in the afternoon, Maria Eugenia went into Adele's study.

Since she had talked to Eunice, she had reflected a lot and had conclude that she had no choice but to talk to her mother.

As she entered her room, her heart felt heavy, her legs were shaking, but she tried hard to control her anxiety.

Seeing her enter, Adele stood up and, after exchanging a light kiss on the cheek, she stared at her firmly, saying:

- You don't look well. Has something happened to Dionisio?

- No, he's fine.

- Sit down. You never come looking for me here. You must have something serious to tell me. What is it?

Maria Eugenia felt like making an excuse, saying nothing and going away. But the memory of Pierre and his threats made her control herself.

- Sit down. You look pale. Are you ill?

- No. I must talk to you.

- Go ahead.

- Before getting to the point where things are now, I have to say that all my life it has been very difficult to tell you my innermost thoughts. And if I decided to tell you now, it's because I'm in trouble and I need your help. I beg you to listen to me and not to interrupt me, please.

- Speak up. Be clear.

- You are a brilliant, beautiful, admired, successful person, while I have always been a shadow beside you. I admire you, but I recognize that I don't have your capacity and, no matter how hard I have tried, I have never achieved what I always wanted, which was to be better than I am so that you would admire me and be proud of me.

Adele looked at her surprised, as if she were seeing her for the first time. Maria Eugenia paused briefly and spoke of her childhood, of her frustration and anger at not being able to be a mother, of the envy she felt for other women.

- It was very painful and difficult to accept your proposal to save the company. To have to imagine that Henrique was going to have relations with another woman, even if unknown, tormented my days. Having to wear that fake belly was a humiliation and living proof of my incapacity as a woman.

Adele felt like intervening, but held back. She felt that Maria Eugenia needed to get this off her chest.

- When we went to Paris, depression took hold of me. I didn't feel like going out or enjoying myself. But one night I went out to dinner with a French couple that I had met at a fashion show. The two were incurable lovers of bars, parties and social events. Their passion for the Parisian night scene ended up infecting me, and so I decided to forget everything and enjoy my time having fun, because I knew that when I returned I would have to support a child who was Henrique's son with another woman.

Henrique did not like my new friends and did not want to go out with them, but perhaps not wanting me to go back into depression, he allowed me to continue going out alone with them. So, I plunged into evenings where I drank, had fun, forgot all my problems. Henrique tried to show me that I was exaggerating, but I did not listen to him. I was full of hate, of revolt against him, against you, against the company, against the son they wanted to impose on me. Pierre was involving me with charms. He and Jamille, although married, allowed themselves to be with other partners. One night the worst thing happened. I let myself get involved and ended up in bed with Pierre in his flat. At that moment I felt no guilt. On the contrary: I felt I had the right to do it, just as Henrique did.

Maria Eugenia spoke with eyes lost in memories, tears streaming freely down her face, and Adele, pale, eyes watering, dared not intervene. She continued saying:

At that time Pierre found out that I was not pregnant. But I didn't tell him I was wearing a fake belly. I thought that was it. A little later we returned to Brazil and Dionisio was born. It was then that everything changed in my life. This child made the miracle of awakening in me my best side. His attachment, his love for me, preferring to be with me than with anyone else, his arms around my neck, his eyes shining with joy and love when he saw me, all this made me love him truly, as if he had been born from me. I have changed. Today I am ashamed of my past attitudes. You gave me everything, Henrique was always a loving, adorable, polite, respectful husband, and I recognize today that I love my family with sincerity. Dionisio has become indispensable to my life.

Adele came closer and hugged her, moved. Maria Eugenia's sincerity touched her spirit and she recognized for the first time that perhaps she had underestimated her daughter's feelings.

- You said you need help. What's going on now? Why are you telling me all this?

- Because I'm being threatened by Pierre. They came looking for me. They're from a rich family, but they've lost all their money. They're in misery. Pierre asked me for five million dollars. If I don't pay, he will find Henrique and tell him everything. I noticed that he has been investigating our family and, although I didn't tell him anything, he found out our secret.

Adele struggled to control herself. As usual, whenever she had a problem to solve, she did not allow herself to lose her temper. She knew that good solutions only come when you don't lose your temper.

- He's blackmailing you. It was to be expected.

- I don't want Henrique to know what I've done. He may not want to live with me anymore. I love my husband. I don't want to lose him. I was crazy. I'm so sorry.

- Calm down, my child. Don't let yourself be carried away by despair. We'll think of a way to solve this.

- Will you help me?

- Of course I will! I'm your mother. I love you. Then there are our companies. I won't allow a couple of swindlers to destroy what we've spent a lifetime building.

- Forgive me for being so naive and causing all this.

- Blaming yourself now won't solve anything. We need to find a way out.

- He gave me until tomorrow afternoon.

Adele thought for a while, then said:

- Here's what we're going to do: you're going to get yourself together, get yourself cleaned up, get out of here just fine. I guess you haven't eaten anything today.

- I'm not hungry.

- I'll order a snack and you go eat.

Adele called her secretary and told her to bring a snack. While they waited, she took Maria Eugenia into the adjoining room, where there was a seating area and a dressing table, and put her in front of the mirror.

- Look at yourself. Whatever happens, you must keep your dignity. You can't allow yourself this lack of control, which always leads to failure. You must react. You made a mistake, but your life is not over because of that. On the contrary: you like the life you have, you love your husband, your son. That is your truth now. You must not let yourself be destroyed by some blackmailer. Wash your face and put some make-up on.

Maria Eugenia hugged her mother, saying with emotion

- Thank you for listening to me and not condemning me. Now I understand and admire your way of being. What I thought was indifference was balance, lucidity.

Adele smiled and a greater glow came into her eyes. But she limited herself to answering:

- Come on, get ready. Look beautiful and decent. Think of the people you love.

The secretary brought the snacks and Adele put everything on the table where she usually took her meals. A little later, Maria Eugenia came into the room with her make-up on and her appearance was much better.

The fact that she had spoken, that she had been heard and understood comforted her. Her mother's help made her confident that they would overcome this problem.

Calmer, she sat down at the table and ate her snack, drank her fruit juice and felt refreshed. Adele poured herself a cup of coffee and sat down beside her.

- Now you are going to write down the name of this couple, the hotel where they are.

- Do you intend to go and talk to them?

- I don't know yet. We have time until tomorrow afternoon. I want to make some arrangements. Get information about them. In the meantime, go home and act as usual. Be natural. Neither euphoric nor worried.

- If Pierre calls again, what will I tell him?

- He gave you a deadline. He won't call, he'll wait. In any case, if he calls on any pretext, don't receive him or his wife at home. Wait, because I'll come as soon as I can to see you and figure out what we're going to do.

Maria Eugenia said goodbye to her mother, relieved and restored, feeling a new strength inside her. She had become a happy woman and would know how to keep this achievement.

After she left, Adele called a lawyer who, besides being a friend, was the one she trusted with all her secrets, asking him to come to her office immediately.

When he arrived, half an hour later, Adele received him with a broad smile. Dr. Bernardo Gouveia was a man of class, successful in his professional career, who had been Adele's colleague at university.

At that time, he had been in love with her, but had not declared his love because Adele had accepted a marriage proposal from Aurelio Carlos da Rocha, a rich businessman, and he, although from an upper middle-class family, was a recent graduate, just starting his career and felt that he was not yet in a position to give Adele the position that she deserved.

Besides, she seemed in love, happy, and this was enough for him to hide his feelings. Yet they remained friends. Adele knew she could trust him.

Since she had taken over the management of the family's holding company, Bernardo had been her advisor and friend, to the point that Aurelio often felt jealous. When this happened, Aurelio tried to control himself, because he recognized that Adele's charisma made people admire her and he was delighted to observe the admiration she aroused by her class, lucidity and the ease with which she knew how to say the right words at the right time.

After the greetings, she sat down on the sofa next to Bernardo and went straight to the point, as usual:

- My daughter is being blackmailed and I need you to help us.

He made himself available and Adele told him the whole truth. Besides Celia, he was the only one who knew Dionisio' origin. When she finished, he simply asked:

- What do you want me to do?

- It would be interesting to investigate these people.

- I have some informants. We don't have much time.

- If you need it, I'll find a way to extend the deadline.

Adele gave him the names, hotel address and telephone number, and he left immediately to take care of the matter.

When she found herself alone, Adele kept thinking, trying to find the best solution.

CHAPTER 14

Maria Eugenia arrived home and went straight away to check on Dionisio. The support she had received from her mother had made her more confident. On the way home, she thought about how wrong she had been about Adele.

She realized that her muted rebellious attitudes, passively obeying her mother's orders but keeping anger in her heart, were the result of pride, which prevented her from seeing things as they were.

She was jealous of Adele's success because she had become used to seeing herself as limited and incapable. She was not as weak as she had always thought. On the contrary: she had been able to face her fears and expose her inner feelings, without fear of the criticism she had feared all her life. She recognized that Adele knew more, had more experience, and instead of reproaching her, she offered her support and help.

Even though the situation hadn't changed, she felt different: more adult, stronger, more confident.

Dionisio was playing with a little car and, seeing her, went running to hug her.

- Mummy, you're beautiful!

Maria Eugenia's face lit up and she took him in her arms, kissing his rosy cheeks.

- How is my prince today?

- Gud. No white horse.

Maria Eugenia remembered the story she had been told about a prince riding a white horse and smiled delightedly.

- I think we have to buy a horse. A prince can't walk on foot.

She kept playing with him until Elvira went to fetch him for a bath. Maria Eugenia went to her room and called Eunice.

- I'm calling to thank you for your advice. Everything went well.

- I knew it was. Your mother loves you very much.

- When I got there, I was nervous, afraid, but determined to do what you said. I started to talk, opened my heart, shared my feelings and finally told her everything. She listened in silence, didn't recriminate me, and even hugged me. We had never had such a sincere conversation.

- I am glad. Never forget that your spiritual connection with her comes from other lives. For a long time she has been working for your progress and for you to find happiness. It is time for you to realize that.

- I felt that she loves and supports me. She said she will help me. She asked for their name and the phone number of the hotel. But she wants to think of the best way to proceed. She sent me home and will keep in touch.

- I am sure that we are being helped by friendly spirits. Let's trust and hope for the best. I will continue with my prayers. If there is any news, let me know.

- OK. But I want to tell you that meeting you was the best thing that ever happened to me. I'll never forget what you're doing for me.

- Let's thank the divine forces. They are the ones who protect and teach us.

Maria Eugenia hung up the phone and went to play with Dionisio again, being with him helped her to keep calm and contain her anxiety to wait.

After lunch Pierre went into the hotel room and found Jamille in a bad mood.

- I don't think she'll call.

- Of course she will.

- What are you going to do if she doesn't want to pay?

- What I promised. Talk to the husband, tell him everything. Then there's the mother. I've been enquiring about her. She's reputed to be a great lady, well-liked in the best society.

- Where did you get the information?

- From the tourism lady. She knows everything about people.

- What worries me is what we will do if they don't give the money.

Pierre smiled when he replied:

- You'll see. Soon she will be here with the money. We will take care of transferring it to our accounts and then we will leave.

It was after three when the phone rang in their room. Pierre rushed to answer it.

- Mr. Pierre?

- Yes.

- I'm in the hotel lobby on behalf of Mrs Maria Eugenia. I must speak to you.

- You'd better come to my room.

- That's all right.

Pierre hung up the phone and looked triumphantly at Jamille:

- Didn't I tell you? She sent a porter, I think to bring the money. Go into the other room. I'll see him alone.

She went immediately, and Pierre looked at himself in the mirror. He made a point of always looking impeccable. He smiled satisfied.

The bell rang and he went to open it.

- I am Dr. Bernardo Gouveia, attorney for the Malta Organizations, he said in perfect French accent.

- Please come in. Please sit down.

Once seated, Bernardo said in a firm voice:

- You are blackmailing Mrs. Maria Eugenia, my client who is a partner in the companies I represent.

Pierre smiled, trying to hide his irritation:

- You shouldn't use such strong words. After all, I only asked a friend, with whom I had a close connection in Paris, to help me in a difficult situation.

- At my client's request, I made an enquiry into your life. And, from what I found out, I think I'm being too polite.

Pierre stood up nervously:

- Let's get down to business. Did you bring the money?

- Why do you think we will pay?

- Because I can reveal the origin of that boy she says is her son and that can change their whole financial situation.

- Listen to what I'm about to tell you. This child is the legitimate son of my clients and there is the hospital, the doctor, the nurses who assisted her at the time of delivery, people who, if necessary, will certainly not refuse to testify to this. On the other hand, through the information about you that was given to me by our manager in Paris, I was in your consulate this morning and I found out that you are wanted by the French police for having been involved in some scams.

Pierre paled.

- That is a lie! You are trying to intimidate me. But I won't accept it. If they don't give me the money I'll go to the newspapers and tell them everything.

- For your own good, you'd better not do anything like that. You should know that Interpol is looking for you with an arrest warrant and the consulate is preparing everything to send you back to France.

- That can't be! You are lying!

- I'm telling you the truth. You bet. Then, it is good to know that my clients are influential, respected people, whose word is always highly regarded. If you add extortion charges to this arrest warrant, your situation in our country might be worth a few years in jail here before you serve your sentence in France.

Pierre struggled to control his nervousness. Bernardo continued:

- However, Mrs. Maria Eugenia is a kind-hearted person. Even though you blackmailed her, you do not wish her harm and you managed to get her mother, Mrs. Adele, who was very indignant, not to press charges.

Pierre slumped down on a chair, running his hands through his hair, frightened. He never imagined that they could find out what he had done in Paris. He knew that the police were looking for him. That was one of the reasons he had come to Brazil, a country that meant the end of the world to him, where no one could find him.

He did not want to be arrested and deported to France where, besides cheating and gambling debts, there were more serious crimes that he feared would be discovered. If he had some money to leave the hotel and go to another country in South America, where nobody could find him, he would not go to jail.

- I want to talk to Maria Eugenia, he said nervously.

- That's not possible. I'm authorized to take care of everything.

- I have no money. I have to pay for the hotel and go somewhere where they can't find me. Ask her to help me, to get some money.

- That won't be possible. The best thing for you to do is to go back to your country, answer for what you did and be free. Then you can start your life again.

Pierre looked at him incredulously. He would never do that.

- I will follow your advice. I will go back to France. I will do nothing against Maria Eugenia. But I would like you to ask her in the name of good times in Paris to send me some money so I can leave this hotel in a civilized manner, paying my expenses.

Bernardo stood up and said:

- All right. I will talk to her and see what I can do. Goodbye, Mr. Pierre.

As soon as he left, Jamille returned to the room. She had tried to listen to the conversation, but had only managed to pick up a few loose words.

- Well? By the looks of it, he didn't bring the money.

- No. He won't. We're lost.

- What do you mean, lost? Didn't you say you were gonna get it?

- They've been checking up on us and found out the police are looking for me.

- The police? What did you do this time?

- It must have been about those jewels from Nicole. They think I stole them.

Jamille shuddered:

- Was it you?

- She gave me the jewels. You know she had a crush on me.

- But she turned up dead in the flat. What did you do anyway?

- You and I talked about it in Paris. I gave you my word that I had nothing to do with it. She didn't choose her friendships. She had other lovers. Any of them could have killed her.

- I really hope you're telling the truth. I don't even want to think that you could have done a stupid thing like that. What do we do now? How do we get out of here?

- The lawyer's going to talk to Maria Eugenia and see if she can at least get us some money so we can pay for the hotel and get out of here.

- Do you think she'll give it to us after what you did?

- Yes, I do. But, in any case, let's pack our bags and get everything ready to leave.

Once again, Jamille regretted having continued living with him. After he lost everything and got into complications, several times she thought of leaving him. Jean wasn't rich, but at least by his side she wouldn't be in need.

Why had she allowed herself to be deceived, believing that Pierre could make money out of Maria Eugenia?

There was still the case of Nicole. If he was involved in the crime, she might be an accomplice. She shuddered at the thought of it. At that moment she decided to leave before everything got worse.

She went to her room, packed all her things. She had hidden some money. Still, she went to the safe box where he kept what they had left and picked up almost everything. Then she put her two suitcases in the room and said:

- I'm ready now. You'd better go and pack your things. You don't like the way I do it.

He went into the bedroom. Jamille picked up the phone and called the valet. She went into the bedroom and told Pierre:

- I'm hungry. I'll go down and get something to eat.

She went back to the room, picked up her bags and went out into the hall where the valet was already arriving.

- I am going away with a friend, but my husband is staying. Take my bags downstairs.

Minutes later, she took the lift and went downstairs. In the lobby she picked up her bags, went to the exit door and decidedly took the street.

In the room, Pierre packed his bags and went to check the money in the safe box. Startled he realised that it was gone. Nervous, he went into the living room and saw that Jamille was not there, nor were her bags.

He immediately called the reception desk.

- This is Pierre from 1512. Did you see if my wife left?

- Yes, about five minutes ago.

He hung up nervously. Jamille had left with all the money. He was overcome by rage. He felt like smashing everything around him. That coarse deserved to be taught a lesson. But, where to find her?

He had to get out of there, leave, but how? He called the valet. When he arrived, he said naturally:

- Did you accompany my wife with the bags?

- Yes, sir.

- What did she tell you?

- That she was going away with a friend. You didn't know? - he found it strange.

- Of course I knew. I just forgot to ask where.

- That she didn't say.

- In that case, I'll wait for her to call. You may go.

She left and Pierre sat there not knowing what to do. His sense of caution told him it would be good to get out of there as soon as possible, but how to leave with his bags without paying the hotel bill?

He loved his fancy clothes and couldn't bear to go away and leave them at the hotel. The best thing would be to stay calm and wait for some news from Maria Eugenia. The lawyer had left a card on the table for him to call. The man did not want Pierre to speak to Maria Eugenia. In view of what had happened he thought it best not to upset the lawyer.

Bernardo left the hotel and went straight to his office where Adele was waiting for him.

- So, how was it? - she asked as soon as she saw him.

- It was fine. I think this one won't bother us anymore.

In a few words he told how his meeting with Pierre went. He concluded:

- He is a scoundrel of the worst kind. Now all that's left is the last phone call to my friend Homero.

- You can call him now.

- If you allow me, I will.

He picked up the phone, called and, after the greetings, said:

- Everything went well. This is a dangerous guy. I think now is the time for you to call that friend of yours from the consulate and warn him, because he is thinking of escaping.

- I'll talk to her right away.

- Thanks for your help. I owe you.

- You don't owe me anything. You have helped me so many times...

Bernardo hung up the phone, smiling.

- That's it, Adele. I think everything's settled. You can talk to Maria Eugenia.

- Thank you, Bernardo. I don't know what I'd be without you.

- I don't know what I'd be without you either.

He said this seriously, eyes sparkling, in which Adele noticed a flame of emotion.

- You're a great friend.

- I wish I could be more than that.

She smiled, thought for a moment and said:

- In spite of everything, I'm not going to bring this matter to a close until this scoundrel has been taken back to France.

- I have left one of my men at the hotel to keep watch. If he tries to escape, we will know. The hotel security guards won't let him leave with his bags. And as far as I know, Pierre has no money to pay his expenses.

- He can leave his luggage and go.

- I don't think so. From what I've observed, he's snobbish and attached to appearances. He won't want to leave with only the clothes on his back.

- I'm afraid he'll want revenge in some way.

- He won't have time for that. Don't worry. I have to go now. But first I think our victory deserves celebration. Will you have dinner with me tonight?

- We'll see. If by tonight he's properly locked up, then I'll accept your celebratory dinner. Otherwise, I'll move it to when we can really celebrate.

- You got it. I'll call you later to give you an update.

After he left, Adele called Maria Eugenia and told her everything that had happened. She finished:

- You can relax. This one won't bother us anymore.

- Are you sure? What if he runs away and looks for Henrique? I don't want him to know anything.

- He won't have time for that. Soon he'll be arrested and extradited. After that, he'll never be able to enter our country again.

- I will only rest when I know that he is already away and can no longer return.

- Bernardo is standing by and will call me as soon as he has any news.

- If you know anything else, give me a call.

- Don't worry, everything is under control.

She was not used to praying, but she felt that, having been spared, she had received forgiveness, perhaps because she had repented. She joined her hands and murmured a heartfelt prayer in which she thanked God, the higher spirits and Eunice for the help she had received. And, touched by a feeling of gratitude, she decided that she would never again do anything that she could be ashamed of. At the same time, she would try to study spirituality in order to understand life better.

Meanwhile at the hotel Pierre had made a plan. He would wait for night to fall and then try to escape with his luggage. He got ready and went down to the restaurant to eat. Then he strolled around the hotel paying attention to what he had to do to escape.

He had noticed that at dawn the service entrance watchman slept in his cabin. That was the way he thought to escape. Then he would take a taxi and go to any station.

For that, the money would give. Then he would sell his watch or maybe even his rings. With that he counted on going far away. Brazil was too big. Maybe he would go to the Amazon. Nobody would find him there. Once free, he would decide what to do with his life. The important thing was to escape the French police.

He went back to his room willing to rest so that he would be in a good mood when the time came to leave. He placed his bags beside the sofa and leaned back on it. He stretched his legs out on a stool and fell asleep.

He woke up to the insistent ringing of the doorbell. He got up, startled, and, still half asleep, went to answer it. There were two men.

- Are you Pierre Legrand?

- Yes, what do you want?

They did not answer and went in, looking around. Pierre had just come out of his sleep and immediately realized that he was in danger. He tried to get out but they held him back.

- Interpol. You're under arrest.

- It must be a mistake. I'm a French citizen. You can't arrest me like this. I haven't done anything.

- You'll say that there.

- Look at the bags. It's true. He was ready to run away.

One of them took out a revolver and pointed it at Pierre, who, pale, didn't know what to do. The other took the handcuffs, but Pierre asked:

- Please. Let me put on my shoes and my jacket.

- If you try anything funny you will be set on fire.

Trembling Pierre put on his shoes and jacket and they handcuffed him.

- What will you do with my bags?

- They will be kept at the hotel. Unless you have money to pay the bill.

- I don't. What are you going to do to me?

- Enough talk. We're on the service of the French police.

- But I need my things.

- Let's get going.

Between the two of them, with the revolver pointed at his back, Pierre bitterly regretted having sought out Maria Eugenia. A deafening rage invaded him and he thought:

"I'll have my revenge. That damned woman will pay for it."

As they left the hotel, arousing the curiosity of those around, a young man standing in the lobby smiled satisfied. He followed them and saw when they put Pierre in the car and took him away. He immediately picked up his car across the street and followed them.

Inside the car, Pierre tried his last move:

-You are my compatriot. Wouldn't there be some other way to solve this?

- What do you suggest? - asked one.

- Well, I have no money, but I have this gold watch which is worth a lot.

- I thought you were going to offer us a few million, joked the policeman. - Well, you should know that even if you had those millions we wouldn't let you go. Nicole was my cousin and it was a pleasure for me to come here to look for you.

- You are wrong. I had nothing to do with her death.

- You better shut your mouth or I'll lose my temper. I am mad to avenge the death of my dear cousin. It would be a pleasure to end your race right here. After all, we're so far away... Who would know?

Pierre fell silent, frightened. There was nothing to be done. Soon he would be back in France, in jail, without even the money to hire a good lawyer.

The car stopped in front of the French Consulate. The gate opened and they went inside. The young man who was following them stopped in front of the gate. He saw when they got down and entered the house. He put the car in motion and quickly drove away from the scene.

A little later, Bernardo called Adele:

- You can get ready for our celebratory dinner.

- Really? Everything alright?

- Yes, that's fine. I'll stop by your place at 8 and tell you all the details. By now our man must be deeply sorry he got in our way.

- This really deserves a celebration. I'll be waiting.

As soon as she hung up the phone, Adele called her daughter.

At Maria Eugenia's house, the couple was heading to the dinner table. When the phone rang, Henrique said:

- Let me answer it.

Maria Eugenia hurried to say:

- Not at all, dear. I'll answer it myself. You can make yourself comfortable and I'll be right there.

She picked up the phone:

- How are you, mom?

- I'm sure you can't talk right now. But everything went well. You can celebrate.

- Thank you, mom. You don't know how happy I feel.

- So do I. I'll tell you the details later. I'm having dinner with Bernardo to celebrate.

- Give him a hug for me.

She was going to continue, but she saw that Henrique was approaching and she restrained herself.

- Bye, mom. Have a good time.

- Is she going to a party?

- She's having dinner with Dr. Bernardo. It seems they won a cause and are going to celebrate.

Henrique smiled maliciously:

- Bernardo is still in love with Adele. I don't know why he doesn't declare himself.

- I think he's afraid she won't accept him.

Henrique thought for a while, then said:

- You know what? I think he has a chance. He's the perfect man to please Adele. I don't know why she hasn't figured that out yet.

- Maybe mom isn't inclined to marriage. With dad, even though they lived well together, I never noticed any desire on her part to devote herself to the home. On the contrary. When they were together, she was the head of everything. That's why he put her in charge. He didn't do anything without her approval. I always doubted that she married him for love.

- He was very much in love with her. You could see it in his eyes when he looked at her.

- But she, though an exemplary wife, was not given to displays of affection.

- Perhaps you're wrong. Adele doesn't strike me as an indifferent woman. On the contrary. In everything she does, she puts a lot of passion, a lot of drive.

- That could be. Then maybe she never really loved my father. Let's have dinner before the food gets cold.

Embraced, they went together to the dining room.

CHAPTER 15

Marina ran into the house, trying to control her excitement. That unexpected kiss had made her heart race. An uncontrollable feeling of joy overwhelmed her.

She went into the bedroom, took off her shoes and sat on the bed, pensive. Several times Ofelia had told her that Rafael was attracted to her, but she had not taken this opinion seriously. They were just good friends. They liked to talk, go out together, they had an affinity, but she had never noticed anything more in him.

How had they come to that kiss? Why was she so excited? Why did she run into the house without saying anything? Wouldn't it have been better to wait and talk?

A thousand turbulent thoughts enveloped her. Rafael was a wonderful man. Handsome, elegant, cultured and with a charming temperament. Any woman would be happy to date him.

When they went out together, Marina noticed how many women tried to attract his attention. At such moments, she smiled proudly at him for preferring her company. But that was only vanity, not love. Was she falling in love with him?

At that thought, she remembered the kiss, and her heart beat faster. She certainly felt attracted to him. His closeness, his perfume, his lively eyes, his friendly smile, all this pleased her very much.

She had never loved before. She remembered her relation with Henrique. She had felt pleasure in that relation, even without loving him. Wouldn't what she was feeling now be the same thing, just an arousal of the senses?

She needed to think about analysing her true feelings. Then she wasn't sure of anything. What had that kiss represented for Rafael? Wasn't it just a temptation of the moment because of the proximity?

They had had a very pleasant evening, had talked a lot, talked about their inner feelings, about their way of seeing life, now from the spiritual viewpoint which had opened new doors of understanding.

The kiss was spontaneous, it happened naturally. But what did it really mean?

She got ready for bed, but the agitated thoughts continued and she took a long time to fall asleep. She woke up a little later the next morning. Looking at the time, she got up hurriedly.

She took a shower and went downstairs for breakfast. Cicero was at the table talking with Ofelia, recounting the experiences of the previous night. Seeing her arriving, Ofelia remarked:

- From what Cicero says this lady is really good.

- Indeed. I liked her very much.

- Cicero told me he is going to attend a mediumship course. I want to go with him.

- You? I never thought you'd be interested in that subject.

- I never said, but every now and then I see my father's soul.

- Why didn't you say anything?

- You've studied, you have a degree. I didn't want you to laugh at me.

- I would never do that.

Marina had had a cup of coffee with milk and a piece of cake. She got up in a hurry. Ofelia asked:

- Aren't you going to tell me what she told you?

- Now I'm late. We'll talk later.

She left and Ofelia remarked:

- I don't know why she runs so much. She could get sick that way. I didn't even have time to tell her how much better you are.

- I'll tell you myself later. Today, when Mrs. Rute comes, I want to ask you a few questions. She knows all about mediumship.

- Try to study. She is happy when you learn your lesson.

- Leave it to me.

Ofelia smiled. Seeing her children happy was her best incentive. She went to the kitchen to make something tasty for lunch.

Marina arrived at the office and found a few petitions and a contract on her desk.

She put her purse away and sat down ready to put all her attention on her work. It wasn't easy. From time to time she surprised herself thinking about Rafael. What would their relationship be like from then on? What would he tell her about that kiss?

Maybe he would justify himself, saying that it had been a temptation of the moment and would even apologize, since he was a very polite man. And everything would go on as before.

But she knew that nothing could be as before. That kiss had awakened in her a need to love and be loved. Even if it was only a physical need, it existed and would be present between them.

Marina got up, took a glass of water, then a cup of coffee, and made an effort to focus her attention on work. It took all her effort to succeed.

She called her mother and told her that she wouldn't be home for lunch. She needed to get on with her work, which earned her a reprimand from Ofelia, worried about her health.

\- You won't run out of lunch. Try to eat something.

\- I'll do that. I'll order something.

She hung up the phone and plunged into her work, trying not to divert her attention.

It was past six when she left the office and went downstairs. As she stepped out onto the street, she found Rafael waiting.

\- Rafael, why didn't you come upstairs?

He kissed her lightly on the cheek and answered:

\- I didn't want to get in the way. I came because we have to talk. She agreed and noticed that he was tense.

They walked to the car in silence. Once they were settled, he said:

\- Then I'll bring you back to get your car.

He started the car and drove slowly.

\- Where are we going? - she asked.

\- I don't know.

\- I can see you're tense. Maybe because of what happened last night.

They had entered a quiet street. Rafael stopped the car, looked at her and said:

\- I couldn't sleep at all tonight.

\- Neither could I.

\- I don't know what you're thinking about yesterday. I need to be honest. I discovered a long time ago that I'm in love with you. Since I know you don't feel the same way about me, I tried to hold back as much as I could, for fear of losing your friendship. Yesterday I couldn't resist. It was magical because, contrary to what I thought, you reciprocated. Do you think I'm dreaming too much?

Marina looked at Rafael's moved face and felt an immense feeling of love blossom in her cheast. She felt like hugging and kissing him. Looking into his eyes, she answered:

- No. If this is a dream, I don't want to wake up.

He hugged her and kissed her lips several times. They remained embraced, in silence, feeling their hearts beating strong and a sense of fullness that needed no words.

After kissing her again, Rafael said:

- You have no idea how much I have desired for this moment. I have never met a woman who has touched me as much as you have. At your side I feel at ease to be myself, which has never happened before. It's a pleasure to be with you, who respect my opinions, but speak your mind without acting out roles that women like so much.

- Is that the only reason you fell in love with me?

- No. Your beauty was what attracted me at first. I won't deny that from the very first day I felt like kissing you. But you immediately cut off any chance, showing that you weren't the least bit interested in having an affectionate relationship with me. I conformed and even liked being just your friend. We had some good times together, when we exchanged ideas, got to know each other better. But one night when we went dancing, holding you in my arms, your face full of life, excited by the music, I discovered how much you meant to me.

- I did not know. I didn't notice anything.

- It was hard to control. But at no time did you show anything but friendship. I confess that I reached a point where I was very afraid of losing you, so I preferred not to say anything.

Marina stroked his face.

- I was in love and I didn't know it. Yesterday, when you kissed me, I felt so much emotion. I was confused, without understanding my feelings. I even imagined that you had done so by giving in to a temptation of the moment, which can happen between a man and a woman, even when there is no love.

He held her hand and brought it to his lips. Then he said:

- Between us there has always been so much more than that.

- I have been wondering all night what you would tell me about it. But as soon as we saw each other today, I knew the truth.

He kissed her again and they held each other in silence for some time. Rafael cut the silence by saying softly:

- I want to spend the rest of my life with you.

She smiled and asked:

- Are you asking me to marry you?

- Take it any way you like. I know that this word provokes in you a contrary reaction.

- It's not the word, but what people do when they get married. Perhaps because I had a sad example at home. My father abandoned us to live with another woman. My mother was a devoted but passive wife and he always abused her, which made me angry. When he left home I thanked God. But I was small, and mom was pregnant with Cicero. But although we were poor and mom worked hard to keep the house, we could live in peace. It was then that I promised myself that I would never let myself be deceived by a man, that I would dedicate my life to study and graduate so that I could give comfort and well-being to my family.

- Which you have achieved brilliantly.

Marina was thoughtful for a moment, remembering her contract with Adele.

- What was it? You became pensive...

- Nothing. Just some memories from the past.

- The past is gone. We are living today and have a whole future ahead of us. What I want is to live by your side, with or without marriage. You decide how you want to do that.

- I'll think about it. Maybe a contract with no expiry date, but which can be undone if necessary.

- Why are you saying that? I want to be with you forever.

She laughed and replied:

- Don't talk like that. I love you, you love me. Today we want to be together forever. If this happens, it will be good. But if at any time we stop having pleasure in living next to each other, we will have the right to choose another path.

- The way you talk, it seems that you don't trust our feelings.

- It is not like that. What I mean is that being together is only good as long as there is love. I don't want you to think you are stuck with me for the rest of your days. We are free. Even though we live together, we each need to keep our individuality, to be what we are.

He kissed her gently on the forehead and answered:

- You don't exist! And that is why I am sure that we will be very happy together.

That night, when they entered the house, Ofelia was studying in the living room. She, noticing Cicero's progress, who had lost almost all his country accent and was acquiring a vocabulary, had decided to study too. She wanted her children to be proud of her and had asked Rute to teach her.

Seeing them enter, Ofelia noticed immediately that they were different. She liked Rafael and suspected that behind that friendship there was a greater feeling, so she was not surprised when Marina said:

- Mom, Rafael and I are dating.

Ofelia stood up and hugged them happily:

- I knew this would still lead to marriage. I am very happy for you.

- How did you know? - asked Rafael.

- Oh, my son. Do you think I didn't notice how you looked at her?

He laughed good-naturedly and answered:

- And I thought I was disguising it well... But a mother has a sixth sense.

- Marina has never had a serious relationship and I was afraid that she would become an old maid.

- If it's up to me, that won't happen.

- This is an event. We have to celebrate. I'll get a bottle of wine.

Ofelia went to the pantry and Rafael hugged Marina.

- Your mother is happy.

- She appreciates you very much.

A little later, Ofelia returned with a tray of glasses and a bottle and asked Rafael to open it. He obeyed and poured. Then he gave each one a glass, saying:

- I toast to this moment of happiness.

- May our lives always continue this happy, Ofelia added.

- May our love bring us happiness, Marina added.

They touched glasses and drank. Then Rafael hugged them both and kissed them on the cheek.

- Thank you for letting me join this family, which I adore.

Ofelia brought some snacks and they continued chatting for a while longer. Rafael said goodbye and Marina walked him to the door.

When she returned Ofelia said happily:

- I'm sure you two will be very happy.

Marina went to her room and got ready for bed, but one thought bothered her: the secret she kept about her contract with Adele.

Rafael was a good man, sincere. She felt she loved him. Would it be fair to him not to tell her the truth?

He admired her, he was proud of her, he thought she was a winning woman. What would he think if one day he found out that she had lent herself to having a child in exchange for money?

For the first time he regretted having agreed with Adele. She decided she wouldn't tell him. He wouldn't have the courage. But how could you start a serious relationship with a lie?

Maybe it was better to break up. Then she wouldn't have to say anything. They would remain friends as they had always been. But at the same time, having found love, should she spend the rest of her life alone?

What would she do when her brother took full responsibility for his life and her mother died?

At that moment she realized how much she loved Rafael and wanted to live by his side, enjoying his company. Her head ached and she lay in bed worried for a long time. Finally, tired, she fell asleep.

She dreamt that she was in a very beautiful garden. She remembered that she had been there before. She looked around for someone. Soon she saw the same girl she had dreamt of before, who hugged her lovingly.

- I am happy to see you.

- I don't know how I got here. I was restless, and this place has the gift of calming me down.

- Let's go for a walk. Come.

She embraced her and together they rose, flying over the gardens in the starlight. Marina felt a great pleasure and a sensation that her chest was swelling as she looked at the lights of the sleeping city below.

Then Marina noticed that they were on the street outside her house. They went downstairs and entered the bedroom. She could see her own body asleep on the bed.

Thrilled, she clung to her companion, who told her smiling:

- Don't be afraid. All this is natural. You will return to your body and remember our meeting. Remember: everything is right. You did what you promised to do. There is nothing wrong.

Marina looked at her worriedly and she repeated:

- Remember: everything is right. You did what you promised to do. There is nothing wrong.

Marina stirred in bed and woke up feeling the pleasure she had enjoyed in her dream. In her ears the last words of her spiritual friend still sounded:

- Remember: everything is right. You did what you promised to do. There is nothing wrong.

She sat up in bed excited, feeling that sensation of happiness, and thought:

"It was no dream. I have found her again. Her words comforted me. We talked about many things. Why can't I remember everything?"

Marina laid down again, feeling calmer. As for Rafael, she decided not to say anything, just to wait for events to take place. First, she had to understand why they told her that there was nothing wrong with her attitude, even though she had received money from Adele, which in a way was embarrassing.

She remembered Eunice. Maybe she could clarify her doubts.

Two days later, as they had arranged, Marina and Rafael went to a meeting at the centre for spiritual studies run by Eunice. After the conversation they had had with her, they decided to start studying.

During the trip, Marina told him about the astral experience in the company of the spiritual friend that Eunice had mentioned. She said that on the way back she had seen her own body asleep in bed.

- I was frightened, but my companion said there was no need to be afraid, that it was natural.

- How wonderful! I would very much like to experience that.

- It is a wonderful sensation, you gliding over the places, under the light of the stars, seeing the city below, and at the same time inside your heart a joy that cannot be explained in words.

- What else did she tell you?

- During the dream I understood everything she said, but as soon as I woke up I couldn't remember anything.

She did not mention the words that still sounded clear to his ears, so as not to draw his attention to the matter that concerned her.

As soon as they entered the building, they signed up to join the study group. With half an hour to go, they stopped by the small bookstore in the next room.

Eunice came out of one of the rooms and, seeing them, approached them to greet them. Then she asked for Cicero.

- He is well - answered Marina. - He will come tomorrow for the mediumship course. My mother decided to come with him.

Eunice smiled.

- It will be good for her, who already has some knowledge about spiritual life.

- I was surprised when she said she would come with him. She has never been connected to religious matters.

- Don't be surprised. These are things of her spirit. She became interested because she felt that we are here learning about the natural phenomena of life and not creating or following a religion.

- That was the reason I decided to come here to learn, Rafael said.

Marina checked her watch and saw that there were still twenty minutes left before the course began. She asked:

- Are you very busy right now?

- No. I have just finished the service.

- I had an out of body experience the day before yesterday and I would like to ask you a few questions. I'll be quick.

- Ok. Let's go in.

Rafael mentioned accompanying them, but Eunice said:

- I prefer to speak to her alone. I also have a personal message for her.

- Make yourselves at home. I am going to choose some books.

They went in and settled down. Before Marina began to speak, Eunice said:

- You have a great affinity. You understand each other well and will certainly have a happy and fruitful union. Your love comes from other lives. As to this, all is good. You are a loyal person and you are worried because you keep a secret in your heart and don't have the courage to tell him.

Marina looked at her surprised.

- How did you know?

- Your friend Norma is telling me. She is the one you have been meeting when you leave your body.

- That's right. Rafael declared himself and I discovered that I loved him too. My secret involves other people and I promised not to tell anyone. But the doubts bother me. I don't want to start a relationship with a lie.

- Norma is telling me that she has already told you about it.

- She says that she is grateful because I rendered her a service and fulfilled what I had promised. She stated that everything is right, there is nothing wrong.

- She is repeating this to me. So, what is the doubt?

- But it's that I received money to provide this service. That's what bothers me.

- Have you harmed anyone?

- No. On the contrary: I helped a family solve a problem. I agreed to provide this service because I needed the money. My father abandoned us when I was a child and my mother was pregnant with Cicero. They lived in the countryside. I studied, I worked hard, always thinking of a better life for them. My mother sewed until the early hours to support us. I wanted her to have a better life and my brother to study to be someone in life.

- The reasons are noble. You know, my daughter, there is still a lot of prejudice about money. However, it is necessary to do good, to develop science, to alleviate human suffering. There is no harm in wanting to improve your life, to have money. It is value, and it is neither good nor bad. It depends on how we use it. It is good when used intelligently in favour of progress and bad when accumulated without benefit or to the detriment of others.

- Your words do me good.

- Norma is telling you not to worry. When the time is right, life will sort it out for you. Keep your heart in peace. Live your life and be happy.

Marina stood up, her eyes watering:

- Thank you, Mrs. Eunice. Your words have given me back my peace.

- Go with God, my daughter.

As she left the room, Marina felt happy and in a good mood. Rafael was waiting for her. Seeing her, he said:

- You came just in time. I bought two books. I'll show you later.

She held his arm and said:

- Let's go. I don't want to miss this class.

Cheerful and in a good mood, they entered the room, where many people were already settled and waiting. They looked for two seats and sat down.

A young man, tall and clear, entered the room and stood in front of them, saying:

- Let us unite our thoughts seeking to achieve our goals of progress and light. Together we ask Universal Intelligence to open our minds so that, more lucid, we can better understand what life wants to teach us now.

He closed his eyes and remained silent for a few seconds. Then he opened them and said:

- Today we are going to talk about the messages that the facts of life bring us and how to understand them.

With his eyes shining, he began to talk about the subject, and both Rafael and Marina, who had found it strange that such a young professor should be so young for such a deep subject, were captivated by his words, which made them think, amazed at how he expressed himself.

For fifteen minutes he spoke and everyone in the room, as if magnetized, listened attentively. Then he stopped, smiled and invited:

- Now let us move on to the questions.

Immediately some people raised their hands and he listened to them one by one, clarifying doubts, explaining situations, letting them draw their own conclusions.

At the end he thanked everyone for their attention and closed the meeting with a prayer of gratitude to the spiritual friends.

Rafael and Marina left the place enthusiastically. They went to have a snack and all the while they were exchanging ideas about the theme of the evening. They did not see that Norma's spirit was hugging them happily, enveloping them with thoughts of joy and peace.

CHAPTER 16

Six months after these events, we returned to Paris where Pierre was in prison awaiting trial. The evidence against him was mounting day by day and he was in despair.

The friends who had helped him dissipate his fortune had disappeared, his family name was disgraced and those relatives who were left behind refused to help him.

Without money to pay a good lawyer to defend himself, Pierre felt more and more afraid of being condemned every day. It was intolerable to endure the three cell mates, the precariousness of the installations without privacy, always smelling of cheap disinfectant, and the humiliation of the disregard and malice of others.

In addition to drug trafficking and the suspected murder of Nicole, the police suspected that he had also murdered Jamille, since she had disappeared without trace and Pierre claimed not to know her whereabouts.

For them it was inadmissible that a woman who had gone to Brazil with her husband and who did not know the language of that country should decide to disappear for no just reason. Most probably she knew too much and he had killed her to protect himself.

Pierre, when he thought of her, felt his hatred grow. Jamille had abandoned him at the most difficult moment of his life after having enjoyed a luxurious life at his side, frequenting places of luxury.

Of course, she had abandoned him for fear of being accused of complicity. However, besides stealing all his money, she had also left him in a delicate situation. How could he prove that she was still alive, living in Brazil?

The amount of money she possessed would be enough to live on for a month, and that with great economy, which he believed she would not be able to do.

What would she do when the money ran out? To return to France would be impossible, since she had no resources. Since she was unable to work, she would certainly end up prostituting herself.

Pierre's hatred was even more violent against Maria Eugenia. With that air of a good person he had set her that trap. She and certainly her mother, a smart and experienced executive.

When he thought of them, he seemed to suffocate. Then he would get up and walk around the cell from one side to the other like a caged beast, which irritated his companions, who threatened to beat him.

This could not go on. He had to do something. While he suffered for living in that hell, Maria Eugenia enjoyed her quiet little life with her family in that wonderful mansion, posing as an impolite lady of the best society. He had to act. They had to pay for what they had done to her.

Thinking about everything, he decided to change his attitude inside the prison. Having shown himself aggressive, rebellious, he had only made the situation worse. He was watched constantly and the jailers looked at him angrily.

He had to swallow his anger and try to work around the facts. He had always known how to deal with people at any level. He began by being polite to everyone, resigned to the situation, showing himself sad for his companion's ingratitude.

The jailers, relieved at not having to watch him constantly, began to treat him better. And little by little his cellmates also changed with him.

One day he was approached by Jacques, a lawyer that Justice had appointed to defend him at the trial that was to take place three months later.

With the lawyer present, Pierre was able to leave his cell to speak to him alone in a private room. He told him his version of the facts, saying he was innocent.

The lawyer made it clear that as his defender he needed to know the whole truth. Pierre continued to deny the crime and claimed that he used drugs for his own consumption.

- There is the disappearance of your wife, Jacques insisted.

- She left me when she found out that I was wanted by the police. I don't know where she is.

- Do you think she has returned to France?

- Not at all! The money she took from me would not be enough. I imagine she must still be in Brazil. But I don't know where.

Jacques scratched his head despondently.

- In view of the suspicions the police have, your word is worthless. We have to find proof that she is alive.

- I don't know how to do that. Brazil is a very big country.

- You said you have friends there. Couldn't you write, ask for her information? She might have gone to look for them.

- I don't think so. They didn't like her very much.

- It's your only chance. Write them a letter, ask for information. Perhaps they know something.

Pierre looked at him thoughtfully. An idea crossed his mind and he answered:

- All right. Bring me some paper and an envelope and I'll write it down.

After Jacques had left, Pierre returned to his cell thoughtfully. His situation was still bad, but he had found a way to get back at Maria Eugenia.

The next day Jacques took what he had asked for and promised to collect the letter in a day or two. Sitting in a corner of the cell Pierre laid the paper on the table and began to write.

"Dr. Henrique Silveira Couto, I am writing to make a confession. I am in love with Maria Eugenia and know that it is reciprocated. When you were in Paris, she and I fell in love and became lovers. In our moments of intimacy, I discovered that she wasn't pregnant, she was wearing a false belly.

When you returned to Brazil, I suffered a lot with the separation. Since then I thought of going to see her in her country. When we were at her house a few months ago, I intended to reconnect with her, but she didn't want to, because of the boy she says is her son.

I was desperate. My wife discovered everything and abandoned me. She left the hotel where we were staying and took all my money.

Then I was contacted by your mother-in-law's lawyer who threatened me saying that if I didn't stop interfering in Maria Eugenia's life they would report me to the French police.

I didn't believe it, but that same night I was sought out by two policemen who arrested me and took me to the French consulate. I was deported and I am still in prison, accused of crimes that I did not commit. There is even the suspicion that I killed my wife.

Without money, without friends, despised, I am waiting for the trial. I turn to you for help. I have no one to ask for help. If you don't help me, I will be forced at the trial to tell the whole truth. Only in this way will I be able to prove my innocence. Surely the newspapers will not spare you, whose company is very well known here. I say that my only crime was to love a woman and not be able to forget her.

I await your answer. Please help me.

Pierre Legrand."

He read it all over again and, satisfied, put the letter in the envelope and closed it. Maria Eugenia would feel the weight of his revenge. Henrique was a serious man and would not tolerate his wife's treachery. He would certainly repudiate her.

The next day the lawyer arrived, Pierre handed him the letter and said happily:

- I think it will work out.

- It's just as well, because Nicole's friend is going to testify against you and is bent on avenging her death.

- She is angry because I did not want to have relations with her. She is lying because of jealousy.

- You'd better think it over, see if you can find an alibi, because your situation in this case is not the best.

Pierre got serious.

- I'll think about it, doctor. I'll think about it.

After the lawyer had left Pierre smiled contentedly. Besides taking revenge, Henrique would certainly try to hush up the scandal and try to get him off scot-free.

Two days later, on Friday, Henrique called Adele pleased to tell her the good news: finally, after months of negotiation, he had closed a huge deal with a large German company.

- They signed the contract just as we wanted. Everything went fine.

- That's great. Congratulations! You did it! We have to celebrate. Come have dinner with me tonight. I want to know all the details.

- I'll speak to Maria Eugenia.

- Tell her to bring Dionisio. I miss him. I'll invite Bernardo. He helped us a lot in this negotiation.

- Ok. We'll go.

Adele hung up the phone and called Bernardo, who was thrilled not only with the news, but with the invitation.

Dinner at Adele's house was served at eight o'clock. At seven thirty, Bernardo had already arrived, having brought a beautiful box of roses. A little later, Henrique and Maria Eugenia also arrived, bringing Elvira and Dionisio.

The atmosphere was festive. Before dinner, the boy attracted everyone's attention with his jokes, his very particular language and his affectionate way of treating everyone.

Then Elvira took him to the kitchen, where she was to serve him dinner while the adults settled down to eat in the living room.

The conversation flowed happily. When it was time for dessert, they toasted with champagne. Everyone was happy. Maria Eugenia, after the problem she had faced with Pierre, her way of relating to her mother had changed.

She had begun to take an interest in the business and to give her opinion, demonstrating intelligence and clarity, which made their friendship even closer.

Finally, Maria Eugenia understood that a company was not, as she had imagined, just a money-making machine, but rather an organization that provided employment opportunities for many people who, at work, developed their intelligence and at the same time earned money.

to many people, who at work developed their capacity for intelligence and at the same time earned their money to support their family with dignity.

She found that Adele ran that organization demanding discipline and self-effort, but acting with generosity and fairness, offering specialization courses to the hardest workers and support in times when someone was in a difficult moment.

She felt proud to see that Adele was very respected by her employees, who felt good to work for someone they admired.

It was after ten o'clock when Maria Eugenia wanted to leave. They said goodbye, but Adele, who was particularly cheerful that night, asked Bernardo to stay a little longer.

- I'm not sleepy. Let's talk.

- Wouldn't you like to go out for a while? We could go dancing somewhere.

- No. I'd rather stay at home. Let's go to the winter garden and listen to music.

Once there, Bernardo asked:

- What would you like to hear?

- You choose.

She sat down in an armchair and soon a blues filled the air. Bernardo stood up in front of her, then bowed, saying:

- Would you like to dance with me?

She stood up and they began to dance. The music enveloped them, and Bernardo said excitedly:

- It seems that time has not passed, like if we are in the club, dancing like we used to. I keep asking myself: what would have happened if I wasn't so shy?

Adele laughed contentedly.

- You mean that back then, you were interested in me?

- I was very much in love.

Adele pulled away a little and looked him in the eyes:

- Why didn't you ever say anything to me?

- I think you always knew.

- In fact, for a while I was suspicious, but then I thought I was wrong. You were always discreet, you never showed it.

The song ended. Adele poured herself some more champagne while he chose another record. Soon Sinatra began to sing a romantic song and Bernardo wrapped his arms around her again. They danced for a few moments in silence, until Bernardo said:

- Hiding that love was hard for me.

- You have had several relationships. Why didn't you ever get married?

He pressed her against his chest and said in her ear:

- Because I could never love another woman.

There was so much passion in his voice that Adele shuddered. She walked away from Bernardo and went to sit on the sofa. He followed her and sat beside her, concerned.

- I'm sorry. I think I overdid it. You didn't give me the freedom to do that.

Adele looked at him seriously and replied:

- Don't apologize. Knowing that you loved me like that thrills me and takes me back to the past. Maybe if you had been more daring my life would have been different.

Bernardo looked at her in amazement:

- Why are you saying this? Do you think I would have had any chance?

- I don't know. What I do know is that my marriage was not what everyone thinks.

Bernardo was surprised:

- Why? You seemed so happy! In fact, it was that thought that comforted me. In spite of everything, what I wanted most of all was for you to be happy. Dr. Aurelio was a successful, handsome, respected, rich man.

- Aurelio was all that, socially. In intimacy he was cold, insensitive. Everything he did was planned. To be able to live with him I had to bury my passionate side, my fiery temperament, full of life.

Bernardo held her hand in an attempt to support her. Eyes lost in time; Adele continued:

- Even on the honeymoon he would show irritation whenever I had any exuberant, spontaneous attitude. He said it was unpolite. He taught me the way and the time to laugh, to speak, even to cry. But you know me, you know I'm a practical woman. I put my feelings aside and tried to analyse his personality. I swore to myself that he would change the tone in which he spoke to me and make him respect me. I knew that for him business was more important and he admired people who succeeded in their endeavours.

She paused slightly and, noticing that Bernardo was listening to her with interest, continued saying:

- I studied, prepared myself and gradually took over the business. At first, he did not take me seriously, until I proved that I knew what I was doing and managed to reverse the situation. He started to do nothing without consulting me and ended up trusting my ability, leaving the most important part in my hands. When he fell ill, he told me about his father's will and the hope he placed on Maria Eugenia. For him, these companies were more important than his own family.

- Is that why you hired Marina?

- No. If Renato had been a capable man, maybe I would have offered him a partnership. But, irresponsible and a gambler, he'd cause a lot of trouble.

- Indeed. You're right.

- The fact is I enjoyed running the companies. I learned a lot from that, I developed my creativity, I observed human beings better, I was able to exercise my knowledge and develop good work, giving other people the opportunity to grow with me.

- I have always admired the way you lead your employees.

- I respect them. It was more to continue doing this job that I wanted to stay on as president of our organization.

Bernardo squeezed her hand lovingly, brought it to his lips and kissed her hand.

- That is why I still love you.

- I have become a woman without love.

- You're wrong. Everything you do is with love. The whimsy, the dedication, the taste for art, it all shows sensitivity.

- This is a night of celebration. Let's dance Bernardo, forget the past.

She stood up and he wrapped her in his arms lovingly. Soft music lulled them as they danced in silence.

Bernardo felt his heart beating faster and faster and he was overcome with emotion. That long-cherished love longed to express itself and he gave in.

He pressed her against his chest and kissed her lips with passion. The emotion was contagious and Adele surrendered to those sensations, which made her body tremble with pleasure. She hugged him too, responding to his caresses.

They continued kissing until Adele, pulling him by the hand, took him to his room, where, intoxicated, Bernardo said in a voice that passion made him mad:

- If you only knew how I dreamed of this moment! To have you in my arms was what I most desired in life.

Moved, Adele felt that she was awakening again to love, as she had never imagined she would.

She kissed him tenderly. She closed the door as he waited for her with open arms. She nestled into them and together they went to bed to experience that moment of love.

The next morning Adele woke up and looked at Bernardo asleep at her side. She sat up in bed thoughtfully. The memory of the loving moments they had enjoyed filled her chest with warmth.

She remembered having had more champagne than usual, which had certainly made her break the barrier of conventionality.

Bernardo opened his eyes and, seeing her, smiled.

- Am I dreaming or did it really happen?

- It did happen. We danced, drank champagne, talked, and ended up here.

He sat on the bed, looking at her seriously:

- Are you sorry?

- No. But it scares me a little to realize I've lost control.

He smoothed her face affectionately.

- Love needs to be celebrated.

- I want to be honest with you. What happened yesterday was unexpected. I need to think about it, evaluate my feelings.

- Well, I am sure of what I feel. I never told you about my love because you didn't give me a chance. You always treated me as a friend. I didn't want to ruin this friendship. But yesterday I felt that you want me too. Maybe it's hard for a woman like you to give herself to love: used to leading, to speaking according to the moment and acting according to her objectives. It can be scary to let emotions flow freely, to lose control. However, you are still the same person, capable of acting as you always have done, only more fully capable of loving and being loved. Doesn't that make you happy?

Adele smiled:

- It does. When I woke up and saw you lying across from me, I felt a little afraid of losing my freedom, my hard-won privacy. But now I am starting to think that it might be worth it to leave the leader aside a little and just be a woman.

Bernardo hugged her and kissed her on her lips several times.

- Life is not only work, professional success, keeping the flame of an ideal burning, but also joy, pleasure, love. It is moments like those we lived last night that drive us to produce more and better in all the other objectives. Today I feel like a lion, full of strength, of optimism. I am sure that everything I do today will work out.

- So am I.

- Today is Saturday. What about spending the weekend somewhere nice, away from everything and everyone?

Adele's eyes twinkled mischievously.

- That would be wonderful. Where shall we go?

- You choose. We can take a plane and go to Rio de Janeiro or to some city in the south, or we can leave by car, without a destination, stopping wherever it seems best.

- I like the last option.

- How long will it take you to get ready?

- Half an hour, but first we will have breakfast.

- We'll do that on the way. Let's get ready quickly. I know a great place where we can have breakfast. Then we'll stop at my flat, where I'll pick up a few things. Then we'll go out into the world, aimlessly. Just the two of us, free to do whatever we feel like doing.

They both got out of bed and quickly got ready. Adele, face flushed with pleasure, looked like a teenager heading for adventure. She couldn't remember feeling so motivated and excited about going on an outing for many years.

It was great not having to think about attending to the day's appointments, looking for solutions to the business problems that were multiplying, challenging her creativity and her efficient team.

Less than half an hour later, they were leaving. Adele called the maid and said:

- I'm going on a trip and won't be back until tomorrow night. Make sure everything is under control.

Then together they went to the car, eyes bright, faces flushed, smiling easily, joy in their hearts.

CHAPTER 17

On Monday, Henrique arrived at the office before nine o'clock. He had an important meeting with an importer and needed to study the proposal he had made.

His secretary had placed some open letters on the desk, including one that, being personal, she had not opened. Henrique picked up the handwritten envelope and, not recognising the handwriting, looked at the sender and shuddered:

PIERRE LEGRAND

The stamp was from a prison in Lyon. He turned the letter over in his fingers, thoughtful. The letter had been sent from a prison. Was Pierre in prison? Why would he write to him?

Curious, he tore open the envelope, picked up the folded sheet of paper, opened it and began to read. As he read, his face became flushed and his frown tightened. When he finished, he was pale.

So that was it? Had Maria Eugenia even fallen in love with that scoundrel? Had she given herself to him, betraying his trust?

Perhaps Pierre was lying. But how could he doubt if he knew that Maria Eugenia was not pregnant? He could only have found that out if he had been intimately involved with her.

Henrique ran a trembling hand through his hair, as if to push away those painful thoughts that were devastating him.

Maria Eugenia had changed a lot after Dionisio' birth. But this scabrous story had happened before, when she had shown herself insensitive, futile, rebellious.

A few tears streamed down Henrique's face and he did not care to wipe them away. He had been a faithful husband. He had accepted a relationship with Marina to help Adele and, why not say it, because of the possibility of being a father, which would have been impossible otherwise.

Had Maria Eugenia done it to get back at him? When in Paris, she let her rebellion show for having accepted Adele's proposal. But Pierre said that she was in love; that when he had been in Brazil trying to win her back, she had only not gone with him in order not to leave Dionisio.

Henrique recognized that she had indeed become very attached to the boy. This justification was perfectly probable. In that case, she no longer loved him. She preferred the love of that disgraced scoundrel to his, who had always been a devoted and honest husband.

Pierre was in prison, pleading not guilty, but Henrique did not believe this. Moreover, he threatened him, intending to tell this unhappy story to the newspapers in Paris, where they had a branch office and were well known and respected.

A deafening rage took hold of Henrique. If at that moment Pierre appeared in front of him, he would certainly not answer for his life.

He had to do something. But what? What good would it do to pressure Maria Eugenia, to throw all his anger in her face, if she was a devoted mother of his son and, besides, Dionisio only felt good with her?

Should Henrique swallow his anger for the sake of the child and pretend that nothing had happened? He certainly couldn't. One way or another he would end up talking.

He could break up with Maria Eugenia, but he was sure that Dionisio would suffer greatly from this. He loved the boy very much and wanted him to be happy. On the other hand, he did not want to leave home and lose the company of his only son.

Agonized, Henrique got up and walked from one side of the room to the other. A thousand contradictory thoughts crossed his mind.

What if Pierre really did what he was promising? If he went to the newspapers and told the story, besides the scandal, there was the possibility that they would find out that Dionisio was not Maria Eugenia's son, so Adele would have to step down as President of the companies, and they might even have to go to court for breaking the law.

He had to do something, but he couldn't take on this responsibility alone. As much as it hurt him, he had to find Adele and tell her everything. Together, maybe they could find a way out.

He wanted to do that immediately, but he had that important interview later. He felt like cancelling the meeting, but he controlled himself. The person had come from a long way away and he couldn't miss it. Cancelling the interview would give the impression of disorganization, and he couldn't do that.

He took a deep breath and decided to see Adele after he got rid of the appointment. It was hard to wait, but he had no other recourse.

He picked up the business proposal and tried to examine it again, but it was difficult. He couldn't understand what he was reading. It took a great deal of effort for him to concentrate on his work, to pay attention to the person, to show himself kind and in a good mood, when he felt distressed, afflicted, uneasy.

He breathed a sigh of relief when he finished the task. Despite the circumstances, even though he had not been brilliant, he had achieved what was indispensable.

He looked at his watch. It was lunchtime and Adele liked to have lunch in peace and not discuss any unpleasant matters at this hour.

Henrique was undecided. It would be better to wait a little longer, but his anxiety did not let him. He went to look for her.

He found his mother-in-law in the dining room next to the room where she worked. Seeing him, she said:

- Henrique! If you had come a little earlier, you would have kept me company. Have you already had lunch?

- No, thank you.

- In that case, I'll have something brought for you.

- That's all right. I'm not hungry. I've come because we have some serious business to discuss.

Adele cast a glance at him and considered:

- You don't look well. Has something happened?

- Yes. But I don't want to interrupt your lunch. I'll wait in the other room.

- I've finished," she said, getting up. - Come on, let's talk.

They went into the other room and sat down opposite each other.

- And then? - Adele asked.

- Something terrible has happened. I don't know how to begin...

- From the beginning, of course.

- When we were in Paris, before Dionisio was born, we met a French couple. I didn't like them, but Maria Eugenia became very friendly with them.

- I know. That couple were here a few months ago.

- Yes. They came to visit us once, then disappeared without saying goodbye, which I was relieved about. I never liked Pierre. Today, on arriving at the office, I found a letter from him that disturbed me a lot.

Adele felt that something serious was happening. She just said:

- Let me read it.

Without saying anything else, Henrique took the letter from his pocket and handed it to her in silence. Adele began to read it and tried to remain calm. When she finished, she looked at him seriously and asked:

- You didn't believe what that rascal said, did you?

- I wish it were a lie, but the details mentioned made me believe that he is telling the truth.

- He lies. He wants to take revenge on us because we handed him over to the French police, with whom he had a score to settle.

Henrique was surprised:

- Did you have him arrested? Why didn't you tell me?

- We didn't think it was worth bothering you with that scoundrel. He went to Maria Eugenia, tried to blackmail her. She asked for $5 million. When they were in Paris, he found out Maria Eugenia wasn't pregnant, did some research and learned how important the birth of a child was to us. He found out that she had had a boy and from his age deduced that he was not legitimate. Pressured by debts, he came looking for her to get some money.

- Why didn't you tell me? How could you hide all this from me?

- I asked her not to tell you anything. I didn't want you to think that Maria Eugenia might have had an affair with that guy.

- But I think she did. The only way he could have known she wasn't pregnant was if they'd had an intimate relationship.

- Don't believe that. You know how careless Maria Eugenia was. You mustn't forget that my daughter was a friend of his wife's, who may have noticed and told him.

- But Pierre says they had an affair and that Maria Eugenia loved him.

- I can't believe such nonsense. Maria Eugenia married you for love and has never stopped loving you.

- You don't know, I never told you, but when we were in Paris, she changed a a lot. She was rebellious, joined that couple and other friends, went out every night and came back at dawn.

- Didn't you accompany her?

- At first, yes, but I didn't like her friends and I didn't want to go out with them. She was in a bad mood, jealous because of Marina. At that time, I even thought that she would never forgive the fact that I had a relationship with another woman, even if it was not for love. I didn't want to go out with these friends, I worked all day and couldn't go to bed at dawn every night.

- You shouldn't have allowed her to lead that life.

- I think you're right, but at that time she complained about being alone in the flat all day. At night she wanted to go out, to clear her head. I also like to go out at night, but not to stay until dawn, having to work the next day. I stopped accompanying her, I allowed her to go out with them. I think it was a mistake. Disgusted as she was with our situation, she let herself be taken in by Pierre, who took advantage of her.

- I don't believe she went that far.

- What he says in his letter is very plausible and in accordance with the problems we lived through at that time. What hurts me was him saying that Maria Eugenia loves him and only didn't accompany him because of Dionisio. How could he know how attached she is to him?

- He's been to yourhouse, seen how their relationship is. He took the cue.

- I'm desperate. I love my wife. We've been married for eight years and I've never cheated on her. How could she do this to me?

- I repeat; she loves you, always loved you. When he blackmailed her, she became desperate and came to me. So, I called Bernardo, told him what was happening and asked him to get information from Pierre. He contacted our branch in Paris and asked Marcel to investigate his life. We discovered that he was wanted by the French police, including on suspicion of murder.

- Murder?

- Yes. Of a girl he was in a relationship with. I don't know the details. But that was enough to get rid of him. Bernardo looked him up at the hotel, told him that we knew all about him and that the French police already had a warrant for his arrest. Bernardo advised him to leave as soon as possible to avoid arrest. He said we weren't going to give him any money, because he was mistaken and Dionisio is Maria Eugenia's son.

- Did he believe him?

- I don't know. But as soon as Bernardo left, he left a security guard guarding the hotel and came here. He called a friend of his at the consulate to tell him where Pierre was. He was arrested and deported. A few days later, we learned that the French police suspected him of murdering Jamille, his wife.

- She came with him. They didn't take her too?

- No. Our watchman saw that as soon as Bernardo left the hotel, Jamille left carrying a suitcase, took a bus and disappeared. As nobody knows where she is the police suspect Pierre, but we know he didn't kill her.

- I am perplexed. Despite all this, he is threatening us. If he arouses suspicion about Dionisio's origin, he could harm us.

- I know. We must stop it anyway.

- He wants us to help him. But I think that's out of the question.

- I'm not willing to help this scoundrel either. I'll call Bernardo and ask him to come here now. Together we'll find a solution.

Half an hour after the phone call, Bernardo arrived. He read Pierre's letter carefully. Then he said:

- This guy is worse than I thought. I hope you didn't believe what he wrote.

- I confess I'm upset. When we were in Paris, Maria Eugenia's behavior changed a lot. She was angry, mean, futile, unrecognizable. She went out with them every night. She drank too much. She must have let herself be taken in by that scoundrel.

Bernardo put his hand on Henrique's arm and said in a firm tone:

- It is clear that he is angry and has wished to take revenge. Besides not getting the money, Maria Eugenia came to us and he ended up in jail. Don't you think that's enough? I don't believe anything in this letter.

Henrique sighed nervously. Just imagining Maria Eugenia in the arms of that crook was already driving him crazy.

- I don't believe him either, Adele interjected. - I'm sure Maria Eugenia will know how to disprove it. What worries me now is what we are going to do to prevent him from carrying out his threat.

- I'll get in touch with my friend at the consulate. He's a very capable lawyer, trustworthy. I can go to him, talk to him about the letter. Then I'll check the steps of Pierre's wife. I think she is still in Brazil. Without money, I don't believe she has returned to Paris.

- What's your point? - Adele asked.

- I think if she left her husband, she must be afraid or angry with him. Pierre told the police that she had gone away and taken all the money they had left. I think she could be of great value to us.

- Do you really think so? - asked Henrique.

- She might know all about him and tell us.

- Maybe, said Adele.

- We don't know how much money she had. It might even be over. Besides, she doesn't speak our language and might be in difficulty, said Bernardo.

Henrique remained thoughtful for a few moments, then said:

- As for the letter, it is better not to answer.

- I think so too, agreed Bernardo.

- Isn't it dangerous? - Adele asked fearfully. - What if he opts for scandal? It's a way of consolidating his revenge.

- I don't think so, added Bernardo. - He would have a lot to lose by acting like that. I am sure he will give it some time, perhaps send another letter. We must act quickly. I'll leave now and make all the arrangements.

- Good luck, Adele wished him.

- Keep us informed, asked Henrique.

Bernardo agreed, said goodbye and left. Henrique's sad face, sitting in the armchair, worried Adele.

- Let's have a cup of coffee, she said. - You need to wake up. You can't let yourself be taken in by the evil deeds of that scoundrel.

- I'm trying. But it's difficult.

- Try to calm down before you talk to Maria Eugenia.

- It won't be easy. Every time I think of it, my blood boils.

- Aren't you being hasty?

- No. In Paris, I tried several times to show her that Pierre was a scoundrel, but she defended him ardently. She never accepted my reasoning. She must have really been in love with him.

- Why are you torturing yourself like that? This guy, like all rascals, must have been good at talking. It's easy to imagine that he must have showered Maria Eugenia with compliments, dazzling her. She'd always been withdrawn. Beautiful, but she didn't believe in her own beauty.

- That may be. There she seemed like a different person: haughty, vain, daring, provocative, sure of herself.

- He knew how to get her involved, thinking of taking advantage of our money. I don't believe this love story of his, and of hers even less. Think about it, Henrique. Even if she let herself be involved, that's over. After Dionisio was born, she became another person, but this time for the better. You can't deny that.

- Indeed. But that's what hurts the most. Our relationship has never been better. She's perfect in everything, affectionate, and on top of everything, she really loves Dionisio. I confess I was afraid she'd never accept him.

- Think about it. Calm down. Maria Eugenia really loves him. No one can fake a feeling like that all the time. She's constantly proved how much she loves you and Dionisio. It's not fair for you to forget that and believe the words of a disqualified man.

She stood up, approached her son-in-law, put her hand on his shoulder and continued saying:

- Come, let's have a coffee. You need to eat something.

He followed her thoughtfully. They had coffee. To make her happy, Henrique ate some biscuits.

Adele diverted the subject, asking about the business meeting he had had in the morning. With that, they had dived into business matters.

An hour later, Bernardo returned. Adele and Henrique surrounded him anxiously.

- First, I went to Adauto and asked him to look for Jamille. He was the one who kept watch at the hotel and saw when she left and took the bus. He went to the bus company to see if he could find out anything. Then I went to see my friend at the consulate. Rene listened to me attentively. Then he called Paris and spoke to the police. Pierre is still in jail, and it seems that the suspicion of murder is getting stronger every day. There is a friend of the dead girl who testified against him. Pierre is in trouble and will not get out soon.

- What do we do now? - asked Adele.

- We have to wait, answered Bernardo. - Let's see if Adauto finds out anything.

- I'll wait in the office. I need to get busy, said Henrique. - If you hear of anything else, call me.

- Stay calm, everything will be fine, said Adele.

- That's right, added Bernardo. - While the news doesn't arrive, let's keep trying to find a better solution.

Henrique hugged them and left. Adele's support and Bernardo's help had calmed him a little. Maybe he had been too hasty, given too much credit to Pierre's words. He didn't deserve to be trusted.

Maria Eugenia, on the contrary, after their return from Paris, had never given him any reason to suspect him of her affection.

On the way, he thought it might be better not to tell her. But he didn't know if he could keep quiet. Back at the office, he made an effort to immerse himself in his work and forget his worries for a while.

It was after five when Bernardo called.

- What's up? - Henrique asked.

- Well, Adauto talked to the driver who works at the time Jamille left the hotel. He remembered her because she went to the end of the line and tried to talk to the conductor, who had difficulty understanding what she was saying. Finally, one of the passengers, who heard the conversation, understood that she was asking if they knew of a modest boarding house. They indicated one nearby. But the driver did not know if she really went there.

- And Adauto went to that boarding house?

- Yes. In fact, he found her, but he did not approach her because he does not speak French and asked me to get a translator. He doesn't want to scare her.

- I'd like to talk to her.

- Me too. I will stop by in fifteen minutes and we will go together.

Henrique hung up the phone satisfied. He told his secretary that he was leaving and went downstairs to wait for Bernardo. He arrived before the allotted time and they both went to the place where Adauto was waiting for them.

- What's up? Is she inside? - asked Bernardo.

- Yes, she went out, bought some things and came back.

- We are both going in, said Bernardo. - You keep watching. I don't know if it's convenient for her to meet you, at least not yet.

They went in and asked for Jamille, but the woman who received them said she didn't know anyone by that name. Then Henrique explained that she was a French woman and described her.

- Ah, you are talking about Professor Claire.

- A teacher?

- She teaches French. She knows little Portuguese but they say she is great at teaching French. She has many students.

- Is she here? - asked Bernardo.

- Yes, should I call her?

Henrique interjected:

- 'I've been her friend for a long time. We have many things to talk about. I prefer to go to her room. Where is it?

- Come with me.

They accompanied her, went upstairs and went down a corridor. They stopped in front of a door. The woman knocked, saying:

- Claire, visitor for you.

No one answered. She knocked harder and finally the door opened a little and Jamille's face appeared through the gap. She asked:

- Who is it?

Henrique came forward, saying in French:

- It's me, Jamille, Maria Eugenia's husband. I really need to talk to you.

- Go away, she answered in French. - I have nothing to say. I separated from Pierre a long time ago. Whatever he may have done, it's none of my business.

- I know, answered Henrique. - We don't wish to do you any harm. We need your help, and we can help you too.

She opened the door and they entered. The modest room, Jamille's clothes were not at all reminiscent of the pompous life she led in Paris.

She closed the door and looked around saying:

- Look how reduced I have become because of Pierre. I hate him. He has disgraced my life.

- This is Dr Bernardo, a lawyer, my friend.

Bernardo shook the hand she held out to him and said:

- I am not here as a lawyer, but as a friend.

- Sit down, please - she asked, designating a sofa where they settled down.

Jamille took a chair and sat down in front of them. Addressing Bernardo, she said:

- When I was still with Pierre at the hotel, you went to talk to him.

- Yes, he answered. - You must know that he made up a story to get money from Maria Eugenia.

- I know. But I never agreed to it. I knew it wouldn't work. I've done a lot of things in my life, but I've never done anything against the law. I don't want to get involved with the police. When I heard what you were saying to Pierre, I found out that the French police were after him and I was terrified. That's when I made the decision to leave him.

- Do you know why the police were looking for him?

- Yes. Suspicion of murder. He claims he's innocent. There was a time when I believed him. But then I started putting the facts together and came to the conclusion that he might be guilty. I was afraid of being framed as an accomplice.

- If you had stayed with him, it really could have happened. But your disappearance worried the police. They suspect that you were murdered too.

She crossed herself, saying:

- God help me! How awful!

- Fortunately, this did not happen, said Henrique.

- What happened to him?

- He is in jail in Lyon, awaiting trial. The police are gathering evidence. Do you think he really murdered the girl?

She shrugged

- I don't know. He had an affair with her. He got in her ass. Our marriage was free. Both he and I could have sexual relations with other partners. That meant nothing to us. But with her Pierre got into it. He just wanted to be with Nicole, you could tell and I even rebuked him. She was free and didn't like that he kept nagging her, watching who she went out with. Then one day she turned up dead in her bedroom.

- How did he react? - asked Bernardo.

- He got scared. I asked him if it had been him. The day before I had seen him very nervous, walking from one side to the other, you couldn't talk to him. That night I went out with some friends and when I came back the day was already dawning. He was not at home. He arrived shortly after; I was already in bed. He locked himself in the bathroom and stayed there for a long time. I heard the sound of the shower. Then he did not lie down. He just sat in the armchair in the living room. I fell asleep, I was tired.

- What happened next? - Henrique asked.

- Two days later the bomb exploded. Her body was found in her room, but, according to the police report, she had been killed on the night I mentioned. I have to confess that I was very moved by this. I was afraid that he had committed that crime. I spoke to him and he denied everything and forbade me to talk about it. He held my arm and said: "Never say that again. I am innocent. Do you want the police to suspect me? No one can know about my relationship with her." I thought maybe I was wrong. Pierre didn't seem capable of committing a crime like that. But a month later he was summoned to testify and he was terrified, so he prepared for us to come to Brazil.

- What did he tell you then? - asked Henrique.

- Well, he told us about Maria Eugenia's fake belly and said that he could make a lot of money out of it. I doubted it. I never really believed in it. When we were at her house, I saw how Maria Eugenia treated her son. She'd never have been so attached if the boy had belonged to another woman. Pierre was bluffing. I did everything I could to talk him out of it, but he insisted. And that's what happened.

- What would you do if you got the money? - asked Bernardo.

- Going back to France was not in his plans. He wanted to look for a place where we could have a good, luxurious life, as we always had.

- But you preferred to leave him and work for a living, reminded Henrique.

- Yes. When I left the hotel I didn't know what to do, or where to go. Before I took all the money. I thought it was right, since he was the one who threw away all our money, in the game and in other things. When I arrived here, I was received by simple but kind people, who welcomed me with sympathy, helped me. I had never worked and didn't know how to do it. A student who lives here suggested I give lessons and I accepted. She got me some students herself. It was then that I began to learn what it is to live.

- You felt useful, said Henrique.

- More than that. The money I earned was not much, but it had a different taste. I felt alive with dignity. People treated me with respect, invited me to participate in their lives, I made friends, met families. I changed.

- You look better, you have regenerated, said Henrique.

- That's why I ask you to leave me alone. I don't want to get involved with Pierre anymore or to live any of that life. I am happy here as I have never been in all my life. I have been thinking a lot and today I realize how wrong I was.

- As I said, we don't want to hurt you, Henrique said, holding out Pierre's letter.

She picked it up and as she read it her face twitched. Finally, she handed it to Henrique, saying:

- That's good of him. He is good at making up stories, as long as he can get something out of them. I hope you don't believe anything he says there.

- What do you know about it? - asked Henrique.

- Enough to say that Maria Eugenia never liked Pierre. She liked to go out, to have fun, to know the Parisian nightlife, to shine at parties and in fashionable theatres, but she was not a rakish woman. On the contrary. Many times I saw her surrounded by men who were attracted by her brilliance. But she just laughed and was never interested in any of them.

- Do you think he's lying?

- I'm sure of it. He made it up to get back at her for not giving him the money. That's very much his.

Henrique breathed a sigh of relief. What Jamille was saying was more in keeping with Maria Eugenia's temperament.

- Thank you for having us. I would like to return your kindness, offer you some help. Perhaps a house in a better place, more in keeping with your level.

- Don't do this to me. I need to live here, learn lessons of simplicity. I don't mean that living well, in luxury, in comfort is an evil, on the contrary. But at the moment, for me, it is very useful to live here, where I have learned to appreciate sincere friends who take pleasure in being by my side. Thank you for wanting to help me. If Maria Eugenia forgives me, I'd even like to keep your friendship. But, for the moment, I prefer to live here.

Henrique stood up:

- I'll leave my card. If you need anything, call me.

They said goodbye and left.

- Let's go, said Bernardo to Adauto, we have nothing more to do here.

A little later, Bernardo and Henrique said goodbye to Adauto and went to the car. Bernardo left Henrique in the office and said goodbye, saying:

- Forget this unpleasant incident. Go home in peace, hug your wife with your usual affection.

He left and shortly afterwards Henrique took the car and drove home. He was still not sure about what attitude to take. He would think about it when he got home.

CHAPTER 18

Rafael and Marina left the spiritual study centre, commenting in the evening class. It had been a few months since they had been attending these classes, and each day they felt more enthusiastic.

During this time they became closer and more in love. Marina had never been in love before, and the fact that she was loved in return filled her heart with joy. Each day she appreciated Rafael's qualities more, his intelligence, his affectionate manner that did not cancel out his firmness when necessary.

That night, as they did when they got out of class, they went for a snack, during which the conversation was animated. It was on the way back, inside the car stopped in front of her house, that he embraced her and kissed her lips lovingly. Then he said, looking into her eyes:

- I want to marry you. Every day it gets harder to leave. I want to spend the rest of my days at your side. Let's set a date.

Marina hesitated a little and he asked:

- Don't you want to?

- Yes, I do. I love you.

- I sensed that you hesitated a little, but you said you wanted to. Is there something that's bothering you?

- I've worked all my life to reunite the family, and now I wouldn't want to be separated from them.

- I don't intend to separate you from them. I love those two. I have the possibility of buying a bigger house, where we can all live together more comfortably. What do you say?

She smiled satisfied and answered:

- They love you too. I think it will be the perfect solution.

- Tomorrow we'll talk to them and agree on the details.

They exchanged a few more kisses and then said goodbye. Marina entered, and the house was dark. She went straight to her room, but she felt restless. She got ready for bed and went to bed. But a thought troubled her.

She loved Rafael, she was sure that she would be happy with him, but what would he think if one day he found out her secret?

He thought of her as a woman of courage who had fought and conquered her position through her own efforts. He was proud to see her succeed professionally. What would he say if he found out that she had made that contract with Adele, subjecting herself to having a child with a stranger and giving up the baby in exchange for money?

That thought had been bothering her for some time. She understood Rafael so well, they were so close that one spoke what the other was thinking. Keeping this secret even for him started to get heavy, making her feel bad. Several times she thought of opening her heart, of telling him everything, but she kept backing away. It was a secret she had promised to keep for all her life, and it involved other people.

And if one day she and Rafael didn't get along anymore and they broke up, she wouldn't run the risk that he, for whatever reason, would end up talking too much?

She was sure that he was a serious, honest man, interested in doing good. But in her profession, she had seen several cases of legal separation in which a marriage that had started out perfect had ended in fights and much suffering.

She did not want to keep her secret from him, but at the same time she feared the consequences of telling the truth. What if he didn't accept and broke off the engagement?

A thousand thoughts passed through her mind and she rolled over in her bed, sleepless. Finally, she decided to pray, to ask the spirits of light for help. She sat up in bed, raised her thoughts and said a heartfelt prayer for inspiration.

Then she laid down again. Then she remembered Eunice, whom she trusted, and decided to look for her the next day to ask for help. She was sure that she would be able to show her what she needed to do.

Having decided this, she felt calmer, turned over and finally fell asleep.

Henrique arrived home and found Maria Eugenia in a good mood, playing with Dionisio. He kissed them lightly on the cheek and went into the bedroom.

She asked Elvira to look after Dionisio and went to him. She approached him, saying:

- You are not well. Has something happened?

- Nothing's happened. I'm just a little unwell.

She came closer, hugging him and leaning her face against his chest.

- You look sad. I don't like to see you like this.

- It'll pass. I'm going to take a shower.

He went to the bathroom and she waited. Later, while he was getting dressed, she kept talking, telling him Dionisio' latest jokes. But Henrique, looking far away, didn't even seem to hear.

She approached him, hugging him again, and tried to kiss him on the lips. Henrique could not bear it and pulled away from her.

Shocked, Maria Eugenia said:

- Why did you do that? Are you angry with me?

Unable to contain himself any longer, Henrique took Pierre's letter from his coat pocket and handed it to her, saying:

- See for yourself.

With trembling hands she took the letter and, as she read, her face turned pale. Her surprise was such that she sat up in bed so as not to fall. Then she began to cry convulsively.

Henrique could not contain himself:

- Have you nothing to say? That makes me think it's true. You love that scoundrel.

These words had the power to snap Maria Eugenia out of her shock, and she fought back:

- That's a lie! I never loved Pierre. He wanted to take revenge because we wouldn't give him money. Mom and Dr. Bernardo know all about it.

Henrique came up to her and put his hand on her shoulder:

- You say you don't love him, but can you swear to me you never had an affair with him?

She sobbed desperately, unable to speak, and he continued:

- At that time you were unrecognisable. You looked like another woman, angry with me because of the arranged pregnancy. Several times I noticed that you hated me. That came to mind when I read this letter.

Maria Eugenia shook her head negatively and replied:

- It's not true. I've always loved you. I was jealous.

- That's absurd. I didn't even know the girl. If I see her on the street, I won't even know who she is. Everything was done so as not to endanger our relationship. It was just business.

- Now I understand that. But back then I was dying of jealousy. I used to imagine you in her arms. It tormented me. But I've never loved a man other than you.

He seemed calmer and remained thoughtful for a few moments. Then he asked:

- You didn't love him, but answer truthfully: did you have an affair with him? Is that how he found out you were wearing a false belly?

Maria Eugenia stood up, took a deep breath, approached her husband and answered:

- Yes. I can't deny that. I was angry, we had been drinking. He had been courting me for some time. One night I gave in to his impulses. I think I did it for revenge, because afterwards I felt less resentful about our affair. But I swear, I never loved Pierre.

Henrique sat up in bed, gloomy and sad. Maria Eugenia hastened to say:

- It was only once. Later, I regretted it very much. I hated what happened. After Dionisio was born, I realized how ungrateful I had been. You gave me the privilege of motherhood. This boy is all I love most in this life. Please, Henrique, forgive me. I'm ashamed, sorry. You've always been a great husband. I behaved like a spoilt and capricious child.

Tears streamed down her face, but Henrique, lost in his own private world, devastated, sad, shaken, did not even notice.

She put her hand on his shoulder.

- Look at me, Henrique. Say you forgive me.

- Leave me, Maria Eugenia. I need to think.

- Please, I know I made a very serious mistake, but at that time I was crazy. You're witness that I've changed. I'm back to the person I've always been, or even much better than before. Say you forgive me.

- I can't do that now. I'm going out for a while, to cool off. Then we'll talk.

He got up, picked up his jacket and left. Maria Eugenia threw herself on her bed, sobbing disconsolately.

The next few days were a torment to Maria Eugenia. Henrique never mentioned the matter again, but had moved away from her and gone to sleep in the guest room.

She had tried several times to break the ice, to get closer, to talk to him, but Henrique avoided her and asked her to leave him alone.

Not knowing how to proceed any longer, Maria Eugenia went in search of Adele to get off her chest and ask for advice.

- He does not talk to me, mom. He leaves very early in the morning and only comes back late at night. He hasn't eaten at home. He goes to the guest room and doesn't answer when I knock. I'm desperate. He doesn't care about me anymore.

- Calm down, my child. You must be patient. Unfortunately, he found out what you did and he is suffering from it. He has lost his confidence. He questions his own feelings.

- If he doesn't forgive me, I won't be able to live anymore.

- Don't be dramatic. What did you expect after what you did? Despair won't improve the situation. Think that Henrique loves you, admires you for being a good mother. Give him time to regain his balance.

- Do you think that will happen?

- Henrique is an intelligent man. He has discernment. He loves his family. I don't think he will destroy everything for a moment of madness that you committed. Afterwards, he knows that you're sorry, that you won't do it again. All that will carry weight and he will eventually forgive you. In these cases, time is the best remedy. You need to be patient, to wait.

Despite Adele's advice, Maria Eugenia did not calm down. She arrived home and Dionisio ran to hug her, wanting to play. But she didn't feel up to it.

Shaken by the sleepless nights, her face creased with worry, she sat in the boy's room while tears streamed down her face.

Dionisio hugged her, saying sadly:

- Is Mama mad at me?

She hugged him and hurried to answer:

-No dear. I have a headache.

- Mama has a hehe, he answered, smoothing her face tenderly.

Elvira came over and Maria Eugenia asked her to take Dionisio for a snack and then put him to bed, as he did every afternoon. Then she went into the bedroom. Elvira took the boy and after a while went to look for her:

- He slept. You haven't had lunch, you haven't eaten anything. Can I get you a snack, a juice?

- I am not hungry.

- I couldn't stay without eating. I'll get it anyway.

A little later, Elvira returned and put the tray on the table.

- Excuse me for meddling, but it's just that I really like you. I saw that Dr. Henrique has been sleeping in the guest room and that both are sad. Even Dionisio has been crying and irritated.

- Things are not good between us, answered Maria Eugenia, sad.

- I feel that the atmosphere here is tumultuous and sad. Why don't you go to Mrs. Eunice? She can help.

- I don't think there's any remedy.

- Everything is remedied when God helps. You liked her.

- I did. She gave me good advice. She gave me her phone number, but I don't know if I still have it.

- I know it by heart. I'll call and you can talk to her.

Elvira made the call and passed the phone number to Maria Eugenia.

- Mrs Eunice? It's Maria Eugenia, Dionisio' mother. Do you remember me?

- Of course, my child.

- Some things have happened, and I'd like to talk to you. May I come to your house?

- You're distressed, afflicted. I prefer you go to the study centre. There, I'll have more resources to help you.

- What time can I come?

- Be there at half past seven. I'll give you the address. It's not far from here.

Maria Eugenia wrote everything down.

- Don't miss it, asked Eunice. I will be waiting for you.

She thanked her and hung up. Then she asked Elvira:

- Do you know how this study centre works?

- It's a place where she assist people. I've already been there for spiritual treatment. It was very good. If I could, I would go with you.

- No. You have to stay with Dionisio.

Five minutes before the agreed time, Maria Eugenia entered the study centre. Answered by a young woman, she gave her name and was taken to a room where Eunice was waiting for her.

Seeing her enter, she embraced her saying:

- How are you, my daughter?

- Badly, Mrs. Eunice. My marriage is falling apart and I don't know what to do.

- Sit down. Let's talk about it.

- It was my fault. I made a mistake, now I'm paying for my mistake.

- Don't say that. You're just learning a hard but necessary lesson.

- But I'm sorry. I'm sure I'll never do that again. Isn't that enough?

- No. Experience, knowledge, has its price. No one gains wisdom without learning the value of each feeling.

- I need your advice. I don't know what to do.

In a few words, Maria Eugenia told her everything between tears. Then she finished:

- He won't talk to me, he's sleeping in the guest room. He doesn't want to forgive me. I love him so much. We lived so happily together!

- You are both happy. You love each other and love covers the multitude of sins. Let's trust each other. You're being sincere. Don't despair. Don't let a moment of past folly turn into a tragedy.

- But he doesn't forgive me.

- Have you forgiven yourself?

- Have I? Of course I haven't!

- That's the first step.

- But I can't forgive myself. How could I have been so blind? I had a wonderful husband and I didn't value it; I ended up getting involved with a scoundrel, blackmailer, self-interested.

- Don't be so strict with yourself. Now you have the purpose of not making the same mistake again. This is a sign that you have already understood what life wanted to teach you. This attitude is fundamental.

- But Henrique doesn't think like that.

- That is his mind. Let's see how he reacts. It is good to know that it is no use you insisting, wanting him to change his way of seeing. What might work is if you change your inner attitude towards yourself. The moment you understand that you were weak because you did not yet have the discernment to act better, that today you would act differently, and let his generosity forgive you, you will feel relieved. The despair will disappear, giving way to a serene waiting for events.

- Of course, today I would do no more. I am sure of it.

- So, my child, be benevolent. Understand that you have grown up. You were a naive, spoilt and shy girl who did not have the courage to dare in front of your mother's personality, a woman who shines because she has charisma, beauty and light. But you also have all this within yourself. Your spirit is light, beauty, brilliance, capacity. You just have to learn to value your potential and allow it to come out.

Maria Eugenia sobbed without stopping, and Eunice continued saying:

- You cannot feel diminished because you made mistakes. That was the price of growing up. Now you are a more experienced woman and that should comfort you.

- How nice it would be if Henrique thought like you!

- Do your part. Show him that you are aware and know what you want from now on.

- How can I do that?

- Do not condemn yourself any longer. Respect yourself. Think of yourself with love. Don't force the situation with your husband. Give him time to reflect. Act as if nothing happened. Have a dignified attitude.

- I feel you're right. Do you think I'll make it?

- I'm sure you will. I will refer you to a treatment to rebalance your energies. I want you to come twice a week to receive this treatment. I am sure you will sleep better tonight.

She made some notes and gave her the paper.

- Let's trust in God.

Maria Eugenia thanked her and went out.

A young woman was waiting for her outside and she showed her the paper. In silence she was led into a dimly lit room, lit only by a blue light, where there were some chairs and behind them a person was standing in prayer. Soft music filled the air, bringing peace to the room.

Maria Eugenia was led to a chair and sat down. The girl behind her stood in front of her, held her hands up for a few moments, then placed them on her head.

This girl was Marina. She had been working as a volunteer at the study centre for some time, donating energies, and she felt very comfortable taking part in this work.

Eyes closed, concentrated in prayer, as she stood in front of the person to whom she was to donate energies, she was overcome by strong emotion. She controlled herself and tried to mentalize light and love on the patient, who was sobbing heartily.

When she finished the donation, she opened her eyes and, startled, recognized that, already a little calmer, sitting in front of her was Maria Eugenia, her eyes wet with tears.

Excited, Marina lightly touched Maria Eugenia's arm to indicate that the treatment was over. She stood up and Marina asked softly:

- Are you feeling better?

- Yes, thank you.

After she left Marina couldn't continue.

- I'm going out for a while, she explained to the leader of the meeting.

She left the room and went to the restroom, trying to calm herself down. As soon as she entered, she saw Maria Eugenia, who was in front of the mirror trying to redo her make-up. She made an attempt to leave, but she had already seen her and asked:

- Was it you who assist me in that room?

- Yes, it was.

- I have to thank you. When I arrived here today, I was desperate. Now, thanks to Mrs. Eunice and you, I am much better. May God bless you both.

Deeply moved, Marina answered:

- No need to thank me. By coming here, I have also received much more than I could ever imagine.

Maria Eugenia stopped in front of Marina and asked:

- Does it still look like I cried?

Marina smiled.

- That's better.

- Thank you. I have to go. I've been away from home for a long time and my son is very attached to me. He must be missing me. Do you have any kids?

- No, not yet. But I'm getting married soon and I intend to.

- That's wonderful. I'm going, but we'll see each other again soon. I'll get my treatment right.

- Go with God.

After she left, Marina took a deep breath. What was life doing to her, putting Maria Eugenia in her way?

With so many places to go, so many people in that house, why had Maria Eugenia sat down exactly where she was?

What was going on that she was so distress and had cried so much?

A thousand unanswered thoughts were racing through her mind. She tried to push them away. They could never come closer. She had promised Adele that she would never make contact with them.

It had happened by chance, and she shouldn't make a big deal out of it. The fact that Maria Eugenia attended the study centre did not mean that they would maintain a friendly relationship. That could never happen between them.

A feeling of loss enveloped her and she tried to push it out. Maria Eugenia had said that her son was attached to her. A sign that they really loved each other. That thought comforted her.

Maybe it would be better to stop going to the study centre for a while. But she and the rest of her family were so entwined there that she soon dismissed that idea.

Ofelia and Cicero were at the school studying mediumship feeling very happy. Rafael and she preferred scientific research and felt good about donating their energies as volunteers.

Marina tried not to give too much importance to that meeting. No one could know, and everything would remain as it was.

When she left the bathroom, she found Rafael in the corridor.

- They said you left before you finished.

- It was nothing. I was moved when assisting someone and I went to clear my head for a while. I'm fine.

He hugged her and they left. It was later, lying in her bed, that Marina thought about Maria Eugenia again.

Although she didn't want to make a big deal out of that meeting, she wondered:

"Why had life put Maria Eugenia in her path?"

Perhaps it was to remind her that, even though she tried to forget, she had had that child. Why would that be so?

Lately she had been wondering if it was fair to Rafael to marry him without telling him this secret. What would he think of her if one day the truth came out? How could she keep his trust knowing that she had lied about such an important fact?

Her head was full of doubts. She still wasn't sure if it would be better to tell him and face his reaction. She was afraid of sharing with him this secret that did not belong to him, and then, if they were ever separated, he might reveal it to others. Rafael was trustworthy. But at the same time, she knew that the guarantee of a secret lies in never trusting it to anyone.

- I won't tell anything - she decided.

She struggled to sleep.

CHAPTER 19

Maria Eugenia came home determined to talk to Henrique. As on the previous day, he had been away all day and did not come home for dinner.

Though sad, she tried to act as usual: she played with Dionisio, tried hard to banish thoughts of fear and insecurity from her mind.

She had made a mistake, but she understood that at that time she was inexperienced and insecure, judging herself less so by the fact that she was sterile, wanting to prove to herself that she was capable of being loved even so.

It was vanity, illusion. But she recognised that, within this process, she had not been able to act any better. Now, after everything, she was sure that she wouldn't have let herself be taken in by Pierre or anyone else. She regretted it, but that would not change the fact itself and it would be impossible to go back, so there was no point in continuing to martyr herself for what was hopeless.

She was sure that during all those years of marriage she had given her husband enough proof of love. If he could not forgive, understand her moment of weakness, she could do nothing more. Despite the sadness that this thought caused her, Maria Eugenia felt that there would be no other way.

It was past eleven o'clock when Henrique finally arrived. Seeing her in the living room, he said good night and went up to the guest room.

Maria Eugenia got up and went after him. She knocked and went in. He had taken off his coat and looked at her surprised.

- I want to talk to you, she said in a calm voice.

- I'm tired. I want to sleep.

- I'll be quick.

- Ok.

She designated an armchair and sat down in the other.

- I have thought about everything that happened and I must tell you that I am very sorry for having acted that way. That attitude made me revisit my entire adolescence and youth, when I felt unable to be for my parents the person they expected me to be. The brilliance and success of my mother, whom I always admired, made me want to be like her, but at the same time I looked at myself and believed that I didn't have the capacity to do that.

- You were always shy, he said.

- It wasn't shyness, it was a lack of faith in my ability. I thought that no matter what I did, I could never be what she wanted me to be.

- But Adele never demanded anything of you. She has always loved you and accepted you as you are.

- I realized this not so long ago. But in my head, I imagined that to be loved I had to be equal to, or better than, her. I wanted her to admire me. When I met you, fell in love, I got over that a little. Your love gave me joy and a certain security, although I had not changed my way of seeing myself. After our marriage, instead of wanting to shine to please her, I added this need as a condition for you to continue loving me.

- I didn't know you felt that way.

- I used to hide it even to myself. When I found out I couldn't be a mother, I was devastated. I felt crippled and useless. The fact that I needed to have a child to ensure my mother's continuity as president of the companies made me feel like the last of the women. For the first time my mother was depending on me for something, and I had no way of help her.

- You're not to blame for that.

- But I felt terrible. With difficulty, I managed to master the jealousy, the anger of that stranger who was more competent than I was, who could give you the child we both wanted so much. When we were in Paris, I hated that fake belly, because it reminded me of my incapacity.

- Why did you never open up to me? I would have understood.

- It was humiliating. And then I was disgusted with life, with the situation, powerless to change the facts.

Henrique ran his hand through his hair, thoughtfully, and asked:

- Go on.

- With what I am saying, I do not intend to justify what I did. The desire to prove to myself that people could like me made me plunge into vanity. When I remember the parties, where I drank too much, provoking men's attention on purpose, I feel ashamed. However, the truth is that I never accepted the courtship of any of them. What happened with Pierre was an occasional involvement, I would even say a certain curiosity, that I justified as revenge for you having a relationship with another woman.

- That hurt me a lot, since I never imagined it could happen.

Maria Eugenia sighed deeply and considered:

- It's hurting me too. Especially now that I can clearly see how much I was deluded and mistaken. I've discovered that inside me, there's a woman who loves her family. That, despite my weaknesses, I have been a good wife, dedicated myself to you, giving you the best of myself, especially after Dionisio was born, and I learnt the value of maternal love. It is a feeling that has filled my soul with happiness, ever since I took this child in my arms, and he held my finger with his tiny little hand.

Henrique lowered his eyes, trying to cover a tear that was about to fall. Maria Eugenia, eyes shining with emotion, continued saying:

- With him, I discovered that the most important thing is love, because it feeds our life, gives motivation, and makes everything more beautiful.

- It's a pity what happened.

- I regret having hurt you, but at the same time I recognise that this experience has made me grow and see the good things that life has given me and that I did not see before. You, mom and even the stranger who agreed to lend her body so that I could enjoy this achievement deserve my gratitude. Dionisio taught me to live and to value my life.

Henrique, head down so that Maria Eugenia would not notice his emotion, did not know what to answer.

- That is what I needed to tell you. I always remain the same woman who loves you and who loves our son. Nothing is more important to me than that we continue together as always. But I know that this is a decision that depends on you. Think, analyse. If you can understand and forgive, I'll be waiting. But if you feel that you are not able to forget, then I will accept your decision without complaining. All I ask is that you don't separate me from Dionisio. That I could not bear. I've done my part, now it's up to you. You have all the time you need to decide.

She got up and left the room. Henrique, overcome by emotion, allowed tears to run down his face and sobs to vent his sorrow for some time.

Then, somewhat relieved, he felt tired, went to the bathroom, washed his face, put on his pyjamas and lay down. He wanted to sleep and rest. It seemed to him that he was empty and unable to think. He closed his eyes and then fell asleep.

Maria Eugenia passed Dionisio' room, who was sleeping, kissed his blushing face and went to her room.

Although the situation remained the same, she felt different. Inside her a living force had arisen that made her hold her head high with dignity. For the first time, she was sure that she had adopted the right posture.

The awareness of her mistake, the analysis of her feelings had removed the weight of guilt that tormented her, leaving in its place the certainty that she was no longer a child dependent on her mother's approval, incapable of resolving her own conflicts, but a courageous woman, aware of her own strength to choose the most appropriate path.

What she wanted most of all was for Henrique to understand and forgive her. But if he could not do this, she would be strong enough to accept his decision.

The certainty of her love for him comforted her, and at the same time gave her the courage to keep hoping that he would be able to overcome his pride and let love speak louder. Thinking of the love that united them, she felt a soft warmth envelop her heart.

She got ready for bed. Before going to bed, she knelt beside the bed and said a prayer, thanking God for having shown her all these things and for having allowed her to experience the greatness of love in her life. Then she laid down and fell asleep.

During the following days, Maria Eugenia tried to be natural, doing everything she had always done. Henrique remained quiet, only talking about the essential, not coming home for lunch.

In his work meetings with Adele and Bernardo, he had not mentioned the subject again. She, discreetly, waited for him to open up.

One afternoon, Henrique was in Adele's office when Bernardo entered saying:

- I talked to Rene today. I have some news about Pierre.

They both looked at him curiously and he continued saying:

- It seems that his situation has become complicated. The prosecution witness was conclusive, and his statement coincides with some data that the police had. The trial is scheduled to start in a week's time.

Adele was thoughtful for a few moments, then said:

- He must be afraid. Do you think he'll be able to carry out his threat against us?

- I don't think so. First, it's the word of a thug, a possible murderer, against the word of good people like you. Then, he must be so preoccupied with defending himself that he won't have time to think about anything else.

- Do you think that if they find out that Jamille is alive, that will help him in his defence?

- As for the crime on trial, no. I have spoken to Rene about it, but he prefers not to talk about it to the French police until after the trial. For the time being, despite the doubts as to Jamille's whereabouts, there is still no formal charge regarding her disappearance.

Adele turned to Henrique and asked:

- You're so quiet... What do you think?

- I want to forget that this guy exists.

- Me too, but now he is threatening us. Even if he doesn't, it's a possibility we still can't despise.

- This guy has never fooled me. Even under the social veneer, I never accepted him.

- I notice that you still haven't got over what happened, Adele said. - Have you spoken to Maria Eugenia about it?

- Yes, I showed her Pierre's letter that very day.

Adele looked at him, trying to penetrate his thoughts. As he remained silent, she said:

- She didn't come to me, so I thought you hadn't said anything to her. But if she knows and didn't come to see me, she must be so devastated that she doesn't have the courage for anything.

Henrique looked at her seriously and replied:

- You are mistaken. When I told her, she was desperate. But I needed to reflect. So, I decided to stay away from her during the day and stay in the guest room at night.

- I don't understand why Maria Eugenia hasn't come to me. She must be sick, depressed.

- She's not. One night she wanted to talk to me. She opened up, talked about her inner conflicts in her youth and finally said she was sorry for her mistake, because it hurt both of us, but she also understood that this mistake made her mature, to realize all the good things that life had given her. Finally, she said she was not going to pressure me to forgive her because that is something that only depends on me. She said that she has always been a good wife, faithful, a devoted mother to Dionisio, whom she loves like a son, and that she is willing to accept whatever my decision may be. She only asked me not to separate her from the boy.

When he fell silent, Adele, who was listening in surprise, eyes shining with emotion, replied:

- Finally, my daughter has become a woman!

- She surprised me, Henrique said. — But, on the other hand, she threw all the weight of the decision on me. It was her who made the mistake. I did nothing.

- But she has put herself, and she did it with dignity. I'm sure that what Maria Eugenia wants the most is for you to forget what happened and return to your family with the same affection. But she knows that this can only happen when you conquer your pride, your jealousy, your resentment. And that is an inner work that only depends on you. She has no way of doing that.

- The way you say it, it sounds easy, but I don't know what to do. When I think of her with that rascal, my blood boils.

Adele came over and put her hand on his arm.

- Give yourself some time. Until you're sure of what to do, don't do anything.

- I know this is a family matter, interrupted Bernardo, but since I am going to be part of it, may I make a suggestion?

Henrique looked at him surprised.

- Of course. As a friend, it is as if you are already family.

Bernardo looked at Adele and asked:

- Can I tell him?

- I will. Bernardo and I have decided to live out a courtship we couldn't have in our youth. We are going to get married.

Henrique's face lit up a little.

- Thank God we have good news! I always wondered why you hadn't realized how happy you would be together. Congratulations!

- Thank you. But let's go to my suggestion. I have a psychiatrist friend, Dr. Rafael Vilardi. He is wonderful at solving emotional problems.

- I am not sick. I'm devastated, but not crazy, said Henrique.

- Don't be prejudiced. He is an experienced professional who can help you understand your emotions better. I also feel that you and Maria Eugenia love each other. And you have a wonderful son who needs the support of both of you. You are suffering for an event that, although painful, has passed and has no possibility of repeating itself. Making a wrong decision at this moment can make you unhappy for the rest of your lives.

- I don't know if I want to be separate from her.

- Fine. But what will your life be if you stay together, and you hold so much pain in your heart? Do you think you would be happy?

- Bernardo's right. Maria Eugenia, I don't know how, has managed to keep a firm attitude, but you are very hurt. You've never been through a more serious emotional problem, and you don't know how to deal with it. Be humble, Henrique. Seek the help of a good professional to regain your balance.

Henrique remained thoughtful and Bernardo intervened:

- Let's talk to him. Besides being a competent professional, he is a pleasant person. You will enjoy talking to him.

- I will go. I will go.

Adele hugged him happily:

- What I wish most is for us all to be happy. I'm sure we will.

- I will call him and find out when he can receive us.

Bernardo picked up his briefcase, looked for his address book and called. The secretary answered and passed the phone to Rafael. After the greetings, Bernardo said:

- I have a friend who is going through a difficult problem, and I would like you to talk to him and help him.

- OK. I need to check my schedule.

- I know it is packed, as usual, but the case is urgent. See what you can do.

- One moment.

Bernardo waited. A little later, Rafael said:

- If it is urgent, I can see him after work. Around seven o'clock. Is that ok?

- Thank you. I knew I could count on you. We'll be there at seven. I will take the opportunity to hug you and introduce Henrique to you personally.

Bernardo said goodbye and hung up the phone, satisfied.

- Generally, Dr. Vilardi's office is very busy. The wait for an appointment is usually between one and two months.

- It was very kind of him to extend his appointment hours to see you, said Adele.

- Indeed. We've been friends for a few years now, since he treated a businessman who went bankrupt, fell into depression and attempted suicide. Fortunately, he did not succeed. At that time, I was working for that company. I followed Rafael's work, the results of which surprised me. The businessman managed to accept the situation and was motivated to start again.

- It is easier when it is a matter of material loss, said Henrique. - But when it is about the heart, it is worse.

- That's for you, who value family more than money, said Bernardo. - But for that businessman, whose power, money, came first, it was terrible.

Adele invited them for coffee in the next room.

- You need to take care of your health, she said to Henrique. - I suspect you're not eating well. I'll order us a snack.

- That won't be necessary. Just a coffee, answered Henrique.

- I'm hungry too, she lied. - I almost didn't have lunch. You two will keep me company. Then there are some company matters I would like to talk to you about.

After receiving support from them and getting some food, Henrique felt better.

Just before seven o'clock, Henrique and Bernardo entered Rafael's clinic. Half an hour later, they were led to the doctor's room.

Rafael hugged Bernardo, who introduced Henrique. The room was spacious and tastefully decorated. Rafael asked them to sit in a corner of the room, where there were comfortable armchairs. Once they were seated, Bernardo said:

- It is better to leave you at ease. I will wait outside.

- There is no need, said Henrique. - You know more about my life than I do. I prefer you to stay.

Bernardo looked indecisively at Rafael, who agreed.

- Stay. I want to know the situation and you can help.

Henrique hesitated. He did not want to tell Adele's secret. But how could he explain the case by omitting this detail? Rafael waited calmly.

- I don't know how to begin, he said finally. - It happens to be a delicate matter in our lives, a secret that I cannot mention because it involves the lives of other people.

Bernardo intervened:

- Perhaps you cannot omit this point. It is important that Raphael knows the whole truth. I am sure that whatever you tell him will never leave these four walls. I know him and I know that you can trust him.

- Your doubt is natural. You don't know me. But I can assure you that I will respect your wishes. The aim of my work is to help you see all sides of the issue and make the best decision. To do this,

I need to know all the facts and discover and show you even those that you have not yet realized.

Bernardo added:

- When we are involved in an unpleasant situation, we do not see clearly. Dr. Rafael is a master at opening our eyes at such times. Now I think you'll be more comfortable alone with him. I will wait outside.

Bernardo got up and went out. Rafael waited calmly for Henrique to speak. He began to tell how he had met Maria Eugenia, the courtship, Adele's support, the wedding. He told everything.

Rafael listened in silence. When Henrique paused, he showed interest, saying:

- Please continue.

Gradually, Henrique felt that Rafael was supporting him and lost his inhibitions. When he hesitated, Rafael put his hand on his arm to give him strength and he continued. He told everything, without omitting any detail.

He finished by telling of his disappointment, of his fear of losing Maria Eugenia's love, of the anger he felt when he imagined his wife in Pierre's arms.

At last, he was silent. It did him good to get this off his chest. But he felt empty, incapable of any feeling.

Rafael stood up, stood in front of Henrique and said:

- You are out of energy, but it was good that you talked about your feelings. First, I am going to give you some refreshing energies. Close your eyes and relax. You are tired, very tired. You don't need to make any decisions now. I am here to help you. Begin by imagining a ball of very bright blue light. It is in front of you. Concentrate on it as I will help you to receive vitalizing energies.

Rafael raised his hands and lifted his thought, asking for spiritual help for Henrique. Then he placed his hands on his head, radiating light, calm, strength, joy, peace.

He continued mentalizing this, passing his hands around Henrique's body, without touching him, for some seconds. Then he raised his hands again, received new energies, and placed them on Henrique's head. He lightly touched his arm, who opened his eyes and said:

- What a good thing! I felt a pleasant warmth, as if someone was hugging me and telling me to be at peace. Never anything like this.

Rafael smiled:

- Meditation, relaxation, prayer really help.

- What would you advise me?

- I must tell you that you are married to an enlightened woman. In the midst of the conflict, she managed to take the right attitude. Rarely do they succeed. That's the good thing about everything you told me.

- She surprised me. She spoke to me not as a guilty, wrong, distressed person, but as one who recognizes that she made a mistake, repented and made the decision never to repeat it. In addition, she recalled her dedication as a wife and mother and said that I should take this into account.

- She is absolutely right.

- I recognise all that. But when I think of her in Pierre's arms, the anger comes back with full force.

- That's what we have to work on. It's better to stop here for today. Go home, rest. When you remember this unpleasant fact, turn your thoughts to something else, preferably something pleasant.

- My son! He is my greatest joy.

- That's right. Come close to him, feel his love, give him your affection. It will do you good. I want to see you in three days. It can be at seven, like today. Here are my phone numbers. If you don't feel well during this time, call me, whatever the hour is.

Henrique said goodbye and left. Outside, Bernardo, seeing him, asked:

- How are you?

- Tired, but calmer. I should be back in three days.

- Do you want to go somewhere for dinner?

- No. If you can drop me off at the car park, I'd appreciate it. I want to go home.

Once in the car, Bernardo asked:

-Did you like him?

- He had the patience to listen to me. At the end he said that I needed to receive positive energy. He told me to think of a ball of light, close my eyes and did a laying on of hands.

- I didn't know that doctors used this type of treatment. What did you feel?

- At the beginning, nothing. Then I began to feel a pleasant warmth, which was very good. After the tension of the last few days, I think I relaxed. I feel empty, tired, and I can't wait to stretch out on the bed and rest.

- I think, for a first date, it was very good. I am confident that we are on the right track.

Henrique arrived home earlier than on the previous nights and, although he was tired, he went to find Dionisio who, seeing him, ran to him with open arms.

- Daddy! Daddy!

Henrique embraced him tenderly, while, eyes shining, Dionisio said:

- I missed you. Do you have a present?

Whenever Henrique was away for a few days because of work, on his return he used to bring him a little present. Then he remembered that, having arrived late every evening, the boy had imagined he was travelling.

- Today I didn't bring anything. But I have a surprise for tomorrow.

- Yay! Did you see, Mama? Tomorrow there's a present.

Maria Eugenia, who was watching the scene, smiled.

- We've already had dinner. I didn't know if you were coming for dinner. But I'll have it warmed up and served.

- Thank you, but there's no need. I'm not hungry.

- I'll go to the kitchen and make you a snack. I don't think you've eaten anything.

She left and Henrique remained playing with his son. He had not looked directly at Maria Eugenia, but he noticed that she was tidy and her face was serene. He didn't know why, but he couldn't face her.

It was silly, since she had made the mistake, not him. Why did he feel ashamed? Perhaps because he thought that because he loved her so much he was being too condescending with what she had done. After all, a betrayed husband needs to react, to show offended, to prove that he has pride. But he did not feel strong enough for that.

He remembered Rafael's words and tried to concentrate all his attention on Dionisio, who was trying to show him how a new toy his mother had bought him worked.

The boy, in his funny language, tried to describe how the toy worked and Henrique ended up laughing because, when he could not find the words, he made eloquent gestures showing his enthusiasm.

When Maria Eugenia returned and invited him to eat, Dionisio went along. Henrique shared part of the sandwich with him. Then he asked the boy:

- It's almost ten o'clock. Shouldn't you be sleeping?

- I was sleepy, but you arrived and I forgot.

- I'll take you to bed.

They went upstairs and Maria Eugenia accompanied them, preparing Dionisio for bed. Henrique kissed the boy on the forehead, said good night to Maria Eugenia and Elvira, who were in the room, and went to the guest room.

After accommodating Dionisio, Maria Eugenia went to the bedroom. Noticing that Henrique seemed better, for a moment she hoped that he would sleep in the couple's room. But that did not happen.

She sighed sadly. She needed to be patient. That he had come back early, played with the boy and accepted the snack she had prepared indicated that his attitude was changing. She knew she could do nothing but wait.

CHAPTER 20

From that evening on, Henrique went back to having lunch at home and coming home at dinner time. However, his attitude towards Maria Eugenia remained the same: he only talked about what was essential and continued to sleep in the guest room. On the other hand, he became more attached to Dionisio, staying with the boy most of the time he was at home.

Maria Eugenia continued to go to the centre for spiritual studies, where she received treatment for energetic renewal. When she felt sad, she sought out Eunice to let off steam and seek advice.

When she was told what was happening, the medium said:

- Be patient. He needs this time, and he is supported by the spirits of light.

- Well, in a way, he got better. At least now he has lunch and dinner at home and plays with Dionisio. But he doesn't come near me. Sometimes I think he has stopped loving me.

- But that's not true. It's because he loves you that he finds it difficult to understand what has happened. Only yesterday, a spiritual friend whom I asked to help his case told me that he is being helped. I ask you to avoid thoughts of fear and insecurity. In order to obtain good results, it is necessary that you cooperate. Thoughts of confidence in the spiritual intervention facilitate the connection of the spirits of light with you. Remember that you value your family and deserve that harmony be re-established in your home. Stand firm in your stance, trust in God and wait.

These meetings with Eunice, the energies that she received in that house calmed Maria Eugenia and gave her the strength to stand firm and to wait. However, she began to notice that once a week, on Wednesdays, Henrique would tell her that he would not be coming to dinner. This started to intrigue her. Where was Henrique going?

He would attend the therapy sessions with Rafael, which sometimes lasted more than an hour. When he left, he preferred to have dinner somewhere so as not to disturb the routine of the house. It was also a way to breathe a little, to have moments of reflection on the conversations he was having in therapy.

That night, the session had gone deeper and he had managed to understand his own conflict better.

Rafael had asked him how his relationship with his wife was, to which he replied:

- It hasn't changed at all. I only talk to her about the essentials. Even so, I can't look her in the eyes.

- What would happen if you looked at her?

- I don't know. Something unpleasant.

- Get into it and feel what it's like.

- I don't want to. I feel weak. She's guilty and I'm the one who's ashamed. Because I'm a sincere person, honest, while she...

- She betrayed your trust.

- That's right.

- And for that, she must be punished. A husband cannot accept an attitude like that. She has to suffer and pay for what she has done.

- But your heart does not wish to part with her. You love her!

Henrique's eyes filled with tears and he cried out in despair:

- I love her, in spite of everything! I am weak! I have to wake up.

- No. You have to love. This is your truth. You love her.

- But I don't want that. I can't love her.

- Why not? That's what your soul wants.

- No, I can't. It's not right.

- You've lost your trust, and you're afraid she'll do the same thing again?

He thought for a moment and then shook his head negatively:

- That, no. She has changed too much, she wouldn't be able to.

- In that case, what's stopping you from continuing to love her?

- I don't know... A husband doesn't forgive an offence like that!

- You're not a husband. You are a man who loves, is loved and understands that the mistake your wife made was occasional and will not be repeated.

- Even so...

- Close your eyes, forget your pride, feel how much you love her.

Henrique obeyed. Rafael waited a few moments, then continued saying:

- Your heart does not desire separation. But your pride thinks you must assume the role of "husband" and it is this conventional role that is pressuring you not to forgive. It is your vanity that wants to punish her, make her pay for the pain you are feeling. That is the anger you feel when you think about the situation.

- It's true. I get very angry.

- Anger is a natural force, but it needs to be properly channelled so that it does not harm us or hurt others. Indignation, anger, when properly used, can propel us forward. It is the same force that makes us react to injustices, defend difficult causes, face dangers and win.

- Perhaps. But I don't know how to do that.

- All right, then. Then go home and separate from her. Who will have custody of your child? What will your life be like after that?

Henrique shuddered:

- No! I wouldn't know how to live away from Dionisio. Nor would I have the courage to separate him from her. He is more attached to her than to me. I would suffer a lot.

- Everyone would suffer. But your pride would be satisfied. She would be punished.

- I would suffer more. My son is not to blame for anything. He would be punished too.

- So, acknowledge that you don't want a separation.

He thought for a while and answered:

- No, I don't want it. We would all suffer.

- Say that again.

He repeated.

- Say it again.

Henrique obeyed. Until he cried out in an emotional voice:

- I don't want to part with them!

Tears streamed down his face and Rafael silently handed him the box of tissues. Henrique took one and wiped his eyes, but the tears stubbornly kept falling.

- Cry, Rafael said. - Throw away all your sorrow.

Henrique allowed the tears to flow. When they stopped, he wiped his face.

Rafael put his hand on his arm and said:

- It was clear that you love each other and everyone would suffer with the separation. Think about what is more important for you: satisfying your pride, suffocating your feelings, or understanding that to make mistakes is human and part of personal maturation.

- Understanding would be the best solution. But I still don't know if I can manage it.

- Today we have managed to analyse the situation better. But despite this, you don't have to decide anything yet. Go home, start observing what you like best when you are there. That's enough for now.

Henrique stood up.

- Remember that you can call me if you need me.

They said goodbye and Henrique left. He walked to the car park, picked up his car and drove home. He didn't stop to eat. He was not hungry and thought that his appearance was not the best.

He arrived home and went straight to the guest room. He didn't feel like seeing anyone. Fortunately, Maria Eugenia was in Dionisio's room and didn't see him arrive.

He closed the door, went to the bathroom and looked at himself in the mirror. His eyes were red and he washed his face trying to improve his appearance.

He could see that he was sensitive. Raphael's words were alive in his spirit.

"What is more important: to satisfy your pride, to stifle your feelings, or to understand that making mistakes is human?"

He stretched out on the bed.

"You think that, as a husband, you should punish her."

"It is your vanity that desires that."

He could not see, but at that moment Norma's spirit approached him and laid her hand on his forehead. From her heart came a blue light that enveloped Henrique, as she said to him:

- Vanity is a bad counsellor. Do not give importance to pride. Let your heart speak.

Henrique did not listen, but he began to remember Maria Eugenia with Dionisio in her arms, emotionally moved, kissing him lovingly.

A pleasant warmth invaded his chest and other moments of affection and joy came to his memory.

Norma's spirit continued with her hand on his forehead. Now, from his heart came a pink energy that enveloped him completely.

Henrique realized that he loved Maria Eugenia and Dionisio deeply. It was a feeling of fullness that filled his chest with joy and pleasure.

In the midst of this sensation, he fell asleep and dreamed that he was in a very flowery garden, where the air was perfumed, and a young woman approached him saying:

- How are you, Henrique?

- You? - he answered. - It's been a long time!

After hugging her, he asked:

- I know we know each other, but from where?

- Before you reincarnated. We have been friends for a long time.

- I don't understand what you are saying. Reincarnate?

- Born on Earth. You were born again; I wasn't. But that doesn't matter. I want you to feel good. I'm going to take you to a very beautiful place. You'll like it.

She slipped her arm through his and they glided off into the gardens. The starry sky enchanted Henrique, while the pleasurable sensation in his chest gave him inexplicable joy.

For a while they walked back over a town, then they returned to the garden and she asked:

- And then? How do you feel?

- Floating. I would like to stay here with you.

- It's not time yet. You have to go back.

Henrique remembered his problems with Maria Eugenia and his face contracted.

- Don't fall into sadness again. Think that nothing happens by chance. Life's challenges are precious opportunities to mature. Remember that understanding elevates, brings discernment, matures, while judgment limits, hinders, attracts suffering.

Henrique awoke, but her last words still rang in his ears:

"Remember that understanding elevates, brings insight, matures, while judgment limits, hinders, attracts suffering."

In his memory the scenes of the dream were alive. As he recalled, he again felt the gratifying emotion of those moments.

It did not seem to him like an ordinary dream. The woman's face drew itself again in his memory, and he thought:

"I know her. But from where?"

She had asked him for understanding. How could he understand his wife's betrayal? He remembered the words that Maria Eugenia had spoken to him:

"What happened with Pierre was an occasional involvement that I justified as revenge for you having had a relationship with another woman."

At the thought of this, Henrique's hurt reappeared and he frowned.

"It's hurting me too."

"I'm sorry I hurt you, but I recognize that this experience has made me grow, value the good things I have."

"I am still the same woman who has always loved you and loved our son."

Henrique stirred in bed, restless. He remembered their courtship days, their marriage, how devoted she had become after Dionisio' birth.

He felt indecisive, insecure. The phrases in his dream blended with Rafael's and everything Maria Eugenia had told him. He wanted to sleep, to forget, to rest.

He did not notice that the spirit of the woman he had dreamed about was at his bedside. With outstretched hands she prayed, asking God to help him find peace.

Gradually he calmed down and finally managed to fall asleep.

He woke up the next day to a knock on his bedroom door. Startled, he looked at his watch and saw that it was past noon. He jumped up and opened the door. Maria Eugenia said:

- I'm sorry I knocked on the door. But you don't usually sleep this much. I was worried. Are you ok?

- I had trouble sleeping and lost track of time. I'll take a quick shower and get out.

- I'll have lunch taken away. Or would you prefer a strengthened coffee?

- I'm not hungry. A cup of coffee is enough.

She nodded affirmatively and went downstairs. Henrique went to the shower. After his bath, he noticed that he felt much better. The restlessness of the last few days had passed.

He seemed to have woken up from a nightmare. He sat down to drink coffee. Dionisio saw him and ran to him, who took him in his arms.

- Beautiful Daddy! I want to stay with you.

- I want it too, but I have to go to work. But you'll stay with me until I finish eating.

- Yay! I want your bread!

Henrique laughed happily and gave him a piece of bread.

- Is that all? - complained the boy.

- You are going to lunch.

- No. I've already eaten, haven't I, Mama?

- Yes.

- Eat this and if you want more, I'll give you some.

Henrique finished eating and Dionisio walked him to the door.

- I want to stay with you!

- I can't now. Daddy's going to work. Today, when I come back, I promise we'll play a lot.

- Don't take long.

- Look, while I'm gone, play with Elvira.

- I will play with mummy.

Henrique hurried out and Maria Eugenia hugged Dionisio, while he complained that he wanted to play with his father.

Henrique arrived at the office and put all his efforts into work matters. For the first time, after having received Pierre's letter, he managed to take an interest and solve the company's pending issues without his personal problems interfering. At the end of the afternoon, he ordered a snack and decided to stay late to catch up on what he had left behind.

It was seven o'clock when Maria Eugenia entered the spiritual study centre for her usual treatment. She had gone a little earlier because she wanted to be seen first so that Henrique could find her at home when he returned from work. As the treatment would only begin at seven thirty, she went to the bookshop with the intention of buying a book to study spirituality.

Rafael and Marina were there. They used to frequent the bookshop of the centre, interested in continuing their studies on the subject.

Seeing her enter, Marina shivered and tried to hide her nervousness. She noticed that Rafael was looking at Maria Eugenia curiously.

When they left the bookshop Marina couldn't help herself:

- Do you know that girl?

- By sight. Her husband is my client.

Marina didn't answer and thought scared:

"It was too much of a coincidence that Henrique was Rafael's client. Why is life bringing us together? I have studied that all events in life have a message. What does it want to tell me with that?"

She entered the room for her voluntary work, but was still puzzled by what had happened.

"Maybe it's a way of life telling me that I need to tell my secret to Rafael before we get married. I can't share my life with him without telling him the truth. But at the same time, how do I do that? He will think I am a gold digger, that I gave my son away for money.

At this thought, she felt indisposed. The work had not yet begun and she asked the leader to excuse her and went out. In the corridor she saw Eunice, who was saying goodbye to someone.

She waited for her to finish and approached her:

- Mrs. Eunice, I am not feeling well.

Eunice looked at her and invited her to come into my room:

- Come into my room. Let's talk.

She obeyed. Marina opened her heart. She said everything she was thinking and asked:

- What will Rafael think if he finds out what I did?

- Let's talk about you first. Do you feel mercenary for having accepted Adele's proposal?

She hesitated a little and answered:

- I confess that I accepted the proposal for the money. As I told you before, it wasn't so that I could enjoy a life of leisure without working. It was for the chance to achieve my goals, to be able to become independent, to give comfort to my mother, who supported us by sewing until the early hours, to provide a better life for my brother. I did my part: from an early age I tried to prepare myself, I studied hard to graduate, I gave my best at work.

- Has what you have done harmed anyone?

- No. On the contrary. It was sad to have to part with my son, but on the other hand, besides helping Adele protect her family's assets, I provided another woman with the joy of motherhood, and a man with the right to be a father. I heard that they form a happy family and love each other very much.

- If you think so, what are you afraid of?

- I am afraid that Rafael will see me as a mercenary. Besides, I don't know if I have the right to reveal to another this secret that does not concern only me.

Eunice put her hand on Marina's.

- Calm your heart. If you don't know what to do now, don't do anything. Wait and life will show you the next step.

- I think that is already happening. This girl is frequenting this house. A little while ago we met in the bookshop. I noticed that Rafael was looking at her with a certain curiosity. When I asked him if he knew her, he said that her husband is his client. I was terrified. What does life want to show me with this?

- You have nothing to fear. Pray and trust. I have been following Maria Eugenia's case. I can only tell you that she and her son really love each other.

- Do you know him?

- Yes. They live near my home and she came to me because the boy was unwell. He is very handsome and healthy. It was just a bit of heavy energy that enveloped him.

Marina was moved and a few tears streamed down her face.

- My daughter, don't be sad or enter into negative thoughts. The spirit that reincarnated through you is linked to this couple.

You were the instrument that life used so that he could return to help them in this incarnation. You will still have other children who will give you many joys. So, connect with the light, trust and let life show you what it wants from you.

- Your words relieve me. Adele, when she asked me to accept, she told me all this.

- My spiritual friends are saying that this woman is a trustworthy person and is very grateful to you for everything you have done. Don't think about it anymore. If one day you feel you must tell Rafael the whole truth, do it without fear. You haven't done anything to be ashamed of.

Marina thanked her for her words and said good-bye. That conversation made her feel very good.

Outside, Rafael was waiting for her.

- I saw that you left our room quickly. What's wrong? Did you feel ill?

- It was a slight indisposition. It's over now.

He hugged her.

- I've noticed that sometimes you get thoughtful, you look worried. Is something wrong?

- Not at all. It's all over now.

- You're very important to me. I'll do anything to make you happy. If you need anything, don't be shy.

- Thank you, but it's all right.

They left and went for a snack, as usual. They talked, exchanged ideas on several subjects, and Rafael did not touch the subject again.

Marina was curious to ask him about Henrique. Even though she knew Rafael would never tell her anything about the therapy sessions, she would like to know what the father of her son was like, why he was seeking psychiatric help. But she restrained herself. She had never asked questions about any client, and surely Rafael would find her sudden interest in Henrique strange.

Later, alone in her room, Marina decided she would never ask him about this.

She went to bed, but even though she had decided to forget that night's meeting, it was still on her mind. She felt that the circle was closing. First the fact that she would have to give Maria Eugenia energy treatment. Secondly, Henrique, among so many psychiatrists, had chosen Rafael.

She had not provoked their approach. In fact, she preferred to remain distant. The possibility of approaching her son frightened her. How would she react if she were face to face with him? No matter how hard she tried not to get emotional, what would it be like?

Then there was the formal promise she had made to Adele. She did not wish to give her any reason to doubt her word. Adele had been so correct, so frank at the time of the agreement, and so delicate in dealing and keeping what she had promised her, that she wanted to live up to that trust by doing her part.

That case was closed. What she had to do was forget the past, move on, get on with her life. Rafael had appeared, he knew how to win her trust, her love. At his side, for the first time, Marina thought of forming a family.

The memory of the pregnancy, of Dionisio' birth, of the emotion she had felt, had made her want to be a mother, to be able to give all the love she had felt when she heard the boy's cry for the first time.

The difficulty, the pain she felt when she was separated from him made her realise how happy she would be if she could have him by her side, to see him grow up. But she could not go back.

She had to swallow her pain and move on, thinking of the good she would do to her mother and brother.

But it was this experience that made her want to get married, to have another child from whom she would not have to be separated.

She recognized that, although she had done it all for the money, the greatest benefit was the fact that it made her change her way of thinking and make her realize that more important than a successful career was the feeling of love that this child had awakened in her heart.

Rafael had insisted that they should set a wedding date. She wanted to wait longer. However, at that moment it was decided.

The next day they would set the date, and it would be as soon as possible. They loved each other, they had the financial resources to maintain a family. Why wait any longer?

Soon they would be married, she would have other children and everything would be forgotten. Making plans for the future, Marina finally fell asleep.

The following afternoon, when she told Rafael the news, he was very happy.

- The other day I was offered a very beautiful house in Planalto Paulista. Today we can go and see it. If you like it, I'll close the deal.

She smiled satisfied:

- You didn't tell me you were looking for a house for us.

- In fact, whenever anyone told me about a house for sale, I immediately thought of us. A few days ago, I was offered this one. I think it might do.

- You went to see it.

- No. I just saw some photos. But I'll make an appointment, and we'll go see it today.

- It's already late. Set it for tomorrow. First, we have to set the date.

- We don't need much time. We can file the papers tomorrow.

- Just like that?

- We don't have to wait any longer. We'll see the house, then go to a travel agency to choose where we'll spend our honeymoon.

- That's fine. We'll talk to mom tonight.

- If we like the house, we can take Cicero and her for an opinion. I want them to like the house, since they are going to live with us. We will be a very happy family.

Marina gently ran her hand over his face, caressing him.

- I love you!

He kissed her longingly on the lips. Marrying her was what he wanted most of all.

They left the office and went to Marina's house. They were radiant, and Ofelia noticed immediately:

- What happened? You two are lit up.

- Today we're setting the wedding date, Rafael said.

- When will it be? - asked Ofelia.

Sitting in the living room, Rafael spoke of their plans for the future: the purchase of a house, their desire to live together. Ofelia said:

- You are like a son to me. Cicero appreciates and respects you. But I think that people who marry need privacy. You must live alone. We'll stay here, but we'll always be together.

- Not at all, Mrs. Ofelia. I love being with you. We have a rare affinity. We understand each other, we're happy together.

- I agree, but I still think a couple should live alone.

- That works when people have no affinity. I missed my family a lot because we always live so far apart. I am very happy to think that we will all be together, living in a beautiful house, with joy and love. I know that Marina wishes the best for you and Cicero. I would like to contribute so that you will be happy every day.

- Mom, Cicero is very young. Together we can offer him the security he needs until he can decide for himself how to lead his own life. Afterwards, all I have ever wanted in this life is to live beside you, to repay you in some way for everything you have done for me, with your love, your dedication, sewing until late to support us.

- I don't know... I can take care of myself. I don't want to be a burden to you.

- You are great at taking care not only of yourself but also of all of us, the house, the food, everything. By taking you with us, we are also thinking of having a good administrator of our home. I work, I am away a lot; Marina too. Do you want us to leave our things in the care of strangers?

Ofelia bowed her head thoughtfully. Marina looked at Rafael, who winked mischievously. He had touched her weakness.

- Indeed, Ofelia answered. - A house without good management is an abuse. From this point of view, it would be good if I went.

- You know, mom, I don't know anything about houses. Then, as Rafael said, I work outside all day. Who would take care of our things?

- All right. We will go. We'll take Rosa. She'll help us. Let's celebrate. I'll get a bottle of wine.

They toasted. Dinner was served and they did not get tired of making plans for the future. None of them saw that Norma's spirit embraced them happily, but they all felt happy. That was a moment of joy and peace.

CHAPTER 21

Three months later, on a sunny afternoon, Rafael and Marina gathered their friends in a beautiful and spacious venue to formalize their civil union, where a dinner would be served afterwards. Everything had been planned with good taste and care.

Marina arrived at the place, where the guests were already gathered, together with her brother, who accompanied her proudly. They were happy.

Rafael had bought the house he had mentioned, after having taken the whole family to see it. It was a spacious, beautiful and comfortable house, built in the middle of a beautiful garden, with six bedrooms and other facilities, offering comfort and space for the children who would surely come.

When Marina entered the hall holding Cicero's arm, the musicians began to play a romantic song. Rafael, with his eyes moved, was waiting for her at the back, next to the judge and the clerk, near a table full of flowers.

When they were close, Rafael went to receive her, and they stood in front of the judge's table.

Cicero stood next to Rafael's mother and family who had turned up for the ceremony. They had arrived the night before and, although they wished to stay in a hotel so as not to disturb them, Marina and Ofelia would not allow it.

After knowing them, they understood why Rafael missed his family so much. His parents, Diva and José Luís, were educated and classy, but very simple people. They radiated sympathy and soon won everyone over.

Ronaldo, Rafael's older brother, was somewhat reserved, but gentle and affectionate. Dora, a teenager, easy smile, irreverent, good humoured and very willing, livened up the atmosphere.

The engaged couple, surrounded by their families, listened to the words of the judge, who spoke for a few minutes about their married life and, after the usual questions, declared them husband and wife.

Then, Eunice came up and took the floor, said a beautiful prayer asking for the divine protection for the couple, while music played softly, touching those present.

Then the greetings began. The clients and friends of both approached to embrace them. At a certain point, Rafael touched Marina's arm and said:

- I want to introduce you to a special friend, Dr. Bernardo Gouveia, accompanied by his fiancée, Adele Figueira Rocha.

Marina looked startled. Had she heard right? She looked up and her eyes met Adele's, who, smiling, hugged her and said:

- Pleased to meet you.

Marina, trembling, murmured a "thank you" and Adele continued looking into her eyes:

- I wish you happiness and that everything continues to work out in your life.

Marina couldn't hold back her tears and hugged her:

- I am so happy to have you here on my wedding day.

Adele returned the hug with affection. Marina would like to ask her many questions about Dionisio, if they were happy, but she restrained herself. Bernardo greeted her:

- You knew how to choose. Rafael is a wise man.

- Why do you think I chose him? - she replied, smiling.

Bernardo and Adele stepped aside so that others could greet the couple. Marina, while paying attention to the guests and dissimulating her interest, watched them the whole time.

Rafael introduced Bernardo and Adele to their parents and siblings, and then took them to Ofelia.

- This is Marina's mother. Ofelia is my second mother.

Watching Adele chat animatedly with Ofelia, Marina felt her excitement grow. If only her mother knew! But she would never know.

Marina thought once more about the fact that life had brought her face to face with her past just when she thought she had resolved this issue forever.

She had decided not to tell Rafael about that part of her life. But now, faced with this reality, the doubt reappeared: was she doing the right thing by remaining silent?

What if one day, one of these unexpected facts brought them face to face with the truth?

Marina shuddered just thinking about it. But it was Adele who dispelled her doubts. While Rafael was talking to Bernardo, she took advantage of a moment in which Marina was in the toilet touching up her make-up and went over to talk to her.

- I have followed your life from a distance, said Adele. - I knew you would be a winner.

- Seeing you here today moved me and brought back many memories.

- For me too. When Bernardo invited me here, I wanted to see you, to know what this experience was like in your life. And to know how you are now.

- I am well. I love Rafael, my family adores him. I think we will be happy together. Before I didn't think about marriage. But after that time, I felt awakening in me the desire to be a mother, to have a son and to be able to give him the love I felt and could not express.

Adele was thoughtful for a few moments, then said:

- That experience humanized you. I must say that after that we all changed. Maria Eugenia became another woman. The coming of her son awakened her maternal love and she matured; she became a better woman. What moves me most is that Dionisio is more attached to her than to his father.

- It's good to know that they are happy. I was afraid she wouldn't accept him.

- He made her awaken to love. And even I have changed since he arrived.

- Rafael and I go often to a centre for spiritual studies, where we study and do voluntary work. A few months ago, while assisting people, I came across Maria Eugenia crying in front of me.

- What? Did you know her?

- I had been following the social news and had seen photos of her, her husband and her little boy. That night I recognized her immediately. But she was very distressed. Mrs. Eunice, that lady who said the prayer at the wedding ceremony, is a blessed person. She founded and is the director of this centre, where she attends everyone with love. My brother is a medium and she has been guiding us.

- I did not know that Maria Eugenia had taken this approach.

- When I saw her, I was scared, especially because she was crying. But I restrained myself, I prayed for her, I gave her energy to calm down, but I was afraid that there was something wrong with the boy. But then I looked for Eunice so that I could calm down.

She knows all about my life. For her I have no secrets. She is my spiritual counsellor. She is the only person to whom I opened up.

- We can't stay here too long. I would like to tell you why she was distressed. The boy is doing very well; it is her problem with her husband.

- She has been going regularly to the centre, but we never talk. Eunice sometimes receives her in her private room.

- Marina, one day I will go to see you and tell you everything. You are part of our family, although it is not advisable to get close to us. Let's go now. We can't attract attention.

Adele left first and Marina left a little later. The next evening, the newlyweds were to travel to Italy for their honeymoon. Marina would have liked the conversation with Adele to be before then, however there was no time for that. She was keen to find out more about them. Adele had said that Maria Eugenia's concern had nothing to do with her son. She believed it. Adele was a trustworthy person.

Despite the emotion, Marina felt happy about that meeting. Adele continued to show her respect and appreciation. That reassured her. By accepting the contract, she had done nothing wrong and the experience had changed them for the better.

The party was a joyous affair and the newlyweds' antics amused everyone. Later, when saying goodbye, Adele asked naturally:

- I hear you are going to spend your honeymoon in Italy. It will be wonderful. How long are you planning to stay?

- A month - replied Marina.

- It's not much, Rafael added, but it's the time we can settle our work.

Bernardo seized the moment:

- Rafael told me that you are a brilliant professional. One day we shall exchange our experiences. As far as I know, we both work in the business area.

- It is very kind of you to speak in exchange, since I would have nothing to add, only to learn. I know your capacity, I have followed some of your cases. The advantage would be all mine.

- I heard about you back when you worked for Dr. Olavo. As a matter of fact, at that time you were already well known in our midst, and some colleagues even tried to hire you. If it had been me, I wouldn't have let you go.

Marina blushed a little, remembering what had happened later. He continued saying:

- Now you have found your own way. And, from what I hear, you're doing very well.

Marina smiled happily. A compliment from Dr. Bernardo was gratifying.

They said goodbye and left. Once in the car, Adele said:

- I liked that we came. You were a little worried about our proximity, but it was good. Marina is very correct, and this meeting will not harm us.

- I liked it too. They are good people, they are happy. Do you think Rafael knows?

- No. Marina said that the only person she has shared this secret with is her spiritual advisor, Mrs. Eunice, who gave that beautiful prayer. I don't believe she has spoken to anyone else.

Adele told her in detail the conversation they had had in the toilet and finished saying:

- She was frightened recognizing Maria Eugenia, seeing her distressed, weeping. But she managed to contain herself.

- It can't have been easy for her.

- Next week I'm going to visit this lady. I think she was the one who advised Maria Eugenia to tell me about the blackmail. And also advised her to stand up to her husband, as she did.

- We've distanced ourselves from religion. But faith comforts and helps.

- I'm not religious. I don't like the ideas that limit us, and all such beliefs are limiting. I prefer to believe in the higher force that rules this world, takes care of our lives. When I feel the need for support, I connect directly with it and always find a good answer.

- Have you noticed that although the situation between Maria Eugenia and Henrique is still bad, she has managed to keep her serenity and not complain? Do you remember how depressed she used to get during her adolescence?

- Yes, I do. She wouldn't talk. Or she would get euphoric, pretend to be happy, which was even worse, because she couldn't convince anyone. Now she's become more of a woman. I had a feeling a child would do her good.

- Why are you going to look for this Mrs. Eunice?

- I want to meet her, to know more about what she does and hear suggestions on how I can help to improve their relationship. But first I am going to inform myself. I want to go on a day when Maria Eugenia doesn't go, nor Marina.

He was silent for a few minutes, then said:

- Hasn't the happiness of the bride and groom inspired you to set a date for our wedding?

- Yes. If I haven't set it yet, it's because for me, our wedding would be like a celebration. And for the celebration to be complete, I would like Henrique and Maria Eugenia to have recovered their happiness.

- Today I asked Rafael how the treatment is going, and he answered that little by little Henrique is becoming aware of the truth. He is already able to analyse the facts without resentment. But he still has barriers to accept what happened.

Adele sighed and answered:

- Why can't men forgive a moment of weakness? Women are more condescending, or more practical. They recognise that forgiving, giving a second chance, is better than losing their partner.

- Let's not wait any longer. Our example of happiness will do them good.

- It might. I'll consider it. We'll see.

Two days later, Adele left the office in the late afternoon and went to visit her daughter. She found her in the living room reading, while Dionisio, sitting on the floor, was playing with a toy car next to Elvira.

Seeing her enter, Dionisio got up and ran to her, hugging her legs. Adele smiled, left her purse on the small table and took him in her arms, kissing his blushing face.

He kissed her on the cheek in return.

- Grandma, how nice! Do you have a present?

- I brought you two beautiful storybooks.

- Yay! Look mummy. There's a dog, a cat and a bird.

Maria Eugenia, who had just stood up, hugged her mother.

- How lovely to see you! Dionisio, this other book has a castle, a knight, a prince and fairies.

- Does it have a spell?

- I don't know. We'll read it later.

- I want it right now.

- Now I'm going to talk to my mother.

- She's not your mother, she's my grandma!

Adele interjected:

- I can be both. I am her mother and your grandma. – Seeing Elvira approaching, she continued saying: - Ask Elvira to read the stories to you.

Elvira greeted Adele and picked up the books. Dionisio, interested in hearing the stories, agreed to accompany her to his room.

Adele sat down on the sofa next to her daughter and said:

- What are you reading?

- Spiritist Facts, by Sir William Crookes.

- Is it interesting?

- Very interesting. There was a time when materialization phenomena were taking place. Some journalists went to ask this scientist for his opinion. He was interested, but said that he could only give an opinion if the medium who produced the phenomena agreed to stay at his house, at the disposal of his research, for a certain period of time. Only after that he would give his opinion.

- Curious. And what did he discover?

- His research is described in this book, and he proved that there is life after death, that we continue living in other dimensions, that reincarnation is a fact.

Adele looked at her in amazement.

- Are you sure he has verified all this?

- Yes, I'm sure. There is a picture in the book in which he is with his arms crossed with the materialized spirit of a woman. I've almost finished the book. If you want, I can lend it to you.

- Yes, I'd like to. It must be interesting. Now let's talk about you. How are things with Henrique?

- A little better. He comes home regularly, is more accessible for conversation, plays a lot with Dionisio, but he doesn't look for me and keeps sleeping in the guest room. I don't think he has managed to forgive me completely yet.

- At least he's still here, your relationship has improved. I'm sure he'll end up coming back to you and everything will be as it was before.

Maria Eugenia sighed:

- That's what I want most of all. Sometimes it's hard to bear the distance. It's like there's a wall between us that we can't cross.

Adele changed the subject:

- Why did you become interested in reading this book?

- I met a lady who lives in this street, Mrs Eunice. She is a medium, studies spirituality, is the director of a centre for spiritual studies. One day, Dionisio was not feeling well. He was restless, crying. The doctor didn't know what was wrong with him. Elvira, who knew Mrs. Eunice, suggested that we take him there so she could say a prayer. We went. It was great. He got better and we became friends. She has been counselling me and helping me a lot.

- She must be a special person.

- She really is: intelligent, kind, lucid. I have been going to her centre for an energetic treatment, which does me good, calms me down, comforts me. I always leave better.

- You never talked about this with Henrique?

Maria Eugenia looked at her surprised:

- No. We haven't talked about other things than necessary ones. Then, I don't know if he would believe me. We've never talked about it. Why do you ask?

- Because, as you know, he has been having therapy sessions with Dr. Rafael, Bernardo's friend. I notice that he is improving, but maybe what is being good for you would also be good for him.

- I do not know. I would even like him to go, because it is a philosophy of life that makes us see events in a better way, but until now I have not had the opportunity to talk about it.

- What does this Mrs. Eunice advise you?

- She said he needed some time. That I should not pressure him. That I should be patient, keep on doing my part as a good wife and mother, because at the opportune moment life would take care of the best.

- Interesting way of thinking. I understand that pressuring Henrique would have even increased his resistance to forgive.

They continued talking. As Adele said goodbye, she asked her daughter for Eunice's centre phone number.

- It is for an acquaintance of mine who lost her husband and is inconsolable.

- I am sure that Mrs. Eunice will know how to comfort her.

The next afternoon, Adele went to visit Eunice at home. She had called to introduce herself, saying that she wanted to meet her and talk to her about her daughter. She did not want to meet with people she knew.

As soon as Adele entered, she was led to Eunice's office, who, seeing her, stood up smiling:

- Welcome to my home.

- It is with pleasure that I come to greet you. I am very grateful for the help you have given Maria Eugenia. She is doing much better.

- She has made a lot of effort and progress. But please sit down, returned Eunice, indicating an armchair, and sitting down on another.

- Maria Eugenia told me she has no secrets from you ma'am.

- Mom, no. Eunice, please.

- Sure, Eunice. I know that Marina and Dr. Rafael are also attending your spiritual study centre. I confess that surprised me, but at the same time it scared me a little.

- No need to worry. Marina is a special and trustworthy woman, as you must know. She is a high spirit; there is nothing to be afraid of.

- I like Marina. I have only received benefits from her. I trust her, but what scares me is that life is bringing us closer together. Why is that?

- That is also nothing to worry about. Life promotes progress, works for the evolution of spirits and only acts for the better.

- Do you know why this is happening?

- No.

- You are a medium, you could ask your guides.

- I don't usually do that because I know from experience that they only speak what they can, when they want to. I also know that when we need to know something, the truth comes to us, one way or another.

- That is what I am afraid of: that it will come out and get us into trouble.

Eunice shook her head negatively:

- It won't be like that. These revelations happen within each one at the moment when the person needs them. The spirits are subtle when they wish to show us the truth, and it can appear to us in various ways: an unexpected thought, someone who tells us a phrase that touches us, a book that comes into our hands, etc. Life is wise and does not play to lose. When it brings a challenge, it is because the person is mature enough to overcome it.

- Your words are comforting. There is the fact of the blackmail, of which we were victims on the part of that Frenchman. You certainly read that letter.

- I know the contents of Pierre's letter. He will be tried, convicted of murder. He will get many years in prison, he will be sent far away to an island where he will never get out alive.

- You mean he's really guilty of that crime?

- Yes. And also, of another that the police don't know he did.

- How do you know?

- I see him surrounded by spirits that cry out for revenge. Both the girl he killed and the young man he drowned in the Seine are by his side. These spirits will not give him a moment's rest. They will do anything to take him out of his body, that is to say, to provoke his death.

- How horrible! Is there such a thing?

- What is the wonder? People are free to choose their own way. The situation he is in now is a result of his attitudes.

- Does that always happen? Does the murdered stand by the criminal?

- Not always. Soon after death, these spirits are assisted by good friends who wish to help them overcome the difficult moment. But in order to receive this help they must agree to go to places of treatment, make an effort not to hold grudges, because nobody is a victim and nothing happens by chance.

- But this is not easy.

- It really isn't. Those who have more understanding accept it, but those who do not want to are left free for this experience, which will certainly bring them more suffering.

- Then there are those who accept and do not wish to take revenge. In that case, will their murderer go unpunished?

- Not at all! By committing the crime, he accumulated heavy energies and they will attract to him backward spirits that cultivate evil. The divine justice answers each one according to what he gives. It is the law of life.

Adele thought for a while, then said:

- Interesting. I have always questioned justice. Human justice is precarious and partial, and I thought divine justice was late and distant. Your words change my way of seeing things. I feel like understanding more.

- If you wish, I can indicate some books to you.

- Thank you very much.

Adele paused slightly, then continued saying:

- I don't know if you know, but Henrique, my son-in-law, is in therapy with Dr. Rafael. He has been improving, but wouldn't it be good if he also came for the same treatment that Maria Eugenia has been receiving at your centre?

- That would be great. He will come when the time is right.

- Maybe Maria Eugenia should invite him.

- Not yet. Our spiritual friends are looking after their case. We'd better not interfere. When they think it's appropriate, they will bring him.

Adele looked at her in admiration.

- Your faith impresses me.

- There is nothing strange about it. It results from my experiences. Since I was a child, I have lived with this reality. For me it is natural, it is part of my life, and I wouldn't know how to live without this understanding. It is comforting to know that life goes on after the death of the body, to realise that nobody is alone in moments of difficulty. And that there are other worlds of different levels of knowledge and there are places where happiness is constant and we all have the chance to one day go and live there.

- You are describing a wonderful world. Is it really that?

- For me it already is. But unfortunately, there is no way to convey my certainty to you. The materialistic beliefs of the world form a barrier that many still cannot cross. But I am sure that if you seek the truth, it will be revealed and all your doubts will disappear.

Adele looked at her thoughtfully. She had gone to that interview interested in helping her daughter's marriage, but she had found much more than that.

Many times she had seen evil taking the best, good people being harmed, and at such moments she used to question God and religions. She seized the moment to learn more:

- You assure me that no one is a victim and that divine justice responds to each one as they give, but I have seen good people being harmed by evildoers and many miscreants who, despite their wickedness, continue to have a good life.

- You are looking only from the material point of view. It is necessary to go deeper. To do that, you have to study reincarnation.

- Reincarnation? I've read some things about it. But I find it somewhat fanciful.

- At first sight it may seem so, because most people don't remember having lived other lives, keeping only subjective impressions of them. He who is steeped in wickedness may remain so for a long time, living a few incarnations where life first tries by means of everyday situations to make him perceive his weak points and to modify them. To do this it gives him a certain time, after which, if he is resistant, it allows him to receive the consequences of the evil he has done.

- Those who are in evil are not easily convinced, I know that. In that case, why wait so long?

- Because after living a few more incarnations, even while retaining the evil, the spirit is modified. Setbacks, illnesses, the limits of old age, physical dependence, sensitize the most hardened spirit, undoing his illusions, showing him the reality. This is how the universal divine intelligence acts. Every day we receive messages from life, with which it teaches us how to live better. However, if we resist the good and remain in evil, it will allow the results of our evil deeds to reach us.

- But I have seen kind people who suffer a lot. You say that there are no victims.

- As we grow in awareness, we realize that evil is not just about hurting others or harming them. It goes beyond that.

- How so?

- When you reincarnate, life is offering you an opportunity for progress, for improvement, but it determines that you need to value it and cooperate with it.

- In what way?

- Firstly, by taking care of the body that was given to you as an instrument of progress, without which you could not live on Earth. When you become depressed, when you don't accept yourself as you are or relax with your health, you are in evil.

- I never thought about that. How far does this concept go?

- Much further. In the sphere of thoughts, it's worse. When you give importance to negative ideas, when you enter into the slander and judgment of others, you are in evil.

- I can see that it is not easy to stay in the good.

- That's why we take so long to reincarnate on Earth. And there's more. When you enter into the illusions of the world and want to appear to be what you are not, you are denying your spirit, your truth. This type of evil is one of the most common and is what brings the greatest suffering. Then there is collective responsibility. We need to repay the benefits that the Planet offers us, respecting nature and every living being, making the world more beautiful, cleaner, more habitable.

- You haven't mentioned helping others. Isn't this fundamental?

- It's a pleasure to help others, but help only works when we feel love in our hearts. It's not easy to help with intelligence and in favour of what the person needs. Sometimes, in the attempt to help, we get involved, we interfere in other people's lives, and without wanting to, we aggravate their problems.

- You are right. I myself have had some problems because of that.

- That's why I said: it only works when we feel love in our hearts. In my experience, I have noticed that when the person really needs it and I can do something for them, I feel an intuition, the will to do it. Then I do it. But if I don't feel anything, I don't try.

- Thank you for your words. They enlightened me and did me good. I will think about it.

Adele thought for a while, then stood up:

- Thank you also for all you have done for my loved ones. I'd like you to show me the books.

- Thank you very much. It was a joy for me to receive you. I'm sure we'll see each other a lot.

Eunice said these words looking her steadily in the eyes and Adele suddenly felt that one day, somewhere, she had been with her looking her steadily in the eyes as she did at that moment.

Eunice wrote the names of two books on a piece of paper and gave it to her, then hugged her lovingly.

- God bless you.

Adele thanked her and left. She couldn't forget Eunice's eyes and her memory that she was repeating a scene she had already experienced. Where had it happened? When? Try as she might, she could not remember, but the scene was still vivid in her memory and she was sure she had met her before.

CHAPTER 22

Henrique entered Rafael's room for another therapy session. After the greetings, he sat in the armchair and waited. Rafael sat down in another one in front of him and, looking at him, asked:

- So, how are things going?

- More or less. The last few days I have had trouble sleeping and when I do, I have terrible nightmares.

- When did it start?

- Since we have been spacing out our therapy sessions.

Rafael was thoughtful for a few moments, then said:

- What happens in those nightmares?

- I am lost in a dark place, I feel afraid, it seems that something bad is going to happen. I try to hide, but a pale woman appears, maddened, with a child in her arms. Her presence causes me horror. No matter how hard I try to hide, she always appears.

- Didn't she say why she is chasing you?

- She raises her arms, in which the child seems fainted or dead, I am not sure, and screams calling me a murderer.

- Are the dreams always the same?

- No. Although the woman is the same and the child too, she shouts at me and I cannot always understand what she says. I am terrified, in a cold sweat, panicking. I wake up worried about my son and go to his room to see if he is ok. But then I can't sleep. I get anxious, afraid to see her again.

Rafael stood up, picked up a glass of water and gave it to him.

- Drink up, calm down. Don't be afraid. Nothing will happen.

- I wanted to understand. When I was angry, this didn't happen. Now that I am feeling calmer and I have made an effort to improve my family relationship, it happens. I don't know what to think. Would all the treatment here have been useless?

- Of course not! You've really been enjoying our conversations. And to be honest, I think you're ready to be discharged.

- Discharge? This can't be. I really need your help.

- Not as a therapist. During my honeymoon trip, I didn't refer you to another doctor because I thought this time would be useful for us to observe how you feel. Despite what you tell me, I believe that at the moment you need to space out the sessions, give yourself time to assimilate everything you have noticed during our encounters.

- But I've gotten worse.

- The nightmares you've been having don't seem to me to be caused by emotional problems.

- I don't understand.

- You need spiritual help, not therapeutic.

- You want to abandon me just when I'm not well?

- What's happening to you is spiritual harassment.

- What? What's that?

- Sometimes I have mentioned to you that I dedicate myself to the study of spirituality, which involves the phenomena of life after death, reincarnation, communication with spirits.

- You have mentioned your studies, but we have never talked about it.

- The time has come to talk about it. At first sight, it seems that these nightmares have to do with unresolved issues from your past lives.

- Do you think I have already lived other lives?

- We have all lived several incarnations in the world. Not remembering other lives is a protective feature, since we are put face to face with disaffected people from other times. This makes reconciliation easier.

- I am amazed. I never thought that a doctor believed in spirits.

- Those who see life and death face to face are more likely to perceive this reality.

- You mean this woman in my dream exists somewhere?

- Yes. But how, where she is now, we need to find out.

- Can you explain further?

- She is a spirit, and spirit is eternal. So she must be somewhere. She could be reincarnated here, she could be in the astral communities.

- But she looks bad. She must be very bad. And the child? Is there one too?

- Yes. But all this may appear in your dream the way it happened in the past, which means that they may be very different now. The child may be an adult, the woman may be better off.

- All this seems hard for me to understand. I am confused.

- It is that your nightmare may be the reminiscence of an event from other lives that was stored in your unconscious and some need of yours brought up. Perhaps it has something to do with your present problems. Of course, today everything is different. Everybody has changed. But in your dream it appears as it happened at that time.

- Now it is clearer. Do you mean that unresolved matters remain in the unconscious?

- Not only unresolved matters, but everything we experience is engraved in our unconscious. Although we forget everything, it sends us information in the form of intuitions. This is how we mature spiritually.

- When you said that, you reminded me that when I was a student there were things that I already knew even before the teacher taught them. I had the feeling that I knew that subject. And it was true.

- That is very common. On the other hand, there are beliefs learned through education, rules, customs, which we accepted in other lives without ever questioning whether they were true, which get filed away in our subconscious, limiting our progress, confusing our head, and which we resist changing. Sometimes it is necessary a shock, a suffering, for us to wake up to the truth.

- This is a new subject for me. Last night, at home, when entering the living room, a book on the table, entitled Spiritist Facts, caught my attention. I asked the maid whose it was and she informed me that Maria Eugenia was reading it. Now you tell me about it. It is curious.

- No, it is because the time has come for you to study this subject. Your wife never spoke to you about it?

- No. I can understand the problems that caused the crisis in our relationship. The anger gave way to sadness because, despite what happened, I love her very much. Then, the affection she devotes to Dionisio moves me. However, I feel that there is a barrier between us that I cannot overcome.

- You love each other, you have a whole life ahead of you. Why don't you tell her what's in your heart? Isn't that what she did?

- It was. But when I get close to her, my chest feels tight and I can't break the ice. She hasn't told me about the book because I don't give her a chance to talk. We only exchange a few essential words.

- You can break this ice. As you approach her, just remember the good times you enjoyed together.

- I miss it, I miss affection. I often think of looking for another woman, but I can't get interested in anyone.

- You've been distant for too long. That's not good. Think about it. How many times have we men had fortuitous relationships and we know that they always leave a greater emptiness in our hearts?

- You're right. But as for my nightmares, what would you advise me?

- It would be a good subject for you to start a conversation with your wife. Maybe she can find a good solution.

- Why do you think that?

- Because she is studying this subject and the book you mentioned is the result of the research of a great scientist.

- That surprises me even more. Maria Eugenia has never been given to scientific studies.

- People change, they mature.

- I recognize that she has changed a lot. I will try to talk to her. However, I still think I need to continue having therapy.

Rafael smiled:

- At the moment, you no longer need it. But, as a friend, you can come to see me whenever you want. I will be happy to talk to you. But I am not going to take your money unnecessarily.

- I'm embarrassed. You are very busy. It's not fair to take your time like this.

- In that case you can call me outside office hours. Now that you are going to study spirituality, I am interested in exchanging views on the subject. If you wish, I could recommend some interesting books.

- That would be great.

Henrique got up, said goodbye and left. When he went to pay for the appointment, the secretary did not want to receive the payment, which surprised him a lot.

He had felt since the first meeting that Rafael was a trustworthy person. His words were still alive in his mind.

He didn't want to part with Maria Eugenia. She was more of a woman, prettier, more discreet, but in a good mood, and there were moments when he had to control himself not to hug and kiss her.

When that happened, he pulled away, went into the bedroom, trying to overcome the attraction he felt.

What did he expect with this attitude? That she would get tired of him?

That she should seek in the arms of another what he refused to give? Was it not jealousy that drove her into Pierre's arms even without love? What was she thinking of him, since he had not sought her for months?

Rafael was right: the situation was going on too long. Was there still time to try to get closer?

He got home after eight o'clock. Seeing Maria Eugenia reading in the living room, he approached her:

- Good evening. I'm late for dinner. I'm sorry.

- Good evening, she replied, placing the bookmark on the book and closing it. - I'll have it warmed up and served.

She stood up. He picked up the book and asked:

- Is this book any good?

She looked at him in admiration and replied:

- Great. So much that I'm reading it again.

- It seems that you are becoming interested in spiritualism.

- Yes, by studying spirituality I have found many answers to my inner questions. I'll have your dinner served.

- I'm going to wash my hands, but afterwards I'd like to talk about this subject.

She looked at him curiously.

- Did something happen that aroused your interest?

- Yes, it has. But then we'll talk.

He went upstairs and Maria Eugenia felt a soft warmth in her chest. There was a different glow in Henrique's eyes that made her feel that something had changed.

While she waited for the maid to warm up dinner and for Henrique to come downstairs, she raised her thoughts and thanked God intimately. She had long hoped that he would change his attitude, that he would leave the impersonal, cold look with which he stared at her when they talked.

The fact that Henrique was interested in spirituality made her believe that his change was due to the intervention of the spiritual friends in whom she trusted.

Shortly afterwards, Henrique came down and said:

- I went to see Dionisio, but he was asleep.

- He played so much and ran that he got tired. He took a bath, ate very well and then fell asleep.

- I was late and he couldn't wait for me.

- He tried, complained that you were late and fell asleep.

Henrique smiled. It had been a long time since he had smiled when he was alone with her. The maid told him that dinner was served. Henrique asked:

- Have you eaten?

- No. I was not hungry.

- Then come join me.

Maria Eugenia blushed with pleasure. And she accompanied him. Once in the room, he held out a chair for her to sit in and then sat down.

Maria Eugenia was overjoyed at his change, but dared not ask anything. During the meal, she related Dionisio' latest arts. Henrique gradually became enveloped by her smile and the warmth he read in her eyes.

After dinner they went into the living room and he asked her to tell him about the book. Maria Eugenia summarized the content of the work. Henrique listened to her in awe of the enthusiasm with which she spoke, showing a deep belief. When he asked questions, she answered with clarity, conviction and pleasure.

Impressed, he realized how much she had matured. She did not even remotely resemble that retracted, shy girl, incapable of saying "no" to her mother or of maintaining an opinion.

In front of him now stood a firm, lucid woman, who courageously exposed her ideas on such a controversial subject, with practical and true arguments.

At a certain point he said, looking her in the eye:

- It is surprising how you have changed!

Without looking away, she answered:

- I have changed, yes. Life has taught me many things. Today I can see sides of myself that I didn't see before. But my feelings are still the same.

Henrique got up and sat down beside her on the sofa. Then, without saying anything, he hugged her and kissed her lovingly on the lips several times, releasing the emotion he had blocked for so long.

When they had calmed down a little, Henrique said in her ear:

- I love you, Maria Eugenia. I love you very much. I've never stopped loving you!

- I have always loved you too.

- Forgive me if I took a long time to understand what happened to us.

- There's nothing to forgive. The mistake taught me much more than the right ones. It made me value all the good things life has given me: a wonderful mother, money, a husband I love and a son who makes the joy of my life. I discovered that I am a happy person. I am sure that the same thing happened to you.

- Yes, he answered, kissing her again several times. Then he took her by the arm. - Come, let's go to our room.

Embraced, they went up the stairs. Elvira, who was watching them discreetly as they entered the room, smiled contentedly. Then she went to Dionisio's room, sat on the bed, and said a prayer of thanksgiving to God for the happiness of the couple.

Later, in the bedroom, Henrique and Maria Eugenia were in bed, hugging each other and exchanging confidences about their feelings.

Henrique talked about his therapy sessions with Rafael and she about her encounters with Eunice.

- There were times when I feared that you would never forgive me, Maria Eugenia said.

- I also imagined that I would never be able to think about the events without jealousy, pain and sadness dominating me.

Maria Eugenia kissed his hand which she held between her own. He continued saying:

- I was blind. In my imagination I saw you as a naïve, pure young girl, above all mortals, not as a woman who, despite her qualities, had weaknesses like any human being. My vanity could not bear the loss of that illusion. But, even wounded in my pride, I recognized that, although I suffered at your side, I would suffer much more with the separation.

- You did not separate from me because of Dionisio.

- I didn't want to separate from him either, but it wasn't just because of that. I didn't want to lose you.

Maria Eugenia leaned over and kissed him on the lips lovingly.

- Despite what we suffered, it is good to recognize how much we love each other.

- Before I had for you a calm, accommodating feeling, to which I was accustomed without questioning. But then, seeing the concept I had of you crumble, at first I thought you were frivolous. I remembered your evenings in Paris with those futile friends and no longer saw any quality in you.

- I felt how much you despised me.

- But that night, when you came to talk to me and took a stand, exposing your inner feelings, I began to change. You didn't pressure me to make any decision, and that gave me some relief. I wasn't in a position to decide anything.

- I felt that. But I prayed every night that you would forgive me.

- After that night, without wanting to, I began to observe other sides of you, your qualities as a person, the respect with which you treat our employees, the changes you've made to our house, making it more comfortable and more beautiful without consulting anyone, the natural discretion, the class and, above all, the excellent mother you are.

- To love Dionisio is easy. He conquers anyone. Haven't you noticed that?

- He's a lovely child. Then I began to feel guilty for deliberately continuing to treat you with contempt while you continued undisturbed, taking care of everything with love, even more than before, playing with Dionisio, trying to make his life happier. I watched you covertly and never saw you sad beside him. Then I began to notice your better side, your qualities.

- You said something happened. What is it?

- Today I went to see Dr. Rafael. For almost two months he had been spacing his sessions. Today, when I got there, he discharged me. He said I no longer needed therapy. I was insecure. He was a friend for me, as well as a competent professional who showed me and made me face the truth. But, in spite of this, I stubbornly refused to give in. It was hard to get out of the proud posture I had put myself into.

- He must know what he is doing. You've become used to seeking help.

- The last few days I've been having some nightmares. I told him about them, who surprisingly told me that I need spiritual help. He explained some things to me about mediumship phenomena, life after death. He said I could look him up as a friend, pointed me to some books and, to my surprise, suggested that I talk to you about this subject.

- He works as a volunteer at the study centre I have been attending. We never spoke, but he must have seen me there.

- I was surprised that a doctor could give me such guidance. I always thought that spiritualism was something for simple, uneducated people.

- On the contrary. Life after death, communication of spirits, reincarnation have been researched by educated people, scientists who try to understand these phenomena. There are many interesting books, like this one I am re-reading, proving this reality. The simple people feel faith and accept these facts more easily.

- Tomorrow I will buy those books and get started.

They continued talking for a few more hours until, overcome by sleep, they fell asleep. That night Henrique had no nightmares.

The next morning, they woke up cheerful. They had made plans for the future, exchanged ideas about businesses, and Henrique noticed that although Maria Eugenia had never been interested in business before, she asked questions, gave some practical ideas that even surprised him.

He arrived at the office in a good mood. He thought about calling Rafael and telling him everything. But it was early and he didn't think it was appropriate. He would call later in the afternoon. He wanted to show his appreciation. Maybe it would be good to invite him to his house for dinner. This relationship he wished to cultivate. Bernardo had said that Rafael's wife was a brilliant lawyer, respected in the business world.

In the late afternoon, Henrique went to Adele's office and found her standing next to Bernardo. As soon as he entered, she noticed that her son-in-law was different. His face was distended, happy and in a good mood, as she had not seen him for a long time. She waited for him to speak. But he first discussed work matters. At one point, Adele said:

- I have some good news for you. But first I want you to tell me why you're looking so happy today. Could it be that what I am thinking of has happened?

Henrique smiled:

- Nothing can be kept from you! Last night Maria Eugenia and I made up.

Adele hugged him happily:

- It was about time. I couldn't stand to see you so close and yet so far apart. Would it be indiscreet of me to ask how it went?

- No. But first I want to know what good news you have.

- Bernardo and I have set the date for our wedding.

Henrique hugged them, wishing them happiness. Then he sat down next to them and told them how everything had happened. He concluded:

- I am feeling at peace. In so many years of marriage, we had never understood each other so well. It was wonderful to open our hearts and tell each other how we felt.

- It was a meeting of souls - said Bernardo, touched. - This is true love.

- Maria Eugenia is different now. She even showed interest in our work, asked questions about the companies.

- She is revealing herself. She's intelligent and is taking charge of her own life, said a pleased Adele.

- Have you told her you've set a date?

Adele replied:

- Not yet.

- When is it?

- In December. That way we'll have time for a trip.

They continued talking, making plans for the future. Half an hour later Henrique went home.

As he entered, his heart beat faster, thinking of the pleasure of being with Maria Eugenia and her son. They welcomed him warmly. For half an hour they played with the boy. Then Elvira went to get Dionisio for dinner.

Clinging to her husband, Maria Eugenia said:

- The hours were not passing. I missed you.

- I missed you too. I was with Adele and Bernardo. They set a wedding date.

Maria Eugenia clapped:

- Finally! I thought she'd never accept it.
- Why not? They've always been excellent friends.
- That's exactly why. Since their student days they've been just friends.
- She preferred your father. I think it was a good choice.
- It was. Daddy was a clever, cultured man, but very different in temperament from her.
- I never noticed that.
- I did. Mother is ardent, full of life, does several things well and naturally at the same time. She is quick, while Dad was formal, everything had to be well planned for him to act. He controlled his emotions, he didn't allow himself to show feelings.
- He always listened to Adele before making any decision.
- She was so efficient, so quick, so capable, that he trusted her entirely. So much so that, when he founded the holding company, he put her as president.
- In what he did very well, because she really knows what she is doing. But Bernardo has a different temperament to his father.
- Lucid, cheerful, full of life, intelligent, he likes to live well and in peace. I think this coexistence will be good for her. With my father they spent hours talking about their companies. With Bernardo will be different. He is a man who is very well informed about what is happening in the world. Talking to him is always very interesting. I am sure he will make my mother happy.

Henrique hugged her happily.

✳ ✳ ✳

At Marina's home everyone was gathered in the dining room. She had managed to win a complicated case and was overjoyed. When she finished talking about this event, Rafael said:

- We need to celebrate. Let's open some champagne.

Rosa brought a bottle and the glasses. Rafael opened it, filled the glasses and poured. He raised his own and then toasted:

- Let's toast to Marina's success and to all of us.

- Yes, she agreed. - Mainly because this was a case in which I was able to put an end to a tremendous injustice.

- To the victory of good! - exclaimed Cicero.

They touched their glasses and drank. Just then, Rosa warned that they were calling Rafael on the telephone. He hurried to answer.

- Hello.

- It's me, Henrique.

- How are you?

- Sorry to bother you at home, but I have some good news for you.

- It's a pleasure to hear it. Go ahead.

- Yesterday, after I left your office, I went home and got close to Maria Eugenia. We talked a lot and understood each other. I thought you'd like to know. I'm calling to thank you. You offered me your friendship and I don't want to miss this opportunity. Would you and your wife like to come to my house for dinner next Saturday?

Taken by surprise, Rafael answered:

- It would be a pleasure. But first I need to talk to Marina, make sure we don't have another appointment.

- Talk to her. If you can't, we'll set another date.

- Thanks for the invitation. I'm very happy for you.

Henrique hung up and remained sitting by the phone, pensive. Marina approached Rafael and asked:

- What is it? Did something happen?

- Yes. It's not just you who has to celebrate. It's me, too. I've just learned that a difficult case of a client whom I hold in high regard has been resolved.

- Do I know him?

- More or less. He's married to the daughter of Miss Adele, Bernardo's fiancée. They came to our wedding, remember?

- Yes. I know who he is. How nice! Congratulations!

- He called to thank us and invited us to come to his house for dinner next Saturday.

Marina shuddered and tried to hide her concern. Dinner at Maria Eugenia's house! She would love to see Dionisio, to be with him, but she couldn't go. She had promised Adele never to approach the boy. She had to keep her promise.

Afterwards, wouldn't seeing him be worse? Wouldn't it be useless torture to recognize what she had lost by giving him to another woman?

- What's wrong, baby? You're suddenly serious.

- Nothing. I was thinking that we form an unbeatable duo.

- It's because we do our best, trust life and have God in our hearts.

She smiled and, embraced, they returned to the dining room.

CHAPTER 23

The next morning, at the coffee table, Rafael said:

- That client of mine is calling to confirm dinner on Saturday. What do you think?

- I don't know if I'll be able to make it. There is a client who will arrive from England on Friday. We have scheduled a meeting on Saturday and I don't know what time I'll be free.

- I'd really like to go. He is interested in spirituality and his wife is already attending the study centre. But if you can't make it on Saturday, we'll make another appointment.

- That's fine.

The two left for work.

Marina, at the office, could not keep her attention on her work. Once again, she wondered: why was life bringing them together? Did that mean she had better go to that dinner? How to face the meeting? What if Henrique recognized her? They had met in the dark, but in moments of intimacy. Wouldn't that make him recognize her?

Despite the desire to see the boy, Marina did not feel courageous enough to face this moment. What would Rafael say if he noticed anything different? No. The best thing would be to avoid anything.

The best thing would be to avoid any relationship with that family. But how to do that, if Rafael was interested in getting closer to them?

Rafael was very interested in the cases he dealt with in his office. He liked to study them from a spiritual point of view. He was delighted to observe how life worked on people, leading them to new paths.

At that moment, Marina regretted not having told him the truth. If she had done so, she wouldn't be so worried now. He would understand and would not force a closeness with Henrique.

Marina had always been truthful, except for this secret that sometimes weighed on her when she looked at her family and thought that she had been able to hide such important facts.

In the afternoon, unable to work, Marina decided to talk to Eunice. She left her office and went to the spiritual study centre, where she found the medium working with some volunteers.

Eunice saw her, approached her, hugged her and took her to her room.

- Sorry for coming to see you at such an inconvenient time and disturbing your work.

- You don't have to worry about that. It was good to see you. Sit down. Let's talk.

Marina settled down, then talked about her problem and her doubts. And she finished:

- I don't know what to do. On one hand, I would like to go, but I promised Adele that I would never go near them. Then, I'm afraid of being recognized. I don't know if they ever saw any portrait of me, if Adele told them anything about me. What would Maria Eugenia think if she knew that the woman standing in front of her, in her house, slept with her husband and is the mother of the child she holds in her arms?

- You did not sleep with her husband to steal his love, but to benefit this family, even at the cost of renouncing the love of this child you have engendered within you.

- On my wedding day, I was talking to Adele and she told me that Maria Eugenia, despite knowing that Henrique did not know me and had accepted the deal to help the company, felt jealous that he was relating to me.

- At the time, she didn't want to face her mother. She agreed, but not wholeheartedly. But today she thinks differently. She has learned to love this boy, and I am sure that she thanks you for the gift of being a mother. She herself told me how much this fact has changed her life. Maria Eugenia improved a lot as a wife, as a woman, after Dionisio was placed in her arms.

- Adele told me that she truly loves him. And the curious thing is that he's more attached to her than to his father.

- She took him to my house to be blessed and I noticed right away that they are kindred spirits. His body was generated inside you, but he is more her son than yours, because his spirit is linked to hers. Their friendship comes from other lives.

Marina was thoughtful for a few moments, then said:

- I'm sorry I didn't tell Rafael. If I had, it would be easier now to stay away from them.

- Maybe not. Rafael is an experienced spirit. He would soon realize that life is bringing them closer together.

- That's what bothers me. As I promised Adele, I've never tried to get closer. I've seen pictures of them in magazines, I've been interested in everything about them, but that was it. That day when I was donating energy and saw her sitting in front of me crying, it was a shock. Afterwards, with so many competent professionals, Henrique went to look exactly for Rafael. It could not be a coincidence.

- It was not.

- Dr. Bernardo, Adele's fiancé, was the one who took him to Rafael, and they both attended my wedding. I was surprised. But

Adele talked to me discreetly, gave me news of Dionisio and said she was grateful that I had accepted her proposal. I have been wondering what life wants with this. Why is it bringing us closer together?

- It must have its reasons.

- But I, what should I do? I cannot now come to Rafael and say that I have kept such an important fact from him because I was afraid he would think I was a selfish woman who sold herself for money.

- Of all you have told me, that is the most important point. You accepted Adele's proposal, but not wholeheartedly.

- What do you mean?

- There's a side of you that condemns yourself because of the money you received. You didn't look at the good side of your attitude because you see money in the wrong way. You think you are mundane because you agreed to give your body, to give the child you conceived in you in exchange for money.

Marina's eyes filled with tears and she let them flow freely.

- That's why you didn't have the courage to open up to Rafael. You imagined that he would judge you as you are judging yourself. Would he really do that? Is he also prejudiced against money?

Marina looked at her surprised and answered:

- But money is something material.

- Everything on earth is material, including the body of flesh. This is the world of forms. Money, like everything else on this planet, serves to allow the spirit to interact with things and to make possible the achievements of inner maturity. Without it, just as without the body of flesh, no one would be able to accomplish anything on this planet.

Marina frowned thoughtfully.

- Looking at it this way...

- This planet is only one side of reality. The other is the essence, what lies behind the material world. Money is value. When well used, it provides progress, comfort, well-being. There are countries where people already know this, so much so that when someone can't progress financially, he is doing something wrong and doesn't have God's approval.

- But here people don't think like that.

- Unfortunately, our culture values poverty, makes it a quality, a proof of honesty, without realizing that both honesty and all good qualities are attributes of the spirit. It is it that commands the material world and it is on it that depends the good or bad use that is made of everything here. Think about it, Marina. It's time you learnt the true spiritual values. Respecting matter, whatever its state, is proper to evolved spirits.

- Faced with the values of the world, of people, it is difficult to think this way.

- People are free to think what they want, you cannot change this reality and you are not responsible for it. Frivolous judgment, evil, are still present in society. In front of the Divine laws, you are answerable only for yourself, for your attitudes. You made an exchange with Adele. You dedicated almost a year of your life to allow a spirit to reincarnate, a barren woman to become a mother, to help her family, educate her brother, give comfort to her mother. What is wrong with that?

- Adele made that contract to save a company. A business.

- Do you know how many families live off this company? What would become of them if the company went out of business?

- I haven't thought about it, and I don't think Adele has either. What she didn't want was to lose the presidency.

It may be that she thought that way, but life certainly took the good of all of you into consideration when it allowed you to get what you wanted. You will agree that it was a bold project that had high chances of not coming to fruition.

- It's true. I was afraid, but Adele was very sure.

- Adele thought of saving the family patrimony; you, of looking after the welfare of yours. Everybody won. Even Adele's brother-in-law, who was to inherit the presidency of the companies, was spared because, not having the capacity to exercise that position, he would deplete the entire fortune and end up in misery. So, as a partner, he will have his dividends guaranteed for the rest of his life.

- That's exactly what Adele said.

- We need to understand that to live in this world is to utilize all the resources it offers us for the progress of our spirit and the well-being of all. You once told me that having had this child changed your perspective. Before, you did not want to get married. Have you never asked yourself why?

- What my father did by abandoning us, even before he met his second son, hurt a lot. I was a child, I felt powerless to help them. But since then I made it my resolution to study, to work hard in order to be able to help them. But since then I have made up my mind to study, to work hard, to be able to give them what my father did not give us. Throughout my youth, I only studied and worked.

- Even more reason to deserve Adele's money.

- I confess that it was the possibility of speeding up my projects that made me accept this contract.

- Nevertheless, the fact of bearing a child humanised you. Think about all this, look at these facts from the point of view of spirituality. Think about what life would be like for all of you now if you had refused Adele's proposal. You would be struggling to achieve professional success, perhaps you wouldn't have got married; Maria Eugenia would still be bitter, suffering, judging herself less sterile and perhaps even destroying the marriage; Adele would be struggling to guide her brother-in-law, trying to cover his gambling debts and save whatever she could.

Marina sighed thoughtfully. Eunice had been right. Adele had told her that everyone was happy. She felt that way too. She loved her husband and enjoyed good times with her family.

- You're right, madam. But what to do about this dinner? I think it would be better not to go, but what to tell Rafael? Will I have to tell him the truth?

- That's your decision. Think about everything, feel your heart, ask God to inspire you by showing you what will be best. Then observe. I am sure that at a certain moment you will know what to do.

Marina said goodbye and left. Even though she hadn't decided yet, she felt relieved. The conversation with Eunice had done her good. She began to think that maybe she was being unfair in her assessment of the facts.

Rafael's meeting was not yet over and she went to the prayer room to wait for him. That room was a special place in the study centre where people went to meditate and talk to God.

There were some chairs there, on the table a vase of fresh flowers, a tray with a jug of water and some glasses. It was a quiet, simple, clear and pleasant place.

Marina sat down and began to think about everything Eunice had told her. She saw herself as a child, crying, clinging to her mother's skirt, who, unhappy with her husband's abandonment, was struggling to hide her pain in order to spare her daughter.

- Mom, won't father come back?

- I don't know, daughter. He took all his things.

Marina remembered the anger she had felt when she said:

- He didn't love us. He won't be missed. I hope he never comes back. I am here, mom. I love you and our baby. I swear I'll look after you both.

Ofelia hugged her.

- You are still a child. But don't be afraid, because I will never leave you. That I can assure you.

Marina remembered the scene as if it were happening right now. She had raised her hand and answered:

- I'm going to grow up, mother! I'll grow up, study, be somebody in life. You'll see.

That same day, while Ofelia went back to her sewing machine, after leaving school Marina went to look for work. She did what she could to help. She took care of children so that their mothers could go out, carried groceries, helped in the kitchen, was always ready to do any task that earned her some money.

It was with pleasure and pride that she handed her mother the product of her work. Since then, her only objective was to move up in life and fulfil what she had promised herself.

She did not miss her father, who had always been absent, had never given her any affection, complaining about the little money they had almost all earned by Ofelia at the sewing machine.

She thought she had overcome the pain of abandonment, but despite everything she felt that the anger was still there. Why? She did not love her father. She had never felt the affection for him that she had for her mother and brother.

Him leaving them had been better, because they could live in peace, without the complaints he made his unreasonable demands, his bad temper. By leaving, he had done them a favour. So why did she still feel anger?

That was not good. She wanted to be a good person, and that feeling was painful for her. Marina didn't want that feeling anymore.

Looking at the roses in the vase, beautiful, spreading a soft scent in the air, she thought of God, of the life force that created everything. This feeling was stronger than everything and she asked:

- God, show me what I need to know!

A pleasant breeze enveloped her. She did not notice it, but a woman's figure approached her and said in her ear:

- Your father is a weak spirit, who has not yet learned to be better. For now, he can only give what he has given.

Marina remembered how many times she had noticed how ignorant he was. She wished he had been different, that he had been a loving, friendly father.

Norma's spirit continued speaking in her ear:

- But he isn't. Come out of your illusion. Realize that it was you who expected from him what he could never give you. You created impossible expectations and, when life showed you the truth, you didn't accept it.

Marina brought her hand to her lips in surprise. The fact that she wanted to didn't change the reality. Wasn't she being unfair by demanding what he had no way of doing? She was hurt that he wasn't the way she wanted him to be.

- Everybody is only what they are, said Norma.

Marina thought about that sentence, although she didn't know she was being inspired. But it was undeniable. Her father was an ignorant, weak, irresponsible, frivolous, dry man.

She was making an effort to elevate her own spirit, studying the cosmic laws that govern life. In the last few months, she had learned to see beauty, love, she had awakened to the need to harmonize herself, to live in goodness.

This attitude gave her more joy in life, making her value the little things, trying to be better.

How long would her father's spirit take, what challenges would life bring in order to make him mature?

Then Marina began to feel an affection for him that she had never felt before, and all feelings of hurt, of resentment, disappeared.

She felt revitalized, strengthened, and realized how good contact with the truth was.

She left the room after thanking her spiritual friends for the inspiration and went to meet Rafael. His meeting had ended and he was looking for her. Seeing her he approached her:

- You did not stay at work. What happened?

- I was questioning some things and I went to talk to Mrs. Eunice.

- The conversation must have been good, because you look radiant.

- It was great. Shall we go grab some food?

They went for a snack, then went back home.

Later, in bed, Marina, watching Rafael enjoying a peaceful sleep, kept thinking, remembering Eunice's words.

In a certain way, her father's irresponsibility, the anger she felt for having lost the security that his figure represented in her life, had pushed her to study, to work, to conquer a better place.

If she had had the father she wanted, would she have done all this? Wouldn't she have settled in ease under his protection? Wouldn't she have needed a father like him to learn to use her own strength and evolve?

At that moment she understood why she had been born in that home and had gone through all those challenges. Everything became clearer in her mind. Life had given her what she needed to learn to walk with her own legs.

She had learned not to depend on anyone and to take care of herself. So much so that, in marriage, although she loved her husband and lived with her family, she continued to be herself, maintaining a relationship with everyone in which respect and love harmonized her life together, making it natural and pleasant.

Thinking like this, Marina felt at peace. She remembered the dinner at Maria Eugenia's and decided to leave the solution for the next day. She knew that a good solution would appear. She turned to the side and soon fell asleep.

The next day at the office, late in the afternoon, Marina remembered that Rafael, when he got home at night, would certainly bring up that dinner again.

She thought for a while and decided. She picked up the phone and called Adele. When she answered, Marina said:

- Sorry to bother you at your work. But something has happened that I need to tell you about.

In a few words she talked about Henrique's invitation for dinner and finished:

- I don't know what to do. Rafael knows nothing about our agreement and insists on going. He appreciates Henrique, who was his client and wishes to strengthen this friendship. I promised not to get close to them, but it seems that life insists on bringing us together. The other day it was at the study centre, where I bumped into Maria Eugenia. Now it's that dinner.

Adele was thoughtful for a few moments, then asked:

- Would you like to go?

- On the one hand, yes. To see Dionisio, to know how he lives. But on the other hand, I'm afraid. I don't know if they have any information about me. They might recognize me. Before I got married, I felt like telling Rafael everything. But, thinking that this secret is not only mine, I did not say anything. Now, him knowing would be a solution.

- Yes. I don't know if it would be good for everyone if you got so close to them. I'm afraid of your feelings. You may suffer seeing Dionisio up close without being able to show your affection. But living in the same city, going to the same places, I don't know if we'll be able to prevent them from relating, even if it's socially.

- All this has occurred to me. That's why I want to hear your opinion.

- It would be good to talk to you. Can you have tea with me now?

- Yes, I could. Where?

Adele pointed to a teahouse and Marina wrote down the address. Half an hour later, they met. After greeting each other, they sat down and ordered tea. While they waited, Adele said:

- The wedding has done you good. You're even more beautiful.

- Thank you. I am indeed a privileged person.

- You've achieved everything: professional success, comfort for your family, your brother goes to a great school. And you have a lovely man for a husband.

- It's true. Rafael was a light that appeared in my life. He has rare qualities and I thank God for this gift.

Adele looked her in the eyes and said:

- The other day I went to talk to Eunice. A lovely, wise person who impressed me a lot.

- Surely it was Maria Eugenia who told you about her?

- Not exactly. I learned that my daughter is reading about spirituality. I heard that Eunice was counselling her and I wanted to meet her.

- Besides being a wonderful person, she has an uncommon sensitivity. We went to see her because of my brother. He was enveloped by a spirit and we were frightened, since we knew nothing about it. But his teacher understood what was happening and asked us to take him to Eunice.

In a few words, Marina told what had happened in the first meeting they had with Eunice. She concluded:

- Everything she told us was true. We were delighted. Since then, we have been going to this study centre and learning a lot. The knowledge we acquired there made us look at life in a very different way. Finding positive answers to the problems we see in the world relieves us. Knowing that we are not alone, that on our side there is always a good spirit inspiring us, helping us, is comforting.

- Your eyes shine when you say all this. I feel you are being sincere. I am not a religious person, although I have ethics, I try to be true, always do the best. My contacts with religion have not given me the answers I expected. So, I have faith in my own way.

- From what I know of you, I am sure you have a lot of spiritual help. Your confidence in our project from the beginning has been an example to me.

- I believe that when you do your best, seek the good and work for life, it responds positively. But if instead of Dionisio a girl had been born, I would understand that this was not the time to achieve what I wanted. And I would continue trying to reach my objectives in another way.

- The months I spent on the farm at Celia's side were very profitable. I met Isaura, a wonderful person, who taught me many things. My only regret is that I won't be able to see them again. I cherish these two people in my heart and I would like to see them again.

- Who knows, one day? Life takes many turns. Every time I go to the farm, they ask about you.

- What have you been telling them?

- That your son, unfortunately, died young. But that you will certainly have others.

- I've been thinking about that lately. I wish to be a mother, to be able to raise my child, to enjoy this emotion, without pain, with joy.

Adele placed his hand on hers with affection.

- I am sure you will succeed. I want you to know the extent of the good you have done my daughter. I'll tell you a secret.

The waiter arrived, bringing tea and goodies. Adele waited for him to leave. Then, lowering her voice, she talked about Maria Eugenia. She told her everything, including her slip-up in Paris.

Marina listened attentively and said:

- That's why she was crying that night. I can imagine her suffering. From the beginning I was afraid she wouldn't accept our project. I imagined that it would not be easy for her to know that her husband was seeing another woman.

- At the time, that is exactly what happened. But afterwards, when we placed Dionisio in her arms, she changed radically. She humanized herself, became a woman, matured. She loves that child as if he had been born inside her.

- That's good. I'm relieved.

- When Henrique discovered her slip, he was shocked. He went to sleep in the guest room, looking like a zombie. Because of this, Bernardo convinced him to see Dr. Rafael.

He went to therapy and fortunately got along with Maria Eugenia. They are so happy! That's why he invited them to dinner.

- Now I understand.

- I told him everything because I believe that if Dionisio hadn't existed, this marriage would have broken down. He was the link between the two of them at that moment of crisis. Henrique, although shocked, didn't have the courage to separate from Maria Eugenia and, as he told me himself, did so because of Dionisio. He is a passionate father and did not wish to live away from his son, but also, knowing how attached the boy is to her, he could not separate them.

Marina felt her eyes moisten noticing how much good her boy was doing to that couple.

- I want you to know that we are extremely grateful to you. A few days ago, by the way, Maria Eugenia said so.

- She did?

- Yes. She said she's very grateful to you for giving her this son. And that she would like to thank you.

Marina sighed thoughtfully.

- That leaves me at peace. But about dinner, what would you recommend?

- I don't know. I like you very much, your husband. I would like to strengthen our friendship, but I am afraid that, knowing the boy, you will fall in love with him and want to take him from us. He's so beautiful, so loving, so charismatic! It's hard to resist his charms.

- As for that, there's nothing to be afraid of. He loves Maria Eugenia, she's his real mother. I would never have the courage to harm them. I want them to be happy, to love each other and live well.

- I know my fear is unjustified. But sometimes, looking at him, I think of your gesture of offering us a piece of yourself.

- In fact, the separation was painful. I needed all my strength when Celia took him from my arms. But today I know that I only donated a body of flesh, because it was God who destined this body for a spirit linked to Maria Eugenia and Henrique, so much so that they love each other so much.

- Why are you saying this?

- Because I believe in reincarnation. I have no doubt that Dionisio' spirit needed to be born, but since Maria Eugenia couldn't give birth to his body, they used mine. Dionisio belongs more to you than to me. He's a spiritual member of your family.

- Why do you think that?

- Because consanguineous families are not formed at random. Life, in most cases, brings together spirits of different degrees of evolution in the same home so that they may learn from one another. It does the same with those who have had disagreements in other lives, whose unfinished relationship needs to be reviewed by them. Sometimes it does more: it brings together people with the same weaknesses, so that they can serve as mirrors for each other, and so that they can see themselves and seek to improve.

Adele looked at her in amazement:

- That's an interesting explanation. It clarifies the relationship difficulties we observe and which heredity cannot explain.

- But the reciprocal is true. People who have affinity understand each other, feel pleasure in being together. True friendship transcends the death of the physical body and creates bonds that are eternal and form spiritual families. I realize that the love between Dionisio and Maria Eugenia makes one believe that this bond from other lives already existed between them.

- Well, in fact, it's a good explanation, because I have never seen a child as attached to his mother as he is. When he sees her, his face lights up, his eyes shine and express adoration.

- That is why I say he is more their child than mine. You don't need to worry about me. I know my role. To him, I will always be a stranger.

- I knew I could trust you.

- I thought I'd tell Rafael everything. Then he'll understand why I can't go to that dinner.

Adele was thoughtful for a few moments, then said:

- If I can avoid it, it will be better. Henrique has been patient with your husband. Didn't he tell him everything?

- That's a good question. I don't know. Rafael never says anything about his patients. Maybe your son-in-law told him. But what he doesn't know is that it was me who gave birth to this child. One thing comes to my mind now... Henrique never knew anything about me?

- No. We made sure he didn't. Neither he nor Maria Eugenia know your name or have seen any photographs of you.

- That's the fear I felt going to that dinner. I didn't know if I'd be recognized, which would be heartbreaking.

- It was really nice talking to you. Whenever you have any news, be sure to let me know. As for the dinner, think it over and sort it out. I'm sure you'll do your best. If you need to tell Rafael, do so.

The two talked for a few more minutes, then said good-bye. Marina felt comforted to know the other side of Dionisio' life.

On the way home, in the late afternoon, she decided it was time to have a son. A son who would be hers, she could wait for him with love, take care of his trousseau, prepare his room to receive him and breastfeed him with love.

She remembered that, in the first days after giving birth, her breasts would fill with milk, leak, and she would have to pump and throw it away. She was sad, but it was a hopeless situation.

Now she wanted to have the pleasure of breastfeeding her child, to give him all the love she felt in her heart.

That very night she would talk to Rafael about it.

CHAPTER 24

Two days later, in the late afternoon, Marina was at the office when Ofelia called in distress.

- Honey, Cicero is not well.

- What's wrong, is he sick?

- No, I don't think so. But he's acting strange. He went to take a nap after lunch and suddenly he appeared in the living room, talking nonsense, walking in a different way and fighting with me. I think he is receiving some kind of spirit. Rosa and I prayed, asked him to calm down, but he didn't answer. I called Rute and she was at school, teaching. I did not want to call her.

- Keep praying and stay calm. I'll be right there.

Immediately she called her secretary, gave some instructions and went home.

As soon as she arrived Ofelia went to meet her:

- I'm glad you came right away.

- How is he? Hasn't he improved?

- No. I don't understand what he says and he gets nervous. I left a message for Rute, asking her to come here after class. Rafael called and I told him. He's coming here too.

- Where is he?

- Upstairs. I saw you arrive and came down. Rosa is with him.

Marina hurried up and I heard Cicero's voice speaking in a strange language. His voice was deeper and she could not understand anything.

She entered the room and Rosa asked:

- Close the door. He wants to leave and it's better not to let him.

Marina obeyed and approached him.

- Stay calm. Explain yourself better. I don't understand what you are saying.

Cicero paced from one side to the other and, irritated, shouted some words that they did not understand. Ofelia entered the room followed by Rafael.

- Let's unite and ask for spiritual help, he said.

The telephone rang and Rosa went out to answer it. A little later she came back and said:

- It was Mrs. Rute. She is coming here.

Suddenly Cicero started laughing. Everyone looked at him startled. Finally, he said clearly:

- How foolish you all are! You look like silly cockroaches. I have never had so much fun!

As he continued laughing, Rafael said:

- Don't worry about him. We'll continue asking the Spirits of Light for help.

They continued in prayer and Cicero fell silent, but he was still agitated, pacing from side to side.

Rafael tried to talk to him, but got no answer. The bell rang and Rosa went to open it. It was Rute.

- How are things? - she asked.

- Just the same. Everyone is praying in Cicero's room. You can go upstairs.

- No, let's do it differently. Put that vase of flowers on the dining table. Put on it a tray with a jug of water and glasses.

Rosa obeyed. Rute closed her eyes, concentrated for a few moments, then said:

- Now let's call them.

Rute went up and Rosa followed her. In the room, the scene was still the same, but Cicero had stopped walking. In a corner of the room, he looked scared, his eyes bulging, his body trembling.

Rute approached him, held his hand and said:

- Come, let's go down and talk.

He followed her without saying anything. She went down taking him by the hand. She put him on a chair around the dining table and sat down next to him. Then she motioned for everyone to sit down too.

She continued holding Cicero's hand and said a prayer, asking for the assistance of the spirits of light on behalf of all. When she had finished, she stood up, placed her right hand on Cicero's forehead and said:

- You are not well at all. How can we help you?

He did not answer. She repeated the question. Suddenly, Cicero began to cry. Rute let him cry for a few seconds, then said:

- Take advantage of this instant in which we are praying on your behalf and accept the help that is being offered to you.

- I am afraid, he replied.

- You have resisted for a long time, but look: what is the use of running away? How long do you want to remain aimless, disoriented, trying to live a life that no longer belongs to you? Accept the guidance of these kind friends.

- They want to arrest me.

- No. They want you to undergo treatment and recover your equilibrium. Of course, for that you will have to accept the necessary discipline.

- I don't know if I can stand it.

- Try it. Try it, because I'm sure you won't regret it.

- Why do they want to help me? I'm not good. I've done a lot of bad things, taken advantage of people.

- But you can change. I know that inside you there is a suffering heart, angry, but that you still have a good side, that you still love some of the people you left behind.

Cicero began to cry again. After a few moments he said softly:

- All right, I'll go.

- God bless you.

Cicero sighed, shuddered and then looked around, frightened:

- Boy, finally he's gone. He spoke and I wanted him to shut up, but I couldn't.

- Calm down, Cicero - replied Rute. - It's alright. Let's continue praying in silence.

She was silent for a few moments, then sighed deeply and said:

- My name is Norma. I've come to talk to you.

Marina opened her eyes with emotion. Ever since she had begun to see her, the same way she had seen her in her dreams.

Rute's voice had become sweet, yet firm. She continued:

- I had long awaited this opportunity. There are some clarifications which I have permission to tell you and which will certainly make it possible for you to better understand certain facts. For this, I have to go back in time. More than a century ago, in a castle in France, I lived with my husband Antoine, my son Jules and my daughter Marie. Antoine was a hard man, full of religious principles, keeping his family in a strict discipline. Jules, being in the Navy, enjoyed more freedom, but Marie lived in seclusion until she was fourteen.

Then Antoine married her off to Gilbert, a nobleman fifteen years older than her. It was an arrangement between the families, who planned to unite their fortunes. Marie did not want to, but had to obey. Gilbert owned many lands and used to travel the world, staying away for months. Marie stayed in the castle, watched over by her governess.

Gilbert did not marry for love, but out of a need to have a child, to whom he dreamed of leaving his possessions when he died. For this reason, the governess, at his behest, subjected Marie to severe surveillance during his absences.

Marie hated her situation, but had nowhere to turn to free herself. She felt so much anger towards her husband that she decided to frustrate his pretensions.

There was a woman, Sophie, who was received by the governess at the castle to provide clothes, props, anything Maria needed to look beautiful when her husband arrived.

She sometimes stayed in the castle for weeks sewing for Marie. Sympathetic, cunning, she won her trust and became her confidante. She liked Marie, but hated Gilbert for his arrogant attitude, as he treated both her and her husband, a merchant, very badly.

One morning when she arrived, she found Marie crying in despair. She was feeling ill and as soon as she told her symptoms, Sophie realised that she was pregnant.

On hearing this, Marie rebelled:

- I don't want a child from him. I won't do what he wants. I hate him! I won't have that child! He can boss me around, but he doesn't own my body.

Sophie tried to calm her down and promised to help her. The next day, when she returned to the castle, she brought a drink and said:

- I brought you some medicine. Take a cup before you go to sleep and you will get what you want. But no one must know that I gave it to you. If the governess finds out, she can have me arrested.

Marie promised to hide the bottle. That night, before going to sleep, she ingested the abortifacient. The next day, she felt cramps and ended up miscarrying. She felt vindicated. She had won a victory against her husband. Although no one knew it, she felt fulfilled. From then on, every time she became pregnant, she resorted to the abortifacient. She did this for a few years.

There was a time when there was a lot of looting in the region. Bandits were storming the castles, robbing, killing, burning.

Gilbert hired a militia to defend the castle. It was then that Marie met Denis, a handsome, elegant, gentle officer who commanded this group. The two fell madly in love.

Gilbert was still absent. His faithful governess, noticing their interest, increased her vigilance.

Marie and Denis, unable to bear it any longer, planned to run away.

One night, the night before Gilbert arrived from a trip, Marie put a sleeping pill in the governess's tea and they ran away. When her husband arrived, he discovered the escape and had a fit of rage. He had the governess beaten and threw her out in the street wearing only her clothes. Then he hired other soldiers and they set off in search of the fugitives.

But they were far away. Denis had planned everything and left no clues. Disgruntled, Gilbert searched for them for five years. Until one day he finally managed to find them.

They tried to escape, but were arrested and brought before Gilbert, who, blinded by hatred, had Denis killed before Marie's terrified eyes. Then, he locked her up in an outbuilding of the castle and told her that she would meet the same end when he thought it was time, and that she needed to suffer to pay for the harm she had done to him.

Desperate, Marie grieved over the death of her beloved. The scene she had witnessed did not leave her mind. Since then, she swore she would take revenge on Gilbert.

Sophie, the woman who had brought her the abortifacient, had discreetly followed all the events. Wanting to help Marie, she sought out the militia men that Denis had commanded and told them how their leader and friend had died. Outraged, they decided to free Marie and take revenge on Gilbert.

They allied with bandits and together one night attacked the castle, killing Gilbert and freeing Marie. But the bandits looted everything. Marie, taken in at Sophie's house, had lost all her possessions.

She was free, but poor. Having lost the man she loved, she lost the pleasure of living. Sophie tried to help her, making her collaborate in business, and she did well. Beautiful, showing good taste in dress, she managed to attract rich men, with whom she did business.

She hated noblemen because they reminded her of Gilbert. So, she attracted them and negotiated with them, who, thrilled by her beauty, made concessions.

She and Sophie began to grow rich, and Marie became known as a sensual woman. She became hotly contested. Fascinated by using her power and winning easily, Marie lured the rich noblemen to extract what she could from them, then abandoned them when they were ruined.

At that time, immersed in dangerous energies, she sank into obsession, vampirized by dark entities. She had several abortions, until she ended up dying victimized by a generalized infection provoked by one of those abortions.

You can imagine my situation, following this trajectory. I had disincarnated two years after her marriage with Gilbert. During that time, I was helped by spiritual friends, I studied, I learned, but I could not avoid what happened to Marie.

When Denis died, my friends and I collected his spirit. He was so angry, wanting to defend Marie, that it was only possible to remove him from the castle by making him fall asleep.

Taken to our astral community, he received treatment. A good natured man, Denis understood that in order to help Marie he needed to overcome his desire for revenge, to progress spiritually. He made an effort, studied and worked. With joy, I followed his progress.

However, we were unable to help Marie. Her continuous miscarriages had damaged the fertility organs in her astral body, and although she was disincarnated, she still felt a lot of pain. Furthermore, due to her behaviour, she had attracted rebellious spirits to her, who were ceaselessly vampirizing her.

It was then that I met Sophie. She was well, but very worried about the situation of her relatives who lived in the world.

We worked for a long time until we finally managed to get Marie admitted to a treatment colony. She was depressed, with no will to live. Until she received a visit from Denis. For her, it was like a rebirth. She cried a lot and, helped by him, she accepted the treatment necessary for her recovery.

Sophie was extremely devoted. She talked to Marie, trying to make her understand the need to strive for a better life.

When the time came for Marie to reincarnate, on hearing that Denis could not go, she did not want to accept. Her state was not good. She continued to suffer pain, anguish and discomfort. It was necessary for her to reincarnate in order to recover her health, restoring the damaged part of her astral body.

She wanted Denis to reincarnate and they could be together. She was told that Denis had progressed and, because he was in a faster vibration, they could not live as husband and wife. Even if he reincarnated, life would drive them apart. Therefore, before they could resume the love that united them, she would have to free herself from the negative energies she had accumulated, improving her energy pattern. Only then would they have a chance of resuming the love that united them.

Denis wanted very much to help her and turned to his superiors, who, studying the case, said that the only chance Denis had of remaining close to her in the new incarnation would be to be reborn as her son. But this hypothesis was difficult, since she had damaged her reproductive organs and it was almost certain that she would not be able to have children.

It was then that Denis and I asked Sophie to help us. She was preparing to reincarnate. She had met Renan again, the great love of her life, from whom she had been separated for a long time.

He lived in a higher dimension and had obtained consent to have a meeting with her and together programme a new life on earth, where they would have the opportunity, by overcoming some challenges, to continue together forever.

I accompanied their joy. On the evening when the two were happily making projects for the future, Sophie, noticing my sadness over Maria, said:

- I would like to help Marie and Denis. If I can do anything, you can count on me.

She was happy, so I made the request:

- I am afraid that Marie, seeing herself alone, will make the same mistakes again. I feel that if Denis is at her side, everything will turn out well. He wants to be born, however Maria will not be able to have children. But you can.

- What do you mean?

- You can receive him as your son and give him to her. I am sure that if they stayed together, she will come out the winner this time.

Sophie looked at her beloved and said:

- I would very much like to do that. But I don't know if at the time we would want to give our child to someone else to raise.

- I would be incapable of doing that - replied Renan.

I did not have the courage to speak any more on the subject. Renan reincarnated first; Sophie and Maria, three years later.

The years went by and Marie, now called Maria Eugenia, had become an introverted, rebellious and unhappy girl.

We tried to counsel her but she refused to listen to us. When she married Henrique, a good and honest boy, she improved a little. But then, when she found out she couldn't have children, she got worse.

So I remembered the promise Sophie had made to me and to help her and decided to look for her. One afternoon when she was waiting in a room in the twilight I took her out of her body and we talked.

Then I asked her to help us and that when the time came, she would accept the proposal that would be made to her.

Life granted me an opportunity and, faced with Adele's difficulties, I suggested to her a plan of action, aimed at obtaining the good of all, but especially at bringing Denis and Marie together.

Norma paused in her narrative and Marina, unable to hold back her tears, sobbed with emotion. Rafael listened in surprise, identifying with the story that was being told.

Norma continued saying:

- Sophie has fulfilled her promise. She allowed Denis to be born and to live at Marie's side. His presence made Marie see the qualities she possessed and the good she could not see. Having observed her thoughts, her love for life and for people, we believe that she has found the path to redemption and happiness.

I must say that the bonds of friendship that unite us have been consolidated, becoming eternal. Both I and the friends you have in the astral vibrate with joy at your happiness. On your side is a dear friend, who will be the first of the three children you will have. It will be a happy family in which all the members will have a blessed opportunity to progress spiritually. You deserve every moment of happiness you have achieved. Thank you for listening to me. May God bless you.

Rute was silent. Cicero looked around surprised. Ofelia and Marina had their faces washed in tears. Rafael struggled to control his emotion.

They remained silent for a few minutes. Cicero turned on the light and poured each one a glass of water. Rute opened her eyes, picked up the glass and drank the water slowly. Then she looked around and said in astonishment:

- What a strange thing... I slept. I was in a beautiful place, full of flowers. But I feel that something happened here. What is it?

- A spirit called Norma spoke through you. She told me a beautiful story, but I didn't understand it very well, answered Cicero.

The others remained silent. Finally, Ofelia said with a certain euphoria:

- What happened to me today was amazing. While Norma was talking, I saw every scene as if it were a film. And I was there too, sewing with Sophie. I was there! I was one of them! I lived that life!

Marina stood up and hugged her.

- Yes, mom. We were there. I also saw the scenes. While I was selling the goods, you were sewing. I clearly saw the two of us in the castle, talking to Marie, she confiding in us. It was incredible.

Then, turning to Raphael, who looked at them in admiration, she continued saying:

- And you were there too! I felt all the emotion when we met again and agreed to live together as we are now.

Rafael ran his hand through his hair, took a deep breath and replied:

- From the moment she started talking I felt I knew that story. I didn't see the scenes as you did, but I felt every emotion. Even before she said Henrique's name I identified who the characters were. I just didn't know that you were involved.

Marina approached him and hugged him affectionately.

- Forgive me. I know I should have told you everything. But I didn't do it for two reasons: first, because I was afraid you would think I was selfish for taking money to do what I did. Secondly, this secret was not only mine, it involved other people and I had sworn never to tell anyone. But now, after what we have heard, there is no way out. Sit down. It's time for the truth.

Everyone settled around the table and Marina, her eyes lost in the memories, began to speak. She omitted nothing. She told of her revolt at her father's abandonment, her oath to show him that they could live well without him, her efforts in working, studying, fighting to conquer her space. Her meeting with Adele, her refusal, her dreams with Norma and her stay at the farm. The birth of the boy, her emotions, Adele's support and what she had told her about Henrique and Maria Eugenia. And she concluded:

- Now you know everything. I don't deny that the money I received contributed to speeding up the projects I had. I confess that I have often condemned myself for having accepted this money and it was Eunice who made me understand that I felt this way because I was prejudiced, for thinking that money was evil. She taught me that money is a necessary value for those who live in the world to be able to realise their projects. It is only a vehicle, and it depends on us to use it for good or evil. I feel relieved to have told you everything.

Rafael took her hand and brought it gently to his lips. Then, still squeezing it lovingly, he said:

- The first thing I learned, both in the profession and studying spirituality, is not to judge. You did what you felt you had to do. You chose that path. If you had refused that offer, I don't know where we would all be today. While Norma was talking, I remembered the therapy sessions with Henrique, when he told me how much good the birth of Dionisio had done to his whole family, how this child had become more attached to Maria Eugenia than to his father, showing clearly how attached they were. He also said how grateful they were to the woman who had offered her body so that Dionisio could be born. And I feel that this child's spirit is very elevated, so much so that his presence, his love, has brought joy, balance, peace, happiness to all those around him.

- You are right. During the time I lived on the farm and he was with me, inside me, I was very happy. It was a time full of peace, of calm, when I learned a lot. I met wonderful people. Certainly, his presence also did me good.

- I am amazed - said Rute. - Having studied spirituality for so long, I had never taken part in a phenomenon like the one tonight. I think it was extraordinary, but I don't remember anything Norma said. I would very much like to hear that side of the story.

Ofelia stood up and said:

- While someone is telling, I'm going to make some coffee. I think we could all use some after all.

They laughed happily. While she went to the kitchen to prepare the coffee, Marina, hand in hand with Rafael, began to tell what Rute wanted to know.

There were moments when he interfered, pointing out some details, commenting the facts in the light of the cosmic laws which govern life.

When Marina finished, he added:

- Tonight we have been blessed by revelations from our past. For me, they represented a precious lesson on how life reacts to our choices. May they serve to help us continue guiding our lives by trying to do our best, because in this way we will be guaranteeing a future of progress and happiness.

- I agree, said Marina. - Sometimes, in my profession, I find obstacles to this attitude. Human laws try to protect the just and punish the corrupt, but they are executed by people, and it is in this respect that they end up being distorted, covering up dishonesty and spreading injustice. Although I have never condoned them, I have often felt powerless to ensure that justice is done, which always depresses me. However, after I began to study spirituality, I discovered that, despite appearances, nobody escapes the action of divine laws. Today, when I do all I can and I don't win the case as I would like to, although I have done my best and used the case in God's hands, I know that this happened because my client needed to go through that experience.

- I know what you mean, answered Rafael. - Me too, when faced with certain difficult cases, almost insoluble in the eyes of psychiatry, also felt impotent, wondering why these facts happened. I was anxious, nervous, overwhelmed, studying harder to see if I could find a way out. Today I know why I couldn't. In this particular, I am having the same attitude as you. And do you know what I have discovered?

Rafael paused slightly and, seeing that the other three nodded negatively, he concluded:

- That being at peace, trusting in spiritual help, some solutions began to appear in my mind. Some very good ones which, when used, gave excellent results.

Henrique's case was one of them. Some suggestions I gave him occurred to me at such a moment, when I was connected with spirituality and at peace.

Rute considered:

- I have been learning that to solve any challenge, the first step is to try to maintain balance. In those moments, I connect right away with God, try to relax and talk peace, think about the good. Our first impulse is to do the opposite: to imagine every possible evil. Sometimes we have to use all our mental strength to not give importance to those thoughts. When we succeed, the results are wonderful.

- It is not easy to achieve this - said Cicero.

- In the beginning it may not be, answered Rute. - But if you keep trying, you will eventually succeed. You will feel your own strength and this will give you much pleasure and more confidence in yourself.

Ofelia returned to the living room with a tray that she placed on the table.

- Cicero, go to the kitchen and get the plate with the cake.

- The smell of coffee is too good! - said Rafael.

- Ofelia's cake is a must, said Rute, smiling.

Cicero returned. While Marina served the coffee, Ofelia distributed generous pieces of cake.

In the delicious warmth of that moment, they continued talking, commenting on the unexpected facts of that night.

With two spiritual friends beside her, Norma smiled happily. Finally, she said to her companions:

- This is the place where you are going to reincarnate. Not everyone is fortunate enough to find such a favourable environment.

The two agreed and then, embracing, they left and, in a few seconds, disappeared towards infinity.

CHAPTER 25

The following night, in bed, lying next to Marina, Rafael returned to the subject.

- Henrique called me today to renew his invitation to dinner at his place. I told him you couldn't come. He's postponed it to the following Saturday. What do you want to do?

Marina sighed thoughtfully:

- I don't know. I would like to go, to see Dionisio, but I'm afraid.

- Of what?

- Of getting emotional, of being recognized.

- You said Adele never revealed your identity. They never even saw your portrait. After what happened yesterday, I think life wants to bring us closer together.

- I feel it too. But isn't it just my impression, the unconscious desire to see Dionisio?

Rafael shook his head negatively:

- No. If it were that, our spiritual friends wouldn't have bothered to come and tell us about the past. Norma said that we belong to the same spiritual family and that we are united by the bonds of the spirit.

- Do you think it would be good for us to go?

- Everything leads one to believe so. We have learned to observe the signs that life gives us. They have been coming our way insistently.

- I am still unsure. Let's wait a few more days and see what happens.

- All right.

- Norma said we're going to have three children. I think the first one is already on the way.

Rafael sat on the bed and hugged her happily:

- Are you sure?

- Not yet. But everything indicates that I am. Almost two months ago my period disappeared.

Rafael kissed her tenderly.

- We have to be sure. Tomorrow we'll run the tests.

- I'm very happy. At the moment, having a child is what I want most.

- Me too.

- Let's not tell anyone until we're sure. I wish it was a boy.

- Well, I wish it was a girl, beautiful like you.

Embraced, they continued making plans for the future.

***

The next day, the test confirmed: Marina was pregnant.

The news was a cause for joy for the whole family. Marina felt fulfilled. This time, she would have the pleasure to prepare the whole outfit and decorate the room to receive the baby.

Two days later, Rafael made an appointment with an obstetrician friend of his, who examined her and found that everything was fine. He congratulated them for the news, gave some guidelines and ordered some routine tests.

As they left the building, it was after four o'clock and Marina said:

- I'm not going back to the office today. Do you have an appointment?

- I had one, but I cancelled it. I left this afternoon free to take care of you.

- In that case, let's go grab some food. I'm hungry.

- I noticed you've hardly had any lunch. There's a bakery near here. Let's have a snack.

The tea room was elegant and crowded. Some violins livened up the atmosphere, playing cheerful and pleasant music.

Fortunately, they got a table and sat down. The waitress approached them smiling. Rafael asked Marina:

- What will you have?

- Today I want everything I'm entitled to. Then I'll follow the doctor's recommendations and maintain a proper regime.

- Two full teas, Rafael asked with a smile.

Soon after, tea was served and the table was covered with delicious treats. Marina looked like a child. She served herself and began to eat, savouring everything.

Rafael looked at her amused. It was at that moment that a familiar voice said cheerfully:

- Dr. Rafael!

They looked to the side and saw Henrique standing in front of them. Rafael immediately stood up. Marina almost choked on the pastry she was eating.

- Henrique! What a pleasure to see you! This is my wife.

Marina put her cup on the saucer. Henrique, seeing that she was about to get up, said:

- Please, don't bother!

He held out his hand, which she shook gently.

I am looking for a table, but it seems that this place is full today.

- You can sit with us, Rafael invited.

Henrique hesitated:

- 'It's just that I'm with Maria Eugenia and Dionisio. They are waiting in the lobby.

Marina intervened:

- Go and get them. It will be a pleasure to have them with us.

He smiled:

- I'm going to accept because I promised Dionisio that I would bring him here today. I don't want to disappoint him.

- Don't be shy. It will be a pleasure.

When he left, Rafael returned:

- You wanted a sign. What do you think of this one?

Marina had no time to answer: Henrique and Maria Eugenia, taking the boy by the hand, approached.

Once they had introduced themselves, they settled down and asked for what they wanted. Marina watched Dionisio, concealing her curiosity. He was a handsome boy, strong, ruddy, similar to his father, with bright green eyes and a captivating smile.

Maria Eugenia, sitting next to Marina, smiled at her.

- Thank you for giving us this space. We didn't think it would be full. We were taking Dionisio to visit a school and we had promised to bring him here. He came once for a little friend's birthday and he loved it.

- This place is very nice.

Maria Eugenia, sitting next to Dionisio, served him with love, attentive to his every gesture, making sure that he lacked nothing. There was love in her eyes as she looked at him.

Marina was moved to observe that the boy showed her gestures of affection, holding her hand, smiling at her, claiming her attention when Maria Eugenia was amusing herself talking to the others.

She also noticed that there was a special emotional complicity between them, which reminded her of the story Norma had told about them.

Marina had no doubt that they were bound by love. For her, this reality was a reason to rejoice, since she felt happy to have made it possible for them to meet again. Rafael exchanged ideas with Henrique about spirituality, telling his experiences with some cases he had closely observed. Henrique listened with interest, asking questions and expressing his opinions. The conversation flowed naturally and the atmosphere was pleasant.

Marina looked at Dionisio with admiration and interest. Maria Eugenia noticed and Marina hurried to say:

- Your son is very handsome. - And, lowering her voice, she continued saying: - We are coming back from the doctor. We've just found out that I'm pregnant. I'm looking at him because I would like my son to be as handsome and healthy as he is.

Maria Eugenia smiled and replied:

- Congratulations! Is this your first?

- Yes, it's my first.

- Being a mother is a wonderful thing, you'll see. Dionisio has brought us happiness, given new meaning to our lives. For me, he's the most precious gift in the world.

Dionisio amused himself with a bowl of vanilla ice-cream with little pieces of chocolate in it, having fun looking for each little piece, tasting them with pleasure.

While the two men talked about spirituality, the two exchanged ideas about motherhood. Marina wanted to know everything about the first care of the newborn and Maria Eugenia was happy to explain.

At a certain moment, she said with a smile:

- Dionisio! You're soaked! Look at your hands! Let's go to the toilet. Excuse us.

Marina got up:

- I'll go with you.

She wanted to make the most of this unexpected chance to observe the boy.

When they were gone, Henrique said:

- How nice to meet you here. Maria Eugenia and I have many acquaintances with whom we socialize, but few friends. However, with you I feel as if we have been close for a long time. I've never seen Maria Eugenia so at ease, so talkative, as now with your wife. You seem to have known each other for a long time.

- They have interests in common. Marina is pregnant.

- Congratulations! Maria Eugenia is a loving mother. She and Dionisio are very attached. They can't be without each other.

Rafael was thoughtful for a few moments, then said:

- Thinking about our relationship, which went beyond the usual between a patient and his doctor, and the ease with which Marina got on with his wife, I believe we already know each other from other lives.

- That may be so. Studying the phenomena of reincarnation, I have often thought that this attachment between Maria Eugenia and Dionisio reveals that they not only knew each other in other lives but that they liked each other. Ever since he was a little boy, he had shown affection for her. His little face lit up when she took him in her arms or caressed him. And as time went by, he showed her more and more how much he loved her.

- The affection between mother and child is natural. But the reciprocal is also true. I have had cases in which the son, since he was a baby, cried when his mother held him in her arms. There was one that impressed me a lot. When the mother picked the boy up, he cried so much that the husband quarrelled, insinuating that she pinched him on purpose.

- In that case, the son would have been an enemy of hers in other lives.

- That is the only way we can understand such a case.

- That can't be an easy task for parents.

- It really isn't. But, in spite of everything, both mother and son, with the passage of time, will question themselves about this animosity and try to improve this relationship. Sometimes they succeed; sometimes they don't.

- This will depend on many factors, besides the good will of each one.

- I believe that when life unites these people, placing them in the same family, it gives them the opportunity to eliminate badly resolved matters from other lives. Although they do not remember the past facts, in their unconscious the consequences of them are there, interfering in their way of thinking, of acting, hindering their physical, emotional and spiritual equilibrium.

- In this case, knowledge about reincarnation could help them to understand what would facilitate the process.

- On the contrary. Remembering the past could make the relationship more difficult. But sometimes, even ignoring what happened, the rejection is so strong that one life is not enough to end the matter. In any case, knowing that life does not play at losing, when it brings these people together, it is because they are capable of winning.

- This thought helps to discern and to try to improve.

Marina and Maria Eugenia were back with Dionisio, face washed, hair combed.

- How beautiful you look! -exclaimed Henrique, smiling.

- Mom already told me that! - he answered, raising his face haughtily.

- Your mother will make you very cocky! - Henrique joked.

Dionisio hugged his mother, who had sat down, saying affectionately:

- Beautiful Mama!

Marina's eyes sparkled with emotion and she tried to hide it.

- It's time to go, Maria Eugenia said to her husband.

He called the waitress and asked for the bill.

- Leave it to me, Rafael intervened.

Henrique, however, insisted on paying. Rafael and Marina thanked him. At the farewell, Henrique remembered:

- Let's schedule that dinner. Can it be this Saturday?

- I have to look at the schedule, Rafael answered. - I'll call tomorrow, okay?

- I want to show you an old book I discovered about materialization, said Henrique.

- It will be a pleasure.

They said goodbye and left. Rafael sat down again and, seeing that Marina remained silent, he asked:

- Well?

- I'm still perplexed.

- But it was good for you to meet Dionisio, to see how well he is.

- It was wonderful! It's surprising how much he loves her! I think that's what life wanted to show me.

- It was more than that. This meeting brought us confirmation that everything Norma told us was true.

- It is true. In fact, we never doubt, but to be faced with the facts is motivating. It signals that we are on the right track.

He agreed and then they decided to go home.

***

Leaving the teahouse, while they settled in the car, Henrique said:

- It was good that we met Rafael and his wife. I feel very good next to him. And from what I noticed his wife is also very nice.

- Indeed. Seeing her I had the impression that I knew her from somewhere.

- She must be from the study centre. She's a volunteer there.

- That must be it. I really think I saw her there. She is expecting her first child and is very anxious to know how to take care of him when he arrives.

- That's why the conversation between you two got so animated.

- Indeed. The experience with Dionisio was so good that if I could, I would have more children.

- You say that because Dionisio is a lovely boy. It's very good to have him with us.

She smiled contentedly. The boy, settled in the back seat, had fallen asleep. She took a blanket and covered him lovingly.

They arrived home and Henrique took Dionisio to bed. Maria Eugenia took off his shoes and covered him. He is not even awake.

- He played so much that he is sleeping on his own.

They left the room. While Maria Eugenia went to take care of her errands and fix a light supper, Henrique went to the study to get a book and sat down quietly to read.

He was so relaxed, settled in a comfortable armchair, the room in the dim light, that he fell asleep.

He dreamed that he was walking through a place full of fragrant flowers, where a very beautiful woman smiled at him and said:

- Everything is all right. Trust always.

He agreed, but at that moment he found himself in another place. It was dark and a heavy mist made it difficult to see. He was walking a little frightened, not knowing where he was, when suddenly a pale woman, face downcast, hair in the wind, appeared before him:

- It was really you I wanted to see. You live happily while I am suffering in this miserable life. That's not fair. You are to blame. It's because of you that I stayed in this state. I haven't given up. I'll collect everything you owe me. I will never leave you alone.

Henrique felt dizzy and felt an unpleasant smell. He wanted to run away, but he couldn't.

- You won't get rid of me. This time I will get what I want.

He held his hand and dragged him through the mist. He was terrified. Her hand held his and he tried unsuccessfully to pull free.

They reached a small clearing and Henrique saw that they were standing in front of a shack. Without letting go of his hand she pushed open the door and they entered.

The place was poor, sad, with few furnishings. She led him to a bed in a corner of the room, where a boy was lying, apparently dead.

Henrique remembered his nightmare; it was the same woman, the same boy.

- It's your fault, she screamed. - I want my son back. You killed him and took him away from me. But you will pay for all this. I swore. Now you give everything to this boy you got who stole my son's place. But you won't keep him. You will pay for what you did to me. I will do everything to take him away from you!

Henrique thought of Dionisio and felt his horror increase. This could not happen. He thought about God, asking him to take that woman away from his path. Then he woke up.

His heart was beating fast, his hands were cold and he was breathless with horrible fear.

"It was a nightmare! The nightmare is back," he thought.

He tried to calm himself, then went to the pantry to get a glass of water. Maria Eugenia, seeing him, was startled:

- What's wrong, Henrique? You look pale. What happened?

He took the water, then answered:

- The nightmare came back. But this time it was stronger.

- What nightmare was it? You never told me anything.

- A horrible woman chasing me, with a dead boy beside her. She hates me.

- I don't think it's just a bad dream. It's more like a spirit that's chasing you.

- This is the second time I have dreamt about her. I told Rafael about this dream and he advised me to seek spiritual help.

- In that case, we had better go and talk to Mrs. Eunice.

- Talk to her, ask if she can receive us. I will do anything not to have that dream again.

In order not to make Maria Eugenia worry, he did not tell her that his wife had threatened Dionisio.

- I'll call and see if she can see us today.

- You do that.

Maria Eugenia spoke with Eunice, who agreed to receive them. Then she approached Henrique, who was waiting sitting in the living room.

- She will see us today at eight.

-All right. I feel anxious, nervous. I have the impression that something very bad is about to happen, a tragedy.

- You were impressed. Nothing will happen. We are good people, we are protected. Let's trust.

Henrique remembered the woman he had seen in the middle of the flower garden.

- You are right. As soon as I fell asleep I dreamt about a beautiful woman in a wonderful garden who told me that everything was right and that I should trust.

Maria Eugenia smiled and said:

- I felt that we are protected and that we need to trust. Fear weakens us. If we want to avoid bad things, we must not give them strength. Nothing bad will happen to us.

- You are right. I don't know why this fear. I've never been afraid.

- It's okay. It's okay. It's alright.

Henrique did not want to have dinner and waited anxiously for the time to meet Eunice. Time was running out. Maria Eugenia, noticing his restlessness, did her best to entertain him by saying positive and cheerful things.

It was ten minutes to eight o'clock and they were already in the living room waiting to meet Eunice.

Shortly afterwards they were taken to her room, who greeted them warmly and asked them to sit in front of her desk while she settled down on the other side.

Before he could speak, she said:

- The past seeks us out when the opportunity arises for us to resolve old unfinished problems. Resentment, lack of knowledge of the facts create disputes and pride usually ends up pushing us into a vicious circle that, fed, can harm us for a long time. That is your case.

- Why does this woman pursue me? I don't know her, I don't remember anything. But I feel that she hates me.

- Let's say that while you have learned, evolved, changed your mental pattern, she has remained stuck in resentment, nurturing desire for revenge, and this has kept her stuck for long years in a tragic past experience.

- She shows me a dead boy and accuses me of murder. I have studied spiritual phenomena, I know that I have lived other lives, but did I commit this crime? When she accuses me, I feel guilty.

- Don't get into this feeling. It is common for unbalanced spirits to take advantage of the fact that an incarnate person forgets the past in order to demand non-existent guilt, trying to lower the mental standard so as to be able to dominate them.

- Could this be happening?

- It could. But even if it isn't cultivating guilt would be lowering your energy pattern, which wouldn't be appropriate anyway.

Henrique was silent for a few moments, then he said:

- In any case, I wish to say that the problem of a woman mourning her dead son touches me very much. I have a son whom I adore. I can assess how she feels. I want to say that if I have in fact done any harm to her or to that child, I am very sorry and I am willing to do whatever I can to help them.

- That is a good thought. If her case has been brought to you, it is because the time has come for this woman to be helped.

- I don't know how to do that, said Henrique.

- Let's do this: today you will receive an energetic treatment to balance your energies. The restlessness, the nervousness, the uneasiness will disappear. You will be fine.

- And what about the woman's case?

- She is at the limit of her strength. Only hatred feeds her. We have to study the best way to help her. I will consult our spirit guides and ask for guidance. As soon as I have an answer, I will let you know.

- During this time, won't the nightmare repeat itself?

- I don't think so. The woman you saw in the garden was a good spirit. She allowed your meeting with that woman to attract her attention so that she would come to us. Since you got what you wanted, you will wait for us to take action. During that time you will be protected.

- That's good. I would not want to go through that again.

Eunice called an assistant and asked her to take them to treatment. After they left, Eunice thought:

"I will consult, but my part I already know how to do."

Then she lifted her thoughts and thanked God for the opportunity to be able to help.

CHAPTER 26

Two days later, Eunice called Henrique. After the greetings, he asked:

- So, do you have an answer?

- Yes. My spiritual friends have invited you to a special meeting for the case.

- When?

- Tonight at eight o'clock in the evening, here at the study centre. Can you come?

- We will be there.

As soon as Henrique hung up he remembered his nightmare and felt a tightness in his chest. A feeling of fear came over him.

Wouldn't doing a special session attract that woman again? Now that he was feeling well, maybe it would be prudent not to mess with her. What if she came after him again?

Henrique felt some chills and nervously went to get a glass of water. Then he took a deep breath. He felt insecure, afraid. He began to think that maybe it would be better not to go.

He spent the day agitated, without being able to put his attention on his work. At the end of the afternoon, he called Rafael.

- Mrs Eunice booked a session for tonight. I was doing so well, but afterwards I got sick. I feel chills, I can't concentrate on work. Maybe it would be better not to go. What do you think?

- The other way around. Now you need to go.

- What do you mean?

- What you are feeling is not yours. It is they, the spirits that are enveloping you, who are reacting and do not want to go to this meeting. They are afraid of being held responsible for their actions and being forced to leave you alone.

- But it is me who is feeling it.

- I know, but you are picking up their energy.

- Are you sure?

- Yes. When it happens, it feels like you're the one with the feelings.

- I wish I could be that sure.

- If it will calm you down, I will tell you that Marina and I have also been called to participate in this meeting. We will be there.

Henrique sighed with relief:

- In that case, I'll be calmer anyway. Certainly Mrs. Eunice has called you because she knows you are my doctor and I will be safer if you are with us.

- That may be, Rafael said thoughtfully. - Don't worry, we'll be there ten minutes early. In any case, as the time of the meeting approaches, you may feel your uneasiness growing, but stay calm. It is a natural reaction, and I even find it promising. When they show fear, it is because they feel they will not be able to resist the force of the light.

- I will do my best. It was nice talking to you.

- You're in no condition to work. Go home, relax. Trust in the spiritual help and do not let yourself be involved by fear. Everything will work out.

- That's what I'm going to do. Thank you and see you tonight.

Henrique hung up the phone and went home. Rafael's words calmed him down, but in spite of this he felt that fear, anxiety and nervousness were still around him. He struggled to react.

He was not alone. Dedicated spiritual friends were watching over his peace, even though he could not see them. When a thought of fear came over him, he thought that he was protected and that nothing bad would happen to him.

It was quarter to eight when Henrique and Maria Eugenia arrived at the spiritual study centre. An assistant led them to a room where there was a table, some chairs, a sideboard with a vase of flowers and a tray with a jug of water and glasses.

A blue light lighted the dim room. Eunice was waiting for them and, to their surprise, Adele and Bernardo were also there.

Soft music enraptured the atmosphere. Despite Adele's unexpected presence, they remained silent.

Eunice asked them to sit around the table, where a girl and a boy were already. Rafael and Marina entered and were seated as well.

Marina looked around surprised, moved, wondering:

"I wonder why they gathered us here?"

Rafael noticed that she was nervous. He held her hand to show his support.

Eunice sat at the head of the table and said a prayer asking for the assistance of her spiritual friends. Then she said:

- Let us continue praying in silence.

Henrique felt cold in his hands and could not control his nervousness. Maria Eugenia, calmer, felt that something very important was going to happen there.

Adele also wondered why all the participants in her secret, who had promised not to approach each other, were brought together, almost unwillingly, by a greater force, which she felt but could not explain.

Rafael, reverent, raised his thoughts, feeling that a soft and pleasant warmth invaded him, making him feel a sensation of joy and love.

Shortly afterwards, the girl began to cry, saying in distress:

- What do you still want? Why are you all against me? Isn't it enough what they did to me, and are they still persecuting me? It's not fair. I can't accept it.

Eunice stood up and approached the medium:

- How long are you going to keep putting yourself in the position of victim? Aren't you tired of crying and feeding your suffering?

- You say that because it was not your son that he cruelly killed.

- You know it's not true.

- Of course it is! You think I'm lying? Can't you see him here, in my arms?

- That's an illusion you're feeding yourself because you refuse to accept the facts. It's been a long time since your son was in your arms. You carry an image that has crystallized and with it you intend to manipulate people. See what I do with it.

Eunice passed her hands around the medium several times, who screamed:

- No! You will not destroy my memories! This is all I have left. You can't do this to me.

- You imprisoned yourself in revolt and refused to continue on your way. Everyone who lived with you at that time has progressed, evolved, earned a better life. The boy who was your son is now a lucid, loving, happy spirit.

- That is not true. He is still with me, in my arms. I never set him free.

- Illusion. Only illusion. He's long gone. See what I do with this doll that you carry.

Eunice kept passing her hands around the medium, while she screamed:

- No! I won't let you. Please don't take my son away. No! Where is he? Where have they taken him?

- The burden you were carrying was lifeless. It wasn't him.

- You took him. Where did they take him? I already know who did it. He was the killer. Now you want to take him away from me. But it won't stay that way. I'll take his son away from him. They're happy now, but they have to pay for what they did to me. I will take their boy away so that they can feel what I felt when I lost my son.

Henrique trembled in terror, feeling that she meant Dionisio. The others felt the same way. All of them, moved, prayed in silence.

- Threatening now won't help. Despite your hostile attitude, everyone is wishing you well, praying on your behalf.

- I don't think so. They hate me.

- No, they forgave you long ago. It's time you saw the truth.

- I won't forget. They'll pay.

- You're tired. Recognize that you want peace.

- I can't have peace.

- If you accept the help being offered, I'll show you where your son is.

- I can't believe it. He's dead.

- You also died on Earth, but you're still alive.

- You won't convince me. I've sworn revenge and I'm going to finish off that intruder.

- I ask everyone to mentalize the light.

The medium was silent for a few seconds. Then she shouted:

- You have brought him to defy me. I'm going to finish that boy off! Who told you to interfere?

Eunice saw Dionisio in spirit enter the room, brought by two spiritual friends, and stop in front of the complaining woman, looking at her with love and extending his arms to her.

Little by little his face changed.

- Look, returned Eunice. - Don't you recognize him?

- He's my son! He is my son! - she cried, weeping compulsively.

Everyone continued praying, and little by little she calmed down:

- My God! I didn't know! Why did he hide in a different body?

- He has been reincarnated. Look how well he is doing.

- My son! It's been a long time. Can you forgive me?

Eunice saw the boy approach and hugged his mother, who was crying with emotion.

Those present, overcome with emotion, could not hold back their tears. After a few moments, Eunice said:

- Anne, say goodbye to him. He must go away. Thank God for the help you have received.

- No, I don't want him to go. I want to stay by his side forever.

- For the moment it's impossible. But if you agree to undergo treatment, make an effort to get better, one day you will be able to stay by his side.

Eunice saw that Dionisio was taken away and Anne asked:

- Let me see him a little longer. I will do what you ask.

- He cannot stay. Calm down, everything will be all right. Look, the nurse has come to fetch you. Go with her.

The medium took a deep breath, trembled slightly and said no more.

Eunice sat down again and asked:

- Let's continue in prayer.

There was silence. A little later, the boy next to Eunice began to speak:

- I am Norma. Today we have managed to realize one of our projects. You have managed to overcome some unresolved issues from the past and from now on you will be able to enjoy a better time.

You are willing to follow your intelligence instead of going through pain, and that makes us very happy. The other day I told one of the couples here present about the events of the past that gave rise to what is happening now. If they wish, when I am gone, they can tell the others.

I spoke about my daughter Marie; my friend Sophie; Denis, Marie's love; but I still had to speak about Gerard. What I have not yet told you is that after having been cruelly murdered by Gilbert, Denis became angry. He was not satisfied with having been torn from Marie's arms and planned to take revenge.

We tried to convince him to come with us for treatment, but he did not want it. While he was planning his revenge, he followed Marie's steps, despairing at the sight of her relations with other men.

Blinded by jealousy, he joined a band of avengers with whom he made a pact. For years, we were unable to do anything on her behalf. However, the day came when Marie returned to the astral. It was the opportunity he had been waiting for to be together. He went to wait for her anxiously.

Seeing him, she threw herself into his arms, saying that they would never be separated again. But the past had left its marks on each of them, and Denis's jealousy, recalling the debauched life she had led, provoked continual arguments and demands, making them hell. Besides, there were the commitments that both of them had made to groups of spirits who ceaselessly charged them for the favours they claimed to have done them.

Finally, Marie, tired of Denis' suspicions, fled in the company of a group of spirits who besieged her with advantages and promises, feeding her ambition.

After Marie abandoned him, Denis gave himself up to depression and it was then that we managed to take him to a place of treatment.

While Marea continued not to listen to us, Denis acknowledged his mistakes and decided to change his attitudes. He was greatly assisted by Adele and Bernardo, a couple who lived in our astral city and who loved him very much because, although he did not remember, he had been linked to them in other lives. They both really wanted Denis to elevate himself.

From then on Denis dedicated himself to spiritual work, he studied, learned and became better. Then he joined our group and went to live in our town.

Despite his progress, or even because of it, his conscience accused him of the violence he had committed. He recognized that he had given Gilbert cause to take his life when he had stolen the love of his wife, and that he in turn had done worse, because he had turned against people who had done nothing to him.

So he asked God for the opportunity to heal himself. He was willing to do whatever it took to free himself from that torture.

He was allowed to reincarnate in complete poverty, having as his mother Anne, a woman who in his youth had been very much in love with him and with whom he had had a relationship before meeting Marie.

Anne was not a balanced person. Emotionally unstable, she did not trust herself and used arrogance to cover up the defects she thought she had. She went from euphoria to depression with extreme ease. Thus, her affective relationships were short-lived.

In one of them, Denis was born. Her father soon abandoned them and Anne, in the hope of finding a lasting love, would go from one to another blaming all men, without realizing that the cause of what happened to her lay in the way she saw her life.

Then she met Gerard, a handsome, rich man, pampered by women. She fell in love. She employed herself as a maid in his house, thinking of winning him over. He, however, was not interested in her. Anne did what she could to attract his attention, but he did not take her seriously. Until her insistence annoyed him and he fired her.

Depressed, with no desire to react, she did not look for another job. For her, her life was a disgrace and the culprit was Gerard, who had taken her job.

Denis had become a sad, quiet but hard-working boy. He did not like the life Anne led, he tried to study, he dreamed of earning money to take his mother out of her misery.

When they ran out of food, he would go out and try to earn a few coins by helping people. With what he earned he would buy food, but since the quantity was small, he would leave it all for his mother, saying that he had already eaten.

Anne admired him. For her, her son was the only good man in the world. She dreamed for him all the happiness. However, she did not understand the sacrifices the boy made so that she would be well.

Malnourished and undernourished, he grew weaker and weaker. When he fell ill, Anne sought Gerard out. She entered his house, taking advantage of the distraction of a servant, and found him reading in his study.

Seeing her, he became angry:

- How did you get in?

- The door was open... I came because I am desperate. My son is sick and I have no money to cure him.

- It was you who got this son. It's your problem.

- Help me. I need to work.

- Not here. You have no responsibility. Go away. Leave me alone.

- He's sick because of you. You fired me for no reason. I, who have always been devoted to you!

She cried, begged, fought, but he was unmoved. He had her thrown out. Full of hate, she returned home. Her son's condition worsened until he fell victim to tuberculosis.

She, desperate, blamed Gerard for his death. In her mind, unsettled by the loss, she moulded an image of the son she was carrying in her arms, believing it to be his dead body.

Denis, however, had returned to the astral, having left in that small sick body all the energies he had accumulated in his astral body during his previous life.

On his return, he felt better. He remembered some past lives. On learning that Marie continued to refuse our help, he did everything possible to make her change.

At the time, Marie was depressed, tired. Knowing this, we organized a rescue team and went to the threshold, where she resided. We found her apathetic, unresponsive.

However, when she saw Denis, she changed completely. Thus, we were able to take her for treatment.

She wished to live next to him, which was not possible because her energetic level did not allow it. He visited her, stimulating her to do good, motivating her to react.

It was in a memorable meeting that you all attended that, under the guidance of our elder, we studied the possibilities of Marie's improvement.

Adele was willing to cooperate by taking Marie in as her daughter. Denis wished to be born and marry her. He believed that under her influence she could overcome the temptations of the world. However, he was told that this was not advisable. He would be allowed to stay by her side as her son and only in that way could he exercise his influence over her.

Gerard, whom time had transformed into a better person, feeling guilty for the disregard with which he had treated Anne, agreed to take Denis as his son. The problem was that Marie, in her new incarnation, could not have children. Having had many abortions in her previous incarnation, she had damaged the reproductive organs of her astral body and lost fertility.

It was then that we asked Sophie for help, who at first refused, but who ended up helping us.

Today Marie has changed a lot, she has matured and I know that from now on she will continue to progress. I want to say that I am very grateful for everything you have done for my dear Marie and to say that we all form a family and are linked by the eternal bonds of the spirit.

May God bless you all.

The medium fell silent and silence followed. All moved, those present could not hold back their tears.

Eunice said a prayer of thanks and closed the meeting. The light was switched on and the girl next to Eunice stood up and handed out glasses of water.

Immersed in their intimate thoughts, no one felt like speaking, for fear of breaking the serenity of the atmosphere. Adele began:

- I'm impressed. What happened here revealed to me a much bigger world than I thought. I had never attended a meeting like this before. I came with an open heart, wondering what it meant. All I know is that, as Norma spoke, I began to see scenes, places where I lived next to Bernardo.

- That's right, Eunice clarified. - You had memories of your stay in the astral before reincarnating.

- That is extraordinary. How can that be?

- Everything is natural, because in our unconscious all the experiences we live are recorded. Everything is within you. In special cases, these moments come to the surface.

Maria Eugenia, her eyes shining with emotion, said:

- Today I had all the answers I asked God for. Ever since I began to study spirituality, I've been wondering why the chance to have children was taken away from me. Now I know.

I saw myself as Marie. I also saw Dionisio as Denis. I also know who Sophie is, whom I will be grateful to for the rest of my life for having given me the chance to have Denis by my side.

She looked at Marina who shuddered without being able to answer. Henrique, his eyes moist, returned in a voice that changed with emotion:

- I know I was Gerard, the cold, indifferent man. That's why the birth of Dionisio has brought me so much peace. Nothing is worse than remorse. And now it will never bother me again.

The silence lasted a few seconds, then Rafael said:

- It was to me and Marina that Norma told a part of this story. I know that Marina, so emotional, won't be able to tell it now. But I feel that she would like to do it. So, if you want to listen, I can tell you what was revealed to us.

Everyone turned towards him. Eunice answered:

- Speak Rafael. Tonight, all will be made clear. We all want to hear.

Rafael told how Cicero had become medium and Rute had helped them to attend him and then, to their surprise, Norma manifested through her. Then he related everything she had told them and finished:

- I must say that we are blessed people, because we had access to all these things that offered us answers that come to meet our feelings and enquiries. I am very grateful to the source of life for allowing me to be part of this group. I wish to say that in the face of all that we have received this evening, I feel within me the responsibility not only to become better every day, but also to dedicate myself to the study of spirituality.

- You are already doing this, said Eunice. - When we become better, we are improving the world.

They talked for a few more minutes, then got up to leave. After saying goodbye to Eunice and the two people who had attended the meeting, the three couples left the building.

It was time to say goodbye. Adele hugged Marina, saying in her ear:

- Thank you, Sophie dear. You did your part. God bless you. I wish to keep our friendship.

- Thank you, she replied. - I have always considered you one of my family.

Bernardo hugged her affectionately, saying:

- You deserve to be happy. I admire you very much.

Maria Eugenia approached Marina and hugged her, saying softly:

- I know that it was you who gave me the greatest gift I have ever received. I will be eternally grateful.

Henrique also hugged her, saying in a soft voice:

- You have given us happiness. May God protect and bless you.

They left and Rafael held Marina's arm, saying happily:

- See, you don't need to wonder anymore what life wished for by bringing us together. It already answered.

- Yes, mission accomplished. Now I think we can turn the page and prepare to receive our son.

- Or daughter. I wonder who will come to join us.

- For now, we don't know yet. The only thing I know is that in this world nothing happens by chance.

Rafael kissed her affectionately. Embraced and happy, they went home.

THE END

Zibia Gasparetto's Greatest success stories

With more than 20 million titles sold, the author has contributed to the strengthening of spiritualist literature in the publishing market and to the popularization of spirituality. Learn more of the author's successes.

Romances Dictated by the Spirit Lucius

The Life Force

The Truth of each one

Life knows what it does

She trusted in life

Between Love and War

Esmeralda

Thorns of Time

Eternal Bonds

Nothing is by Chance

Nobody is Nobody's

God's Advocate

Tomorrow Belongs to God

Love Won

Unexpected Encounter

On the Edge of Destiny

The Sly One

The Morro of Illusions

Where is Teresa?

Through the Doors of the Heart

When Life chooses

When the Hour Comes

When it is necessary to return
Opening for Life
Not afraid to live
Only love can do it
We Are All Innocent
Everything has its price
It was all worth it
A real love
Overcoming the past

Other success stories by André Luiz Ruiz and Lucius
The Love Never Forgets You Trilogy
The Strength of Kindness
Under the Hands of Mercy
Saying Goodbye to Earth
At the End of the Last Hour
Sculpting Your Destiny
There are Flowers on the Stones
The Crags are made of Sand

Books of Eliana Machado Coelho and Schellida

Hearts without Destiny

The Shine of Truth

The Right to be Happy

The Return

In the Silence of Passions

Strength to Begin Again

The Certainty of Victory

The Conquest of Peace

Lessons Life Offers

Stronger than Ever

No Rules for Loving

A Diary in Time

A Reason to Live

Eliana Machado Coelho and Schellida, Romances that captivate, teach, move and

can change your life!

Romances of Arandi Gomes Texeira and The Count J.W. Rochester

Lancaster County

The Power of Love

The Trial

Cleopatra's Bracelet

The Reincarnation of a Queen

You Are Gods

Books of Marcelo Cezar and Marco Aurelio

Love is for the Strong

The Last Chance

Nothing is as it Seems

Forever With Me

Only God Knows

You Make Tomorrow

A Breath of Tenderness

Books of Vera Kryzhanovskaia and JW Rochester

The Revenge of the Jew

The Nun of the Marriages

The Sorcerer's Daughter

The Flower of the Swamp

The Divine Wrath

The Legend of the Castle of Montignoso

The Death of the Planet

The Night of Saint Bartholomew

The Revenge of the Jew

Blessed are the poor in spirit

Cobra Capella

Dolores

Trilogy of the Kingdom of Shadows

From Heaven to Earth

Episodes from the Life of Tiberius

Infernal Spell

Herculanum

On the Frontier

Naema, the Witch

In the Castle of Scotland (Trilogy 2)

New Era

The Elixir of Long Life

The Pharaoh Mernephtah

The Lawgivers
The Magicians
The Terrible Phantom
Paradise without Adam
Romance of a Queen
Czech Luminaries
Hidden Narratives
The Nun of the Marriages

Books of Elisa Masselli

There is always a reason
Nothing goes unanswered
Life is made of decisions
The Mission of each one
Something more is needed
The Past does not matter
Destiny in his hands
God was with him
When the past does not pass
Just beginning

Books of Vera Lúcia Marinzeck de Carvalhoç and Patricia

Violets in the Window
Living in the Spirit World
The Writer's House
Flight of the Seagull

Vera Lúcia Marinzeck de Carvalho and Antônio Carlos

Love your Enemies
Slave Bernardino
the Rock of Lovers
Rosa, the third fatality
Captives and Freed

Books of Mónica de Castro y Leonel

In spite of everything

Love is not to be trifled with

Face to Face with the Truth

Of My Whole Being

I wish

The Price of Being Different

Twins

Giselle, The Inquisitor's Mistress

Greta

Till Life Do You Part

Impulses of the Heart

Jurema of the Jungle

The Actress

The Force of Destiny

Memories that the Wind Brings

Secrets of the Soul

Feeling in One's Own Skin

World Spiritist Institute

www.ingramcontent.com/pod-product-compliance
Lightning Source LLC
LaVergne TN
LVHW091656070526
838199LV00050B/2182